THE JIHAD NEXT DOOR

THE
JIHAD
NEXT DOOR

The Lackawanna Six and
Rough Justice in the Age of Terror

DINA TEMPLE-RASTON

PUBLIC AFFAIRS
A MEMBER OF THE PERSEUS BOOKS GROUP
NEW YORK

Published in the United States by PublicAffairs™,
a member of the Perseus Books Group.

PublicAffairs books are available at special discounts for bulk
purchases in the U.S. by corporations, institutions, and other
organizations. For more information, please contact the Special
Markets Department at the Perseus Books Group, 2300 Chestnut
St., Suite 200, Philadelphia, PA 19103, or call (800) 255-1514,
or email special.markets@perseusbooks.com.

Text design by Cynthia Young, Sagecraft, LLC
Set in 12 pt Adobe Garamond

Cataloging-in-Publication Data is available at the Library of Congress.
ISBN-10: 1-58648-4036
ISBN-13: 978-1-58648-403-3

First Edition
10 9 8 7 6 5 4 3 2 1

Grateful acknowledgment is made to the following for permission to
reproduce photographs: 1-2, Konrad Fiedler; 3, Courtesy of Rod Personius;
4, Courtesy of Jim Harrington; 5–11, FBI file photographs; 12, Courtesy
of Peter Ahearn; 13, Courtesy of Edward Needham; 14, AP Images/
David Duprey; 15, Dina Temple-Raston; 16–20, Konrad Fiedler;
21–22, Courtesy of Josh Colangelo-Bryan.

To the good people of Lackawanna's First Ward

You are not wood, you are not stones, but men;
And, being men, bearing the will of Caesar,
It will inflame you, it will make you mad.

—William Shakespeare,
Julius Caesar, Act III, Scene 2

CONTENTS

The Route to Jihad

Mosed, Taher and Galab left first, taking a new route from Lahore to Quetta and then on to Kandahar.

Goba, al-Bakri, Elbaneh and Alwan left western New York in May 2001 and traveled from Karachi to Quetta and finally arrived in the al-Farooq camp in Kandahar.

by Lisa Jordan

AUTHOR'S NOTE

The injustice of any one episode—whether it be a crime or a single arrest—looms larger in communities where those kinds of incidents are rare. Before 2002, Lackawanna was the kind of quiet town that kept to itself. Headlines, when they occurred at all, happened in Buffalo, just eight miles away. Lackawanna was perfectly happy to be an afterthought.

When the FBI swooped down on the ramshackle houses in Lackawanna's Yemeni community and arrested a handful of its young men almost exactly a year after the 9/11 attacks Lackawanna's First Ward was transformed. It became the place that spawned this country's first homegrown sleeper cell. Conclusions were drawn before the facts. And Lackawanna's fate was sealed.

Small towns provide a good lens through which to examine American life. The complications of national policy and its points of contention get lost in cities such as New York or Washington, DC. To understand the larger, important issues that affect America, one has to go to the level of the sidewalks and talk to ordinary people put in extraordinary circumstances.

When I wanted to understand racism in America at the dawn of the twenty-first century, I traveled to Jasper, Texas. My first book, *A Death in Texas,* chronicled the aftermath of the racially motivated murder of James Byrd, Jr., a black man who was dragged behind a pickup truck to his death by three white boys who thought they would get away with it. I wanted to look at how whites and blacks in Jasper reacted to Byrd's death and what their response revealed about race relations in this country.

Similarly, after the frenzy surrounding the Lackawanna Six died down, I traveled to Lackawanna and spoke to families and neighbors and friends of the six men arrested to understand what it is like to be Muslim in America today. I wanted to track the uneven, and sometimes rough, justice this country has meted out since the 9/11 attacks as it seeks to strike a balance between civil liberties and security.

There is an expression in the black community that in white America everyone who is black is born suspect. Today, post–9/11, that has come to also define the condition of Muslims here. We double-take when Muslims board airplanes. We subconsciously narrow our lids when they get on buses or subways with large backpacks. The climate in this country has changed, and against that backdrop it seemed a return to western New York, to Lackawanna, provided a perfect way to explore it. I spent two years talking to the people of Lackawanna. I followed in the young men's footsteps, not just in America, but through Yemen, Pakistan, and Afghanistan—from poor villages outside Sana'a to jihadi hotels in Karachi, to what remained of al-Qaeda training camps in Southern Afghanistan. What emerged was a portrait of a community on the fringes of American society, six men who sought to escape it, and this country's struggle with rough justice in the Age of Terror.

MUKHTAR'S BIG WEDDING

September 2002

LIFE CHANGED FOR Mukhtar al-Bakri and five of his friends on an otherwise beautiful crisp September day. He could remember the precise moment when he stepped into the gloom: It started with his hotel room door crashing open. September 9, 2002, was supposed to be the most important day of twenty-one-year-old Mukhtar al-Bakri's short life. His wedding to the teenage daughter of a family friend in Bahrain had been an elaborate affair, something beyond what the al-Bakri family could really afford. His arrival at the wedding hall was greeted by the beating of drums and a cacophony of traditional instruments. The sisters of his bride playfully welcomed each guest with a gentle tap, a sort of blessing, from a stick wrapped in flowers. Attendants donned flowing white gowns and long Arabian headscarves. The bride wore a modest white veil. Waiters lurched under the weight of plates piled high with food. There were dutiful prayers to Allah. It was everything Mukhtar al-Bakri had envisioned. The proceedings were dignified yet oddly fun. It marked a fresh start for him: a new, better phase of his life.

Mukhtar's friends had been surprised, even perplexed, at how seriously he was taking his newfound responsibility. The wedding kindled extraordinary emotions and hopes within him.

Frankly, it wasn't like Mukhtar; he was generally carefree and hardly one to suddenly reorder his life. That might explain why they were alarmed when Mukhtar called one of them before the wedding to say goodbye. "You won't be hearing from me again," Mukhtar said over the crackling of a long-distance connection. Why he sounded so fatalistic just before what should have been a joyous occasion is unclear. Maybe, like many people his age, he was being overly dramatic, as one phase of his life closed and another began. He said later he just meant it as a joke, that he was going to drop out of sight for a while and try his hand at being a dutiful husband instead of a hard partying twenty-something. To his friends, the message sounded ominous.

When they started calling each other recounting Mukhtar's message, a completely different audience was also listening. To the ears of the FBI investigators tracking the call, the talk of a big wedding indicated not a blow-out party in Bahrain but something else entirely. What they thought they heard, all too clearly, was the signature farewell of a suicide bomber—the dialogue of a young man about to meet his maker. As the first anniversary of the September 11 attacks drew closer, America was on high alert. It appeared her enemies—Islamic fundamentalists bent on destruction—were gearing up for something. Mukhtar's phone call fit neatly into a perceived pattern of events. The FBI had worked up a list of potential targets in the days leading up to the anniversary. Attacks on military bases in the Middle East were at the top of the list, and Mukhtar's phone call seemed like a break, a clue amid an ocean of information pouring into the American intelligence community. The military went on Delta Alert—its highest state of readiness—shortly after the intercept. The young man from Lackawanna who was determined to reorder his life had no idea what his talk about a "big wedding" had set in motion.

MUKHTAR AL-BAKRI WAS settled under the sheets for the first time with his teenage bride just before police burst into his hotel room. He had no idea that only hours earlier his name was on the lips of officials at the highest levels of the U.S. government. The FBI and CIA had been briefing President George W. Bush and Vice President Dick Cheney regularly about al-Bakri and his friends. Bush and Cheney then gave the order that would make Mukhtar's big day memorable for all the wrong reasons.

Bahrani police officers swarmed around al-Bakri's wedding bed with their guns drawn, sights trained in his direction. They hustled him from his hotel bed, and snapped on handcuffs. He recalled the sound of his teenage bride in tears as the police bundled him down the corridor, lamenting that he never had the chance to consummate his marriage. He knew that there must be some mistake. It never occurred to him that the Bahrain commandos who arrested him had burst into the room expecting to find guns and explosives, perhaps even a suicide vest, instead of a terrified young man.

A short time later, and nearly halfway around the world, other arrests followed al-Bakri's. Unmarked sedans and police cars came to quick stops in front of houses and malls and delis. One by one, police and FBI agents rounded up al-Bakri's friends and pushed them into the backseats of cruisers. Anyone watching would have said they all looked scared and baffled. To a man, they were all obedient and compliant, nodding numbly when they were advised of their rights. It took only minutes for news of the arrests to filter through the tightly knit Yemeni community. The bulletins were met instantly with shaking heads and clicking tongues. It wasn't the boys about which the residents were worried, it was the authorities. This was racial profiling, neighbors said. We know these boys. They are just like us. We watch them play soccer. We pray with them. We know their parents and their brothers and sisters and wives. If these six are suspects, then so is everyone else.

Someone said something about terrorism. Neighbors were sure that couldn't be right. These men were native-born or naturalized U.S. citizens. Four were married. Three had children. One rode a motorcycle. Another was voted "friendliest" of his graduating class at the local high school. One sold used cars. Another was a telemarketer. They were all registered Democrats. Why had the authorities singled them out?

Mukhtar al-Bakri was a twin, one half of a pair of Yemeni brothers who had lived with their family in a small, two-story, yellow and green wood frame affair on Ingham Avenue. They were part of the second largest Yemeni community in America, just a stone's throw from Buffalo, New York. The al-Bakri household was actually made up of two families: Mukhtar, his twin brother Amin, their mother and father occupied one part of the house; and his older brother, his wife, and their two children comprised the other. It was a typical arrangement. There was no pressure in this community to have the elder sons marry and go off to make their own way. Instead, the families stayed together with succeeding generations and new members—wives, babies, sisters-in-law—simply folding themselves into existing households the way they did in the old country. Home was a place where meals were big raucous affairs with the men of the house eating in one room and the women, more traditionally, taking their meals in another. A look at the al-Bakris during the dinner hour revealed that all the men resembled each other. Mukhtar and Amin were tintypes. Standing five-feet-seven with wiry frames, they looked younger than their years. Their faces were dominated with oversized brown eyes, and they had ears that stuck out at odd angles from their heads. They carried a perpetually vulnerable look, like someone had just struck them from behind without warning.

Their father, Ali al-Bakri, was working class, a twenty-five-year employee at the Sorrento Cheese Factory off Ridge Road downtown. His story was a template for many of the men of his age in Lackawanna's First Ward. He had come to America from Yemen, hoping to find work in the steel mills and to create a better life for his family. The mills inspired such extraordinary hopes that entire clans uprooted themselves for the promise of a better life than the one behind them. The al-Bakris weren't rich, but they had what they needed. The al-Bakri sons had graduated from an American high school with decent educations, and while they didn't have steady work, exactly, they were good boys—or so their father thought.

The truth was that throughout their teenage years the younger al-Bakris were more than a little wild: more of a product of Lackawanna than their native Yemen. Most of the time, their dueling identities hardly bothered them. They played on the Lackawanna High School soccer team (goalie and forward) and drove around the neighborhoods in the rickety cars that teenagers favor. They wore the baggy training pants and hoodie sweatshirts that had become the inner-city uniform among young toughs. They played concussive hip-hop music at ear-splitting levels. They ran with a crowd that paddled through life largely unnoticed. They got by doing itinerant day labor, dabbling in petty theft, trying their hand at drug dealing, laundering money. They gambled with friends across the border in Niagara Falls and smuggled cigarettes from Canada. In the early days, the trouble they got into was of the low-level variety where young men in depressed towns often find themselves: there was pot smoking, carousing, and clubbing. Though they grew into more serious offenses as the boys got older, in the beginning none of their scofflaw antics were serious enough to merit the attention of the authorities.

It was the parents of the First Ward, those who kept their children on short leashes, who worried about the people who surrounded the boys. The al-Bakri brothers and their friends formed the kind of group you hoped your own son wouldn't fall into—not because they were primed to do anything particularly bad or evil, but because the al-Bakri boys seemed to be testing limits more-so than normal, and young men who do that are bound, sooner or later, to miscalculate and cross the threshold of good sense.

The al-Bakri parents, for their part, chose to accentuate the positive when it came to their children. They turned a blind eye to the late nights and suspicious acquaintances. They focused instead on the fact that their sons still seemed to find time to attend mosque. It wasn't so much that they were devout—after all, they partied as much as other teenagers—but it was clear that they found something intriguing about being Muslim. The family's trips back to Yemen every couple of years only fed that inclination. While the residents of Lackawanna's First Ward did not have much money to spare, they always managed to scrape together what they needed for the occasional trips back to Yemen.

Those family vacations to the old country transported the al-Bakri boys and their Yemeni neighbors in Lackawanna, quite literally, from one world to another. When they strode into their villages, deep in the Yemeni interior, they were treated as conquering heroes. Lives that were rather bleak and aimless by American standards took on mythic proportions in Yemen. Relatives there had next to nothing by comparison. They lived in mud huts. They had barely enough to eat. Their clothes were ragged. The boys from Lackawanna seemed to have it all: money, opportunity, freedom. The trips had a soothing effect on Lackawanna's young Yemeni men by reconnecting them with a place they hardly knew and, when they returned, helping them feel oddly grateful for the lives they led in western New York.

When the al-Bakri father decided his two sons would marry the teenage daughters of a friend in Bahrain, the preparations were begun more than six months in advance. Mukhtar flew to the Middle East in May 2002 to plan a September ceremony. Those months in the Middle East were fun for him. He had no work to do, just a succession of social engagements to attend and daily prayers to make at a local mosque. In July, he went to visit his sister in Saudi Arabia. The two took a pilgrimage to Mecca. It seemed, as the September 9, 2002, wedding neared, that Mukhtar had finally found his place in the world.

THE FBI HAD BEEN listening to al-Bakri's phone calls and tracking his emails. His dispatch from Bahrain made the agents swallow hard. The head of the Joint Terrorism Task Force for the Western District of New York at the time was Ed Needham. His job was to bring together federal and state law enforcement officials to identify and investigate international and domestic terrorism. By that fall of 2002, Needham had been working in international terrorism for thirteen years. He had worked for two years with John O'Neill, the man best known as Osama bin Laden's hunter, as a supervisor in the radical fundamentalists unit at the Bureau. It later became O'Neill's famed bin Laden unit. O'Neill and Needham began fighting skirmishes in the war against terror long before it had actually been declared.

In 2002, the FBI's bench of Arabic speakers and Islamic experts was thin. Gamal Abdel-Hafiz was the agency's first Muslim hire and one of a handful of the agency's Arabic-speaking members. He was home with his wife in Saudi Arabia in early September 2002 when his phone rang. The FBI wanted him to travel to the Kingdom of Bahrain and pick up a suspect. Abdel-Hafiz asked the usual questions: what was he looking for, what was the suspect involved in? The answers weren't forthcoming. "Just go there," his supervisor said, "and you'll get the questions you need to ask when you arrive." Abdel-Hafiz would become the first American to interview Mukhtar al-Bakri after his arrest.

About that same time, Mike Urbanski, a state trooper and member of the Buffalo Joint Terrorism Task Force, was aboard a Gulfstream jet that belonged to the Department of Justice. He had picked up the jet in Washington, DC, and began a thirty-six-hour flight from Washington to Naples, Italy, continuing on to Bahrain. "It was the fanciest plane I had ever been on," Urbanski said later. "We knew we weren't going to be in Bahrain long. Just long enough to pick up al-Bakri and bring him home. But it was a nice ride."

As far as Urbanski knew, he was about to pick up America's first homegrown Islamic terrorist, the first American to train in an al-Qaeda camp and then attempt to slip back unnoticed into middle-class American society. So, when al-Bakri emerged from an unmarked car at the Bahrani airport, Urbanski was surprised to see just a kid. Al-Bakri actually looked relieved to see Urbanski. He had been in Bahrani police custody for five days, and it looked like he hadn't slept in weeks. "I think he thought he'd be safer with us," Urbanski said later. The officers searched al-Bakri before he got on the plane, gave him a green jumpsuit to slip on, and handed him a pen and paper.

"Tell us what you know," Urbanski said gruffly.

He recalled that al-Bakri looked so scared that words literally tumbled out of him. In his nervousness he started to speak faster. Like a skater on thinning ice, he seemed to be accelerating to save himself from drowning. He said he'd been to an al-Qaeda camp in Afghanistan a year earlier with five friends from Lackawanna. They had fired weapons, learned about jihad, and had returned shortly before the 9/11 attacks. He drew diagrams of guesthouses. He sketched out the details of Osama bin Laden's residence, marking doors, indicating where there were gardens. He talked about meeting Osama bin Laden in a courtyard in front of a stone hut.

Urbanski and al-Bakri talked all the way to America. The young man looked spent when they were done. Not knowing what else to say, Urbanski turned the tables. "Have you got any questions for us?" he asked.

Al-Bakri looked up and his thoughts slowly evolved into words. "Yeah, how are the Bills doing?"

CHAPTER 1

THE CURSE OF McKINLEY

BUFFALO FEELS LIKE a town that has lost its reason for existing. The streets are deserted. Shopfronts boarded. Residents seem glum.

What a difference a century makes. At the turn of the twentieth century, an encounter with Buffalo was one of boundless optimism. Buffalo and Lackawanna and their environs were basking in the glow of progress. In the fall of 1901, Buffalo hosted the Pan-American Exposition, a global event to showcase the world's most comprehensive collection of technology, architecture, art, and music. At the time, it was lauded as an exposition that would be the "timekeeper of progress." Western New York was abuzz with preparations. Dignitaries were to arrive from the far corners of the globe. President William McKinley had promised a visit. The world was coming to Buffalo to see the wonderful things in store for the new century, and that meant Buffalo, for a brief moment, embodied all that promise.

It took only two gunshots to change all that. On September 6, 1901, Leon Czolgosz, a twenty-eight-year-old independent anarchist who felt that all rulers ought to be killed, approached President McKinley at a rope line outside the Expo's Temple of Music. Czolgosz had bandaged his right hand with a handkerchief. The linen was covering a .32 caliber Johnson revolver.

Czolgosz was able to squeeze off two shots before he fled. Police found him in what would become the town of Lackawanna. The assassin was hiding out in a small cottage set back from Ridge Road in what is today's First Ward, just a short distance from where al-Bakri and his friends would grow up nearly one hundred years later. Police found the revolver in Czolgosz's room. McKinley died a short time later. The assassination, naturally, clouded Buffalo's day in the sun. Some Buffaloians believed the city had been cursed ever since.

LACKAWANNA SITS ON the westernmost edge of New York where the waters of the Niagara River and Lake Erie combine. Before the McKinley assassination, in the late 1800s, it had been six square miles wild with expectation on the edge of the unknown. In the late 1870s, the city had been just a waterfront extension of West Seneca Township. The federal government had provided money to build a long break wall at the east end of Lake Erie. It made the waters along the lake shore smooth as glass. Suddenly, the town was the ideal spot for inexpensively floating the fruits of heavy industry to the Midwest. In 1899, Lackawanna Iron and Steel Company purchased all of the land along the shoreline. It planned to build the most ambitious mill project the planet had ever seen. By its sheer gargantuan size, Lackawanna's new steel mill was poised to change the world as western New Yorkers had known it.

A little more than a year later, the mill's first giant beams shot into the air. Men on scaffolds worked around the clock and by spring of 1901, the mill buildings had swallowed great mouthfuls of sky along the Erie shore. Two years later, Lackawanna Steel had poured its first heat, and, as far as western New Yorkers

could tell, it opened a new era. At the time, the town of West
Seneca had three districts: Gardenville, Ebenezer, and what was
known simply as "the steel plant district." The no-named afterthought belied the plant's importance to the area. Most of the
taxes collected came from the mill and yet, workers groused,
most of those revenues found their way to Gardenville and
Ebenezer, following the votes. The steel workers wanted to form
their own town to keep their homegrown revenues local. It took
nearly a decade, but finally in 1909 the new township took on
the name of its patron. The no-named steel district became
Lackawanna, a Native American name meaning "in the fork of
the river."

Steel mills are Goliaths—long, enormous structures that typically stretch across two to seven square miles of land. In the early
twentieth century, Lackawanna's story was retold in towns all
along the Great Lakes. The idea was to use the waterways to
float steel rails, bars, and sheet metal downriver to car manufac-
turers, railroads, or factories along the eastern seaboard. All
along the shoreline of Lake Erie the waters were illuminated at
night by harbor lanterns and the glare of lights from anchored
ships. The steel towns—from their chaotic streets to their
bustling lakeshores—were transformed.

The sheer bulk of steel mills meant that they didn't just arrive
in towns, they co-opted them. The mills were the sun around
which the people and local businesses revolved. In keeping with
that, Lackawanna Steel built houses and opened company stores.
It provided jobs for tens of thousands of men who came from
far-flung nations just for an opportunity to redefine their fu-
tures. Steel mills became synonomous with the American
Dream.

In the early days, Polish immigrants, dislocated by the First
World War, arrived to fill the mill's ranks. Then, some of the

Irish—rough-hewn men who settled in South Buffalo and opted for mill work instead of union jobs on the waterfront—came to Lackawanna. They built Catholic churches. Bars and delis flourished. Three eight-hour shifts—operations around the clock—meant that there was always the possibility of another customer walking in the door. The times were good for everyone.

The traditional way of making steel—the way Lackawanna Steel and Bethlehem Steel chose to produce it—hadn't changed much from the time it was developed one hundred years earlier. Workers rolled coke and iron into rail cars that rattled down tracks that led to a blast furnace in the middle of the mill. Heated at a hellish temperature, the coke and iron combined to produce liquid iron. It was then rolled into another furnace that transformed the liquid iron into liquid carbon steel, which, in turn, was either poured into great caldrons to solidify into ingots or ladled into a continuous casting machine that spat out a succession of forty-foot-long slabs of metal. Lackawanna's specialty was making rails, tracks for the burgeoning railway industry. Eventually it branched out, adding hot-rolling machines and then cold-rolling machines to make sheet steel used for the defense industry.

The Yemenis first came to Lackawanna in large numbers in the 1950s. They worked the furnaces in the mills and took the menial jobs the Eastern Europeans and Irishmen who came before them no longer wanted. At the time, workers claimed the Yemenis were better suited for the hot jobs because they were used to the blazing heat of the Yemeni summers. By the mid-1950s, there were hundreds of Yemenis in town. They lived together in group homes and pooled their resources. When the United States eased immigration rules in the 1960s, they brought their families, and they settled around the mills in enclaves such as the First Ward. After Detroit, Lackawanna was to become the second largest Yemeni community in America.

Someone should have realized that the boomtimes wouldn't last forever. The process of making steel was anything but efficient. It required millions of dollars in machines, copious amounts of energy, and thousands of steelworkers, at every stage of the process. Making steel was so labor intensive that, in the heyday, nearly the entire male population of Lackawanna was working for Lackawanna Steel. The mill employed twenty thousand people: a small army of hot-metal men wearing hard hats on their heads and silvery asbestos suits on their backs. And they all had that light sunburn—what was called steelburn—that came from working with white-hot metal, day after day. It was a rosy hue that might have been mistaken for a healthy glow by anyone who didn't know better.

From the start, the Yemenis in Lackawanna lived in a world that was part Upton Sinclair, part John Steinbeck. The Yemenis cleaned the enormous vats where the steel was poured and stoked furnaces that one could stand to be next to. They lived in clapboard houses built by Bethlehem Steel and sent money and letters home to their wives and children in the Middle East. They developed a Yemeni enclave on streets named Steelawanna and Wilkesbarre, and they opened the Yemeni Benevolent Association so they would have a place to gather. They bought an old Russian Orthodox church and turned it into a mosque. Their women, when they finally came to join them from Yemen, remained covered, donning *abayas* and headscarves. The men wore beards as long as their fists, as the Koran instructed. The people of the First Ward didn't fit in so much as create their own world, and the continuum of that world depended on steel. When the industry faltered, they, like the Polish and Irish immigrants who arrived before them, became the broken, obsolete men of an outsourced commodity.

THE STEEL EXECUTIVES, the ones who had never set foot in the First Ward or the other housing areas that sprung up in the shadow of the plant, lived like kings. Gold nameplates announced them at the door. There was the Lackawanna Steel Golf Course, a velvety green that was carefully tended only steps from company headquarters. The executive dining room at the mill featured Maine lobsters and fresh Angus steaks from cows raised on the grounds. Such mindless excess was bound to create tension among the workers.

The Amalgamated Association of Iron and Steel Workers, a national group, only began recruiting members in Lackawanna decades after the mill was fully operational. Steelworkers didn't have to work twelve-hour shifts six or seven days a week, the group's representatives told them. They promised better working conditions. National strikes soon followed. In 1919, the largest of the strikes temporarily stopped steel production. Washington called state and federal troops to the mills and forced workers back to their posts. In 1923, the steel industry finally granted eight-hour work days. But more strikes inevitably followed. Between 1945 and 1959 there were five industrywide strikes. The most serious work stoppage happened in 1959 when Lackawanna workers joined five hundred thousand steel men nationwide in a four-month strike to force changes in work rules, wages, and benefits. The industry never quite recovered.

Today, people in Lackawanna still talk about how it all went wrong. Some blame the steel executives. Fewer among them blame the unions. They spend endless hours going over just how they didn't see the decline of the industry coming. They beat themselves up for letting the town become so inextricably linked with steel, allowing Lackawanna's very identity to grow out of the metal. Looking back on it, no one can point to one specific thing that sparked Lackawanna's miserable reversal. It was more a series of unfortunate events. Some said it was the opening of the Saint Lawrence Seaway in 1957. Goods that had previously passed through Buffalo and nearby Lackawanna could now bypass it altogether. Others blamed the flight to the suburbs. At one time, more than half a million people lived in Buffalo and its immediate environs, but as industries declined and people went to try their luck finding work elsewhere, places like Lackawanna just up and died. Buffalo, on whose fortunes Lackawanna had always risen and fallen, had the dubious distinction of being one of the only American cities to have fewer people in the year 2000 than in the year 1900. Even the superstitious who blamed the "Curse of McKinley" never imagined just how bad it would become.

The Yemenis began to look for other opportunities. They pooled their money and lent cash, without interest, to friends and neighbors. They started opening up corner groceries and delis. They sold beer and lottery tickets and pork rinds. Their Muslim beliefs grew dimmer, like the sound of a radio running down, so they could survive in America. Eventually, the Yemenis ended up owning most of the small groceries in Lackawanna and Buffalo. They had cornered the market.

LACKAWANNA'S STEEL MUSEUM has the somewhat musty feel of a finished paneled basement where a boy might set up a train set or a husband might be permitted to store all those things a wife didn't want cluttering up the rest of the house. The walls are covered with signs literally plucked from the bones of the Lackawanna mill. They are metal- and block-letter testaments to the perils of the industry. "Stretcher in the Building," reads one. "Danger 440 volts" and "Steel and Iron Pouring Area," read others. A silver insulated sparksuit, which looks like a primitive spacesuit complete with sparkproof hood, stands with a fire extinguisher in mittened hands in the corner. Wood and glass display cases, like the ones that used to hold trophies or construction paper artwork in elementary school libraries, showcase odds and ends from another time. One display holds an array of Lackawanna Steel hard hats. Another holds sections of rebar and i-beams. An assortment of badges and photographs of the mill: fuzzy images of furnaces and the men who worked them clutter another case. Dinnerware from the plant's cafeteria and the management club sit on a shelf by the door.

Michael Malyak, the man behind the museum, can chronicle the decline of Lackawanna Steel, with all its figures and attendant dates as if they were multiplication tables long since committed to memory. Mild mannered, with the kind of voice that carries best to a small audience, Malyak used to keep the books for Lackawanna Steel. His biggest regret, he says today, is having never seen a live pour of molten steel. "I just always thought there would be another opportunity to do it, so I kept putting it off," he said. "And now there isn't."

As often as twice a week, Malyak lectures on Lackawanna's short brush with industrial greatness in the basement of the Lackawanna Public Library. People who come to visit talk about the slow unraveling of the industry in the same way some people might discuss the breakup of a marriage that no one saw coming, with a mixture of disappointment and sadness that something so wonderful could possibly have to come to an end.

The casualties of the industry, the people who thought they would be followed into the mills by children and grandchildren and great-grandchildren, arrive at the museum in various states of decline, rolling their wheelchairs past Muslim schoolgirls with headscarves scanning the stacks and Yemeni teenagers surfing the Internet or playing video games on the library's public computers. Elder care facility workers wheel some of them in. Others arrive with oxygen tanks heeling obediently at their sides. The youngest among them, usually the spouses of men who came to Lackawanna just to breathe in the mill's acrid odor and stare wide-eyed into its white-hot open-hearth furnaces, liven up Malyak's presentation with anecdotes of their own.

"My husband used to play harmonica for the steelmen he worked with at lunch," one widow offers. "He would climb the ladder up above the furnace and play."

"I worked in that section of the plant," a man says wheezing from a wheelchair in the back of the room. "I was the foreman of the galvanized steel plant," said another.

"I remember as a kid when the Arabs started coming here," one former welder said. "The guy used to give me stamps from his letters overseas for my collection."

The death of the Lackawanna mill was by no means a slow one. As soon as the disease was diagnosed—bad management, no reinvestment, the rise of more efficient mini mills—the signs of mortality seemed to be everywhere. By 1977, Lackawanna Steel employed fewer than eighty-five hundred, laying off nearly eleven thousand workers from their all-time high. Five years later, Lackawanna had only a skeleton crew of five hundred. By 1983, the Lackawanna plant was all but dead. The foreigners who came to America to seek their fortunes were suddenly and dramatically unemployed. Bethlehem closed most of the facility, leaving only the coke ovens and byproducts division, the strip mill, thirteen-inch and twelve-inch bar mills, and the gal-vanizing department. Employment was a scant four hundred workers. The plant's coke-making facilities were sold in 2001. Five years later, Lackawannans working at the plant were in de-molition. The husks of what once was, skeletons of mills all along the lakefront, say more about Lackawanna's decline than locals ever could. They give off an eerie feeling, like some terri-ble disease arrived, killed all in sight, and then disappeared back into the icy waters of Lake Erie.

Mike Malyak's father, brother, uncles, and cousins had all worked at the plant, but he was the only who worked in the back office, keeping careful tally of just how much steel was pouring out of the plant day after day, until it ceased altogether. He recalled walking beneath miles and miles of pipe that criss-crossed the plant. His eyes sparkled as he told the small group of museum visitors that he knew for a fact that forty-two miles of pipe had been removed from the city's dead mills by 2006. They shared his enthusiasm. They nodded in amazement. The steel plant, they all agreed rather wistfully, had been a very wonderful thing before the ovens cooled and the harbor lights eventually winked out.

"I remember looking at the sky as a kid and seeing it shine bright orange. It looked like something out of War of the Worlds," Ed Needham said. "That happened almost as long as I could remember. The plant literally changed the sky, not just the skyline of Lackawanna, but the sky."

CHAPTER 2

WARD RATS

I F SPECIAL AGENT Ed Needham didn't exist, someone would have to create him. An FBI man straight from central casting, he is a neat, attractive package: blue-eyed and solidly built, with short salt-and-pepper hair parted neatly in the center. He exudes a type of Clark Kent earnestness and speaks in such a slow, deliberate way one gets the impression he is always quietly assessing the moment, seeing things others don't see. He is the type of man who takes in stray dogs and provides foster care for troubled kids. It is hard not to like him. And when he says something, you find yourself instantly believing him—or at least wanting to.

Needham grew up in South Buffalo, a working-class, largely Irish-Catholic neighborhood where fathers left their families early in the morning to work on the waterfront as longshoremen or on the line at General Mills. Drive on South Park Avenue by the General Mills plant and open the car window and even to-day there is the warm, sweet-baked smell of Cheerios in the air.

That part of South Buffalo, known as the Old First Ward, was a close-knit place. Everyone knew the name of the man who worked the Michigan Street lift bridge (Rocky Reagan); and scoopers at the grain mill were considered "The Pride of the First Ward." It was a place where men had names like Paddy, Tuffy, and Mikey, and it was an area where young men grew up to become policemen and firemen. The Irish stereotype of being in a fistfight one minute and having a beer with their foes the next was alive and well in South Buffalo.

Needham was a "ward rat," an Irish-Catholic boy who, by his own admission, grew up thinking everyone was a union member, a Democrat, Catholic, and a Notre Dame fan. Needham's father drove a crane for Structural Steel; his mother ran Tricia's Deli, a corner store that sold everything from soda pop to sandwiches. As a boy, he roamed streets with names like O'Connell and Hamburg and Miami and bought milkshakes and pretzels from places like Danny Boy's Tavern and corner stores that were run by Irish families just like his. South Buffalo Fridays were marked by the fish fry—battered cod or haddock—with French fries, macaroni salad, *and* potato salad on a plate the size of a football.

The Needhams lived in a neat, gray two-family house on Hamburg Street that looked much like all the other modest two-story affairs around it. His cousins (forty-three on his mother's side) still lived in the ward and their children now walked the very streets Needham once haunted. A drive in South Buffalo would inevitably mean running into a Needham of some description—a nephew, a brother-in-law, a sister. "I came into Gene McCarthy's one night about 11:30 a couple of months ago," Needham said, "and three people at the bar were related to me. It is just like that around here."

Looking back on it, Needham said he had always seen himself as going into law enforcement. It was what a lot of guys in the neighborhood did. He began taking classes in criminal justice at State University College at Buffalo. At the time, the criminal justice department shared facilities with aspiring social workers, and Needham saw himself drifting in that direction. He started working at the Father Carmichael Community Center in a little neighborhood known as "The Valley," just over the bridge from where he grew up. He ran food drives and mentoring programs. He delivered cheese to the needy and coached at-risk kids in sports. He met his wife in the social work program. The two had talked about opening an orphanage together. "I was going to save the world," he laughed.

The FBI was an afterthought. He had started working toward an MBA at the University of Buffalo and dabbled in commercial insurance when the opportunity to work for the Bureau presented itself. He was what they called a "diversified hire." His background in social work was a novelty. Ed Needham was twenty-nine when he got his badge in 1988.

Needham's first assignment was terrorism related. He was focused on overseas attacks against Americans abroad, covering everything from the New People's Army attacks in the Philippines, to the November 17 Marxist cell that targeted Americans in Greece. The investigation of Pan Am Flight 103, which came to be known as the Lockerbie Air Disaster, in Scotland, soon became one of his highest profile cases. "Pan Am was my real introduction to terrorism," he said.

The bombing was seen as an unabashed assault on a symbol of the United States. With 189 of its victims being American, it had the dubious distinction of being the deadliest attack on Americans until September 11, 2001.

Needham's work got him noticed. In 1995, he was promoted to the supervisor's job of a counterterrorism unit known as the Radical Fundamentalist Unit. The next two years would be busy ones. Bombings in Riyadh in 1995, the Khobar Towers bombing in 1996, and the niggling issue of a Saudi extremist named Osama bin Laden, whom the FBI was tracking in Sudan, were all part of Needham's expanding portfolio. "There were, lots of things going on then," Needham recalled.

Just a month into a Washington posting, and days after his new boss John O'Neill arrived, Ramzi Yousef was arrested and brought to the United States. They knew he had entered the United States on an Iraqi passport in 1993 when he tried to blow up the World Trade Center with a car bomb in its underground garage. Although the attack failed to bring down the tower, it only emboldened Yousef more. In January 1995, shortly before he was picked up, Yousef and his associates were plotting to blow up eleven U.S. commercial aircraft with liquid explosive bombs that were specially designed to pass through airport metal detectors. As luck would have it, while mixing the toxic brew in a Manila apartment, Yousef started a fire. He fled and left behind a computer that allowed authorities to arrest him in Pakistan a month later.

While Needham did well at the FBI, taking on assignments with increasing responsibility, what he really wanted to do was return to Buffalo. His wife, Eileen, now a social worker, felt most at home there, and the old neighborhood was beckoning. The two decided they wanted to raise their children near grandparents and cousins. "I wanted my kids to grow up with the same sense of community I had," Needham said. So he requested a seniority transfer and left O'Neill's shop to land back in his hometown in December 1998, working terrorism leads out of Buffalo and heading up a new unit called the Joint Terrorism Task Force.

In the early days of the JTTF, Needham had been getting the usual reports about drug activity and cigarette smuggling. Both were almost commonplace in Buffalo, given the close proximity to Canada and duty-free goods brought back and forth across the border. Needham had paid little attention to Lackawanna. There were some leads that suggested some people there might be sending money to militant groups, but Needham found he had other fires to put out. It wasn't until al-Qaeda operatives blew up the USS *Cole* destroyer in Yemen in October 2000 that Needham started noticing Lackawanna.

The *Cole* had been on its way to the Persian Gulf to join a naval battle group involved in operations off the coast of Iraq. It had only just arrived in Aden, Yemen, on October 12, 2000, when it was attacked. Though scheduled to stay only about four hours, details of the USS *Cole*'s itinerary must have leaked out. A little more than an hour after refueling began, a small inflatable boat approached the left side of the destroyer. At first the sailors thought the men on board were lost, or just curious, wanting to take a closer look at the ship. Then they detonated their explosives. The blast hit the ship's galley just as the crew was lining up for lunch. Seventeen sailors died and thirty-nine others were wounded.

People in Aden said later they felt a concussion from the *Cole* explosion from miles away. The bomb left a house-sized gash—about twenty feet by forty feet—in the side of the ship. Clearly, the Clinton administration said at the time, whoever had targeted the *Cole* had access to classified information about its visit. The administration vowed to track down the people responsible and hold them accountable. Whether the Clinton administration did enough to discourage further attacks is still subject to debate. What isn't in question is that the battle between the United States and bin Laden had just ratcheted up. The *Cole* bombing was the worst attack on an American target in two years. It had been preceded by the bombings of two U.S. embassies in Africa in 1998, in which 224 people, mostly Africans, were killed. American investigators determined Osama bin Laden was behind that suicide mission too. Thirteen days later, the United States retaliated with missile strikes against al-Qaeda camps in Afghanistan and Sudan.

Special Agent Needham was the only FBI agent assigned to the Joint Terrorism Task Force for the Western District of New York when the *Cole* attack happened. He was focused on working more than a dozen counties in the Buffalo area and the border with Canada. Although he was only one man, Needham was responsible for terrorism investigations in New York's second-largest city alongside one of the busiest border crossings in the country. Buffalo is just twenty miles and a bridge from the Canadian border. When news of the *Cole* bombing reached New York, FBI agents from the Buffalo office began packing for Yemen. They made up one of the many Evidence Response Teams (ERTs) that went to Aden to recover the bodies and review the crime scene. Special Agent Ed Needham, still a one-man Joint Terrorism Task Force Office at the FBI's Buffalo headquarters, went to Lackawanna. He spoke with leaders in the Yemeni community there and told them he was worried about hate crimes and reprisals. The leadership gave him, at best, a chilly reception. "I got the idea they didn't really trust me," he said later.

WHEN PEOPLE TALK about homegrown terrorism in America, they invariably turn to the bombing of the Murrah Federal Building in Oklahoma City. The man behind it, Timothy McVeigh—a former army veteran—was from Pendleton, New York, about six miles from downtown Buffalo. What most people don't know was that, aside from the Oklahoma City field office, the FBI operation in Buffalo was the most involved in the case. McVeigh had more than just grown up in Buffalo. His father, Bill, still lived there. The younger McVeigh had actually applied for a job at the Buffalo Field Office of the FBI. The coincidences were everywhere.

The Buffalo FBI office had been instrumental in building the case against McVeigh: it was in charge of surveillance of his father, and it interviewed his sister. Buffalo FBI provided the early timeline for the life of a man who would be put to death as America's first homegrown terrorist in the modern age. FBI investigators in Buffalo tracked down McVeigh's friends and contacts, trying to ferret out any wider conspiracy that might have existed in the attack. What the agents didn't realize, until much later, was how much the McVeigh case would weigh on the men and women of the FBI's Buffalo office. It showed what could happen if one failed to pick up signs. They blamed themselves for not realizing someone buying huge amounts of fertilizer and plastic barrels was a threat. It showed just what was at stake. And it instilled a deep-seated fear that if one was not thorough enough, something awful could happen.

NICOLE FRICK, a pretty brunette and former cheerleader at Lackawanna High School, was reared a strict Catholic and came from solid Irish-Catholic stock. She celebrated Easter and Christmas. She fasted for Lent. She was the kind of Catholic who might not have gone to church every Sunday but did find time to go to Mass when the schedule allowed or her mother insisted. Her parents could not have been very happy when Nicole began dating Yassein Taher.

On the surface, Nicole and Yassein Taher looked as though they came from different worlds. Taher was a handsome boy, all dark hair and brown-eyed with skin that was a perfect matte olive-beige. Taher's family was devoutly Muslim. His family was from Yemen. Yassein, the youngest of the Taher children, was born in New York, and if anyone had asked, they would say he was more all-American than particularly Yemeni. He was a soccer player, a former western New York soccer all-star, and co-captain of the Lackawanna Steelers' varsity team. His uncles were well-liked youth soccer coaches. Yassein had played for them before lettering in the sport in high school.

The Taher children were reared with many rules that came straight from Yemen. They were not to date or drink (though like most teenagers, they managed to secretly do both). They fasted during Ramadan. And while they were not regulars at the mosque, Islam was a constant presence.

The non-Yemeni community in Lackawanna, where Taher came from, was far removed from the rest of town. It wasn't just that the Yemenis lived on the other side of the bridge that carried cars, literally and figuratively, across the tracks. They did not much like mixing with the locals. It was a conscious choice. And the feeling had become mutual. They had their culture, and the whites had theirs. Nicole and Yassein's long courtship—the high school soccer star and the cheerleader—flew in the face of all that.

That said, Nicole Frick's parents had a hard time not liking Taher. He seemed more white, for lack of a better description, than the other Yemenis they had come across in Lackawanna. And they weren't alone in thinking so. The 1996 graduating class of Lackawanna High School agreed. They voted Yassein Taher "friendliest." Perhaps Yassein worked to get along with everyone because his parents seemed to be so intent on their children fitting into their new home. For all the Islamic rules they enforced, the Tahers did allow a certain American laxness to creep into their lives. For example, they exchanged Christmas presents so the children, Taher and his sisters, wouldn't feel left out or different.

After high school, Taher followed the same route as most of his friends. He attended a local community college, found odd jobs to make ends meet, and lived with his parents in an apartment at the back of their two-story brick house. He found work at a collection agency at one time, pumped gas at a filling station at another. When Nicole became pregnant in 1998, and Taher was eighteen, he did what everyone expected he was going to do in any case: he married her. Shortly after the birth of their son, Noah, Nicole converted to Islam. An *imam* married them in the family living room. At the ceremony, the Tahers said things in Arabic that Nicole didn't understand and she recited some phrases in English. And it was done.

A short time later, for reasons people are still at pains to explain, Yassein Taher started going to the mosque every day, and Nicole Frick began feeling the effects of her conversion. Taher criticized her for watching television ("It didn't encourage clean thoughts . . .") or listening to music. He wanted her covered with an abaya. The twenty-fourth *sura* said women were to throw veils over their bosoms and display their ornaments only to their husbands. When they went to visit his high school friends, Nicole was no longer allowed to sit with the men. Instead, she was asked to stay in a separate room with the women.

"To a lot of this stuff I just said, 'No way,'" she said later. "It was so weird. I hung out with all of Yassein's friends all the way through high school, for three and a half years. I used to bake cakes for these guys. And now that I married Yassein, I have to be somewhere else? I didn't get it."

Taher's newfound devotion to Allah could have been stirred by the birth of Noah or linked to discussions he and Nicole had over whether Noah would be reared Catholic or Muslim. Whatever the trigger, Nicole was painfully aware, by 2000, that

Yassein Taher, voted "Friendliest" at Lackawanna High School, was changing. What began as visits to the mosque on Fridays became nightly prayer sessions. He took photographs off the walls at home, saying it was blasphemy to duplicate the image of a person God made. "Nothing alive is supposed to be represented in a picture," Nicole said, puzzled. "But, why, I wonder, can you have pictures or paintings of flowers on the wall? Aren't those things alive?"

For the sake of peace at home, however, Nicole did try to abide by Taher's new rules. She had a niggling sense that her husband was different, but it wasn't until much later that she understood who was behind the change.

———

IN HINDSIGHT, if there was something that should have tipped off the authorities to a changing sensibility in Lackawanna's Yemeni community, it should have been the bombing of the USS *Cole*. It had inspired an unusual reaction in the First Ward, a reaction that confirmed to the people on the other side of the tracks that the Arabians just saw things differently than the white community did. News of the attack was greeted with whoops and cheers. Residents of the First Ward saw it as the triumph of the little man, a just reprisal for America's arrogance. American troops in Saudi Arabia, so close to Mecca, were an affront. The attack on the *Cole*, a military target, seemed like a reasonable response—proof that America couldn't flex its muscles with impunity.

It wasn't an anti-American thing as much as an anti-military thing, they said. The *Cole* had no right to be in Yemen and was a legitimate military target for the followers of jihad to attack. They were merely defending their oppressed Islamic brethren. What the attack's supporters in Lackawanna failed to understand, though, was that no one had declared war. The USS *Cole* had gone to Aden in a spirit of friendship, in an attempt to forge closer ties with Yemen. The bombing was, in a very real sense, a sucker punch.

It was probably no coincidence that a month later, at the beginning of Ramadan 2000, a group of young men from the Lackawanna mosque had gathered in an apartment on Wilkesbarre Avenue to discuss Islam. It was more of a social gathering of like-minded men than a religious meeting. There was pizza and reading of *hadiths* and general discussion on being Muslim in America.

The one who seemed to be in charge of the group at 21 Wilkesbarre Avenue was a charismatic, bear-like bearded man named Kamel Derwish. Anyone entering the room when Derwish was speaking would naturally stop to listen. He had a way about him that was both winning and engaging. He came across as soft-spoken and passionate, but radical enough to be attractive to the young. He had given some sermons in the local mosque—calling on Muslims to come to the aid of their Muslim brothers at war—that had made Lackawanna's elders edgy. They asked him to take his speeches elsewhere. So he did, down the street to the apartment on Wilkesbarre Avenue.

Derwish had lived on and off in Lackawanna's First Ward since childhood. Born in South Buffalo's Mercy Hospital, he had left the United States and in the 1990s made the occasional trip back to Lackawanna, working at one point in a local plastics factory. He returned to town for good in 2000 and created quite a stir among the young men of the community when he arrived. He appeared with an air of mystery, carrying an intoxicating combination of worldliness and Islamic devotion. Derwish, twenty-three, was steeped in the Koran. He could quote passages at length. He exuded confidence. The young men in the First

Ward had no grand plans for their lives, but they all were look-ing for clarity, for what the Koran called the "straight path." And, Kamel Derwish, with his strong personality and his Islamic devotion, appeared to be offering it, or at least a version of it.

There was something charismatic about Derwish. He talked about going to Palestine as a guerilla fighter. He showed the young men videotapes about jihad in Bosnia. One tape con-tained an interview with Ibn al-Khattab, the mujahideen leader in Chechnya. Another film, called *Five of the Russians*, focused on Russian atrocities in Chechnya. Derwish spoke often about the atrocities leveled against Muslim women in Bosnia and the injustices visited upon the Palestinians by the Israelis. He de-rided the Clinton administration's support of Israel and groused about the millions of dollars sent from America to support Zionists.

When the bombing of the USS *Cole* came up in one of the late-night conversations on Wilkesbarre Avenue, Derwish said he was amazed that one bomb could do so much damage to a naval war ship. He told the group that he knew the men who had planned the attack. It wasn't an act of terrorism, he said. It was an act of defense. It was the obligation of all Muslims to be prepared to help other Muslims in need, he said, and the *Cole* was proof enough that America was vulnerable. A small group of men, working together, could get America's attention, he said.

"I want you to think about something," he said. "Are suicide bombings the right thing to do?" Taher immediately piped up. True jihad, he said, was only in Bosnia, Palestine, and Chech-nya, not in Yemen. Derwish pursed his lips.

"Is it?" he asked.

CHAPTER 3

THE SEARCH FOR CLARITY

FIVE TIMES A DAY, the call to prayer rings out in Lackawanna's First Ward. Residents emerge from their clapboard houses, pulling doors closed behind them. The men walk in bunches, ambling toward a small, one-story converted Russian Orthodox church that sits on the corner of Steelawanna and Wilkesbarre. The women glide along the streets in their black abaya robes, feet invisible as if they are floating just above the surface of the sidewalks. It is one of a handful of times each day when people outside the First Ward can see the Yemeni community in its entirety. The streets are a bustle of activity just before prayer. People melt from the houses like ghosts.

It was in watching this small army making its way to the mosque en masse, crunching through the snow in winter and splashing through the rain in spring, that it became clear to the white residents driving by that the Yemenis in Lackawanna were living in a different world, on the rim of American society. The telltale signs of Islam were sprinkled everywhere—women in *hijabs*, framed photographs of the twelve *imams* (identifying the household as Shia), and shops advertising in a mélange of languages, Arabic on one sign, English on another. The Yemenis in the First Ward may have been in western New York, but only physically. Mentally, spiritually, they were in

33

another place altogether. When the call to prayer rang out, they were transported to another time.

That's why people outside Lackawanna's First Ward referred to the more than one thousand Yemeni-Americans who lived there simply as "the Arabians." Residents of Lackawanna, the people who lived downtown in the ranch houses with manicured yards, saw the Yemenis as foreigners. Never mind that many of them were born in the United States. These people were different. They were as likely to greet each other with *Salaam aleikum* ("Peace be with you"), and a lengthy patter of formal Arabic, as they were a simple "hello." Before the September 11 attacks, the Yemenis in the First Ward only drew the interest of people like Ed Needham and other agents because they might be involved in illegal border trade. Otherwise, the Yemenis barely registered on their radar screens. It hardly mattered to the FBI that many residents of Lackawanna saw themselves as Muslims first, and Americans second. It took the 9/11 attacks to change the calculus: after that, how the Yemen community identified themselves became an issue.

The attacks seemed to give the residents outside the First Ward license to cluck about "how those people lived" and "those poor women" who shuffled around the streets of Lackawanna fully covered. Their dress was seen as a sad commentary on how their husbands sought to oppress them, rather than an indication of their piety. Parents who had groused quietly about the Yemeni youth soccer teams felt free to grumble aloud. Some coaches lied about players' ages, they said, so they could play older, more experienced boys against younger ones. The kind of soccer these young boys played, parents visiting the First Ward would mutter, was the dirty kind. The kindest parents said, "When those Arabians play soccer, wow, they are really aggressive." The more common response was, "They cheat. They play dirty. They just don't think the rules apply to them." The Yemeni sidelines during matches were different, too: the spectators were always men. The women were not allowed to watch. Soccer moms from visiting teams did little to mask their sense of outrage.

And it wasn't just the whites in Lackawanna who judged the Yemenis around them. There was a fierce animosity between the Arabians and the black population as well, a loathing that the black community did nothing to hide. People were at pains to explain where the bad blood began. Some said it was about corner stores and delis. Yemenis seemed to own all of them, and blacks were their customers. One side accused the other of price gouging. Those allegations were countered with claims of stealing. Whites said the conflict was more fundamental than that: the black community had traditionally been on the lowest rung of the economic ladder in Lackawanna. When the Yemenis arrived they were competing for the same ground. There was a sense between the two communities that if one group was down, the other was up. It set up an unhealthy competition.

———

FOR THE YEMENI students at the local high school, the job of navigating between their Muslim heritage and normal American teenage life wasn't always easy. Lackawanna High School, the "Home of the Steelers," sat in a field on Martin Drive just beyond the Father Baker orphanage homes. Students from the First Ward streamed to campus in the usual ways: buses and cars lined up on the drive. Others walked. The high school girls from the First Ward arrived at school early, wearing their black, shapeless abayas and hijabs. Standing outside the girls' bathroom, they would look both ways and then dart into the locker room to emerge minutes later transformed, wearing makeup and skin-tight jeans. After school, the black, shapeless dresses and head coverings were replaced. The makeup scrubbed away. And the girls would shuffle back to a wholly different world where they had little say or control.

The young men felt similarly apart. While their fathers got up at the crack of dawn to mop floors at the school or seal cheese into plastic bags, the boys were left to roam high school corridors where there were drugs and drinking and schoolmates making out between classes. It was unnerving. The kids of the First Ward would be exposed to a typical American high school all day and then return to a place where photographs were forbidden and where they were expected to drop their Western lives long enough to bow and pray toward Mecca five times a day. It was a constant struggle to avoid all of the American temptations that were laid out before them.

Perhaps that was part of the explanation for the tension and restlessness that permeated the First Ward. The young men there were unable to break free of the miseries that accompanied a town in decline, while at the same time they were unable to feel connected to a distant country and strict religion that nagged at them and worried their consciences wherever they went. The push and pull sapped all vitality from their lives. They found themselves looking for a way out: something—anything—to hold onto.

In that unhappy collision of poverty and culture, Kamel Derwish found an opening. Built like a linebacker, Derwish possessed those unteachable qualities of leadership that high school coaches look for in star players. Derwish was more Saudi in outlook than American. It was there that he adopted Wahabi-ism. He attended a *madrasa*. He memorized the Koran. He grew a beard. He wrestled with how the word of the Prophet fit into daily life. He feared God in private as well as in public. He became a very fervent Muslim.

His unannounced return to Lackawanna was like the homecoming of a favorite son. He was at once familiar and mysterious. What little English he knew had long been forgotten. He spoke to people in the community in Saudi-accented Arabic but could tell them things about themselves, little details recalled from his past time in Lackawanna. This only added to his mystic appeal. It is unclear what precisely brought Derwish back to Lackawanna, but what residents recall was that he was visibly upset about its decline. It was unclear whether by leaving at a young age he just remembered the good and not the bad, or whether Lackawanna had indeed gone downhill at such a slow and steady rate that people who had lived through the decline hadn't particularly noticed. For Derwish, the grimness of his old neighborhood was nothing less than shocking, and he thought, in his own way, he could save it. Derwish would say later that he saw Lackawanna as "virgin territory," full of rootless Muslims who were eager to change their circumstances. Derwish thought he could help them do that.

What people in Lackawanna didn't find out until much later was that Kamel Derwish understood his religious calling to be a profound obligation. He wanted to use it to confront the impurities and transgressions of the infidel West. No longer content to simply discuss Islam, Derwish had transformed himself from a naïve young boy into a man of action. Derwish moved in with his uncle and his cousin, who still had a house in the First Ward—and then eventually moved in with a friend, an unmarried man named Yahya Goba whom he had met at a pro-Palestinian rally in New York City years before. They shared his small apartment on Wilkesbarre Avenue.

Goba, twenty-four, just slightly older than Derwish, was a man wrestling with his own questions about balancing his life as an American Muslim. At five-feet-nine and nearly three hundred pounds, Goba didn't move around the First Ward so much as lumber through it. He made an impression when he moved down the street: he seemed big and powerful and bearlike. Children loved him. Parents respected him. Goba was born in Yonkers, New York, but had spent two years in Yemen on a family farm as a child. More than most of the young men in the First Ward, Goba straddled two worlds. He spoke fluent Arabic, but he graduated from Lackawanna High School. He wanted to live a pious Muslim life, but to earn a living he could not give himself completely to his religion. He found his life frustrating and constrained. By most conventional measures, he was defined by a succession of disappointments. He never went to college and was more often unemployed than employed. He managed to scare up odd jobs, but he was clearly too smart and too thoughtful to be pumping gas or doing construction. He taught Arabic to the teenagers and children in the neighborhood and was renowned for his deep grasp of the Koran. But Goba had never found a way to combine those strengths into something that would make the rest of his life more satisfying.

Goba's own malaise notwithstanding, parents in the First Ward saw him as a pious, intelligent man who convinced a number of young people to study Islam. They said he had a much more global vision than the twenty-somethings around him. He was more mature. They respected the fact that he was searching for an authoritative interpretation of the Koran that would identify where he, as a devout Muslim, fit in. Certainly, he had heard about jihad—how it was not just an external struggle, but an internal one as well—but he wasn't satisfied that he understood what that really meant. "How far does a man have to go to be a good Muslim?" he asked himself. "Is it a religious obligation to go to a far-off land to help your Muslim brothers, or is there something you could do short of fighting?" He was in the process of sorting through such questions when Derwish appeared. Derwish told Goba he'd help him establish his priorities. And he offered to help others, various young men in the ward struggling to be good Muslims, find their place as well.

It was easy for Derwish to attract the young men. With his stories, Derwish seemed like a modern-day swashbuckler. He talked of fighting in the hills of Bosnia and sleeping under the stars with fellow Muslims. He spoke with conviction that came with fulfilling a religious duty and a sense of purpose. The First Warders said later that he didn't just offer peace of mind, he seemed to promise something even more alluring: adventure.

———

FOR THE CATHOLICS of Lackawanna, the year 2001 began with the prospect that one of their own, Nelson H. Baker, might, at last, become a saint. Pope John Paul the Second had already named more saints than all his predecessors combined. He had cut the number of miracles required for sainthood from four to one for all martyrs and just two bona fide miracles for all others. Nelson Baker, Lackawanna's favorite son, seemed destined to fall into one of those saintly categories.

Aside from steel, Lackawanna's claim to fame had always been pinned to the inspirational story of "Father Baker." A Buffalo, New York, native, he served as a union soldier at Gettysburg and later ran a very successful feed and grain business. Feeling unfulfilled, Baker entered a Roman Catholic seminary and was ordained at the age of thirty-four. His first assignment was to turn around a small parish in Lackawanna called

St. Patrick's. He renamed it Our Lady of Victory. He used his
own personal grain fortune to retire the parish's debts and began to look for followers.

Baker saw great potential for his little parish. He started taking in orphaned boys decades before Father Edward Flannagan
of Boys Town started his Nebraska orphanage. He invented a
form of direct-mail solicitation to pay for his work. He sent his
fund-raising letters all over the country to housewives who sent
back envelopes with a dollar or two inside. Stories about Baker
took on mythic proportions. Once, apparently, he ordered the
drilling of a gas well where there was supposed to be no fuel.
Legend has it that he struck a rich deposit that still heats many
of the buildings on the Our Lady of Victory campus today. He
reared thousands of young boys at the orphanage and then
helped thousands more by building Saint John's Protectory and
Working Boys' Home, a residence for older charges. He followed
that up with the construction of schools and job-training programs so St. John's graduates could find jobs when they turned
eighteen. The young men came to be known as Baker Boys.

Before Father Baker, downtown Lackawanna on Ridge Road
was announced by a succession of unremarkable Catholic and
Protestant churches on the right and low brick buildings set
back from the road on the left. Visitors were struck right away
by the emptiness of it all. Father Baker changed all that once
he set about creating Our Lady of Victory Basilica that, Lackawanna's Catholic residents will tell you, is the city's crown
jewel. It was a scaled-down replica of Saint Paul's Basilica. It
looks out of place, almost odd, with all its gleaming white mar-
ble, Italian bronze doors, and pews of dark African mahogany.
The massive domed structure seems to have been parachuted
in from an alien—and much grander—world. The town's low-
slung buildings appear to cluster at the feet of the basilica,

almost in homage. It was finished in 1925. Baker died eleven years later, at the age of ninety-five.

Half a million people attended the 1936 funeral. Baker left a legacy. It wasn't just the basilica. The Our Lady of Victory charities replaced the steel industry as the largest employer in Lackawanna. They still are today. With a $30-million-a-year social services business, Baker had built an empire. And it was out of gratitude that the people of Lackawanna wanted the Vatican to make Father Baker a saint. To the Catholics of Lackawanna, frankly, he already was.

For years, the local papers had buzzed with news about Father Baker's possible elevation. There were front-page discussions about the church's requirements for sainthood. The *Buffalo News* reviewed the search for miracles to match the Vatican's "life of outstanding virtue" qualification, which most people believed was demonstratively in the bag. Monsignor Robert Wurtz, the pastor of Our Lady of Victory parish, was the man in charge of the quest for Baker's twenty-first-century sainthood. It was Wurtz who shipped three boxes of Baker's many written documents to the Vatican to testify to Baker's life of virtue. Church officials went over the papers and readily agreed that certainly Father Baker had led an exemplary life. Now, there was the niggling detail of a miracle. The Catholic Church lays out the criteria strictly: a miracle is an occurrence church officials deem completely unexplainable by natural means. A miracle isn't just curing the sick or myths passed along for generations. Instead, there needed to be something bigger. The Catholics of Lackawanna got what they needed in 1999. Father Baker's body was exhumed to move him to another grave site and medical officials claimed that sixty-three years after burial, Baker's blood was still fresh and liquid. Inexplicably, even miraculously so.

Under church rules, beatification is bestowed with one miracle. But a second occurrence had always been necessary to achieve the higher rank of saint. By the end of 2000, Monsignor Wurtz found himself talking to Vatican officials three times a week. The Vatican hinted that the miracle requirement might well be scrapped altogether, something that seemed like the answer to Lackawanna's prayers. By early January 2001, all Lackawannans could talk about was the prospect of this, finally, being Father Baker's year.

For some of Lackawanna's more craven residents this was about more than just giving credit where credit was due. There was a financial incentive to all this. Canonization of Father Baker, community leaders promised, would be a boon to this former steel town. The papers talked about lines of tourists and the placement of special parking lots for the overflow of buses. They talked about busy restaurants and shops with Father Baker, the Saint, key chains and commemorative plates. A brisk sale of snow globes with the basilica inside seemed entirely likely. It was all very exciting. But until the sainthood was official, there was only the waiting.

For the Muslims in the First Ward, all this focus on Father Baker was inexplicable, Catholicism run amok. The local preoccupation with the sainthood of one man only underscored the gulf between the Yemenis of the First Ward and the rest of town. As they saw it, this kind of idolatry of one man was misplaced. And while a goodly portion of the young men in Lackawanna's First Ward would go out of their way to blend in—they drank, they dated—one of their silent fears was that they might end up fitting in too well, that the Islamic part of them would eventually wink out and fade away. They were worried about waking up one morning to find out that they actually cared about

Father Baker's sainthood. The concern was real enough for Taher and al-Bakri and their friends to codify their difference, to put it on display. They took to referring to themselves in the late 1990s as the Arabian Knights. They weren't a gang. Instead, they preferred to think of themselves as a cultural clique of sorts. They made T-shirts and painted the name on the back of jackets as if it would help guard against an erosion of their heritage. Talking to Derwish after mosque was an extension of the same impulse. Many of the men of the First Ward found themselves being more religious than their fathers had ever been. They were, they would proudly declare, better Muslims than the generation that preceded them, and somehow that fact seemed to allay the general malaise they felt. Their ethnicity had become a faintly emabarassing condition for which they hoped Islam would somehow be the cure.

Derwish and Goba lived in a top floor apartment of a house that had been cut up into a number of bite-sized pieces in a neighborhood where a house in decent shape cost just thirty thousand dollars. There was a reason they were so inexpensive. Many of the houses looked as if they were struggling just to stay upright. Most had postage stamp–sized yards, or small weedy patches that looked like no one had sat in them for some time.

The first floor of the Wilkesbarre house was a storefront that had, alternately, been a local deli or food store. "Arabian Foods," the sign outside read.

The apartment was only a short walk from the mosque. There had always been an undercurrent of world affairs in the Lackawanna congregation. Often, it was driven by news from Yemen, some tidbit from the Internet, or news filtered out from a recent visit. Other times, the frontlines moved.

In the 1990s, the focus was on the wars in Bosnia. The congregation was following the news from Chechnya. And with every bulletin, one thing seemed clear: Muslims there were under siege. Islam's *ummah*, or community of believers, were waiting like desperadoes for the day of destruction when the greater powers—the infidels—would wipe them out. In Lackawanna, at night after prayers in the thickest darkness, the news of Muslims in peril sparked discussions about what could be done to help. Derwish told the young men that battles were never won by spectators.

As community centers in the neighborhood came and went, the mosque became a haven, a place of stability. Believers would go there to socialize and learn Arabic and study the Koran after daily prayers. It was during these times that some of the young men in Lackawanna began to realize that their parents were neither as wise about Islam nor as learned about the Koran as they had thought. The young men began to compare notes. They came to the conclusion that Derwish and Goba could explain Mohammed's words better than anyone they had ever met. Derwish's answers to their questions were quiet and confident. In their *halaqa*, or study circle, the young men talked about integrating faith and daily life. Derwish made it sound simple and logical. The groups of men who gathered after prayer to talk found themselves oddly comforted as they retreated into a stricter form of Islam, just as Derwish and Goba had predicted.

Some nights, more than two dozen young men would show up in the Wilkesbarre apartment to share pizza and religious conversation. They discussed politics and current events. And, as these types of groups do, the assembly winnowed down of its own accord. The constants were Derwish and Goba. Then a fixture in the community named Sahim Alwan began to show up.

Yassein Taher started haunting the apartment as did some of his old friends from high school, including a raft of twenty-somethings including Shafel Mosed, Faysal Galab, Jaber Elbaneh, and the young Mukhtar al-Bakri.

A quick snapshot of the men would have pegged them as more Yankee than Yemeni. Sahim Alwan was the son of a steelworker. He was clean-cut, relatively well-spoken, and was one of the few people in the ward who always wore a shirt and tie. He carried a cellphone on his hip and worked with disadvantaged youth at the Iroquois Job Corps Center in nearby Medina. Alwan was held up as a local success story: someone who graduated from Lackawanna High School, maintained a stable family life with three children, had a devout wife, and had a good job. He led Friday night prayer services and often lectured to the men at the mosque about various things, including the proper way to discipline children, always a popular subject with parents concerned about their Muslim children growing up in this Western world.

Shafel Mosed, born in Detroit, Michigan, moved to Lackawanna his junior year in high school when his father, an autoworker, had been transferred to the Ford Motor Company's stamping plant in Buffalo. His father died of a heart attack a short time later, leaving Mosed in charge of a difficult family. His mother had health problems, and he had three younger brothers and sisters to support. Mosed found a job as a telemarketer and started attending a local community college to study computers. Money at the Mosed household was always tight.

Faysal Galab was born in Lackawanna, graduated from Lackawanna High School, and had married a local girl. He was rearing his children in the very neighborhood where he had grown up. His father, James, had worked at Bethlehem Steel. Galab was an underemployed car salesman at a service station on Route 5, just outside of town. He started to hang out at Goba and Derwish's apartment in the evenings at Taher's invitation.

Jaber Elbaneh was born in Yemen and was married with seven children. He, too, had a spotty work history, however, when he began showing up at the Wilkesbarre apartment he was gainfully employed at a cheese factory in South Buffalo. Elbaneh was particularly taken with the evening sessions after mosque. He thought Derwish could help him straighten out his life. If one was looking for what held the group together it would have been an underlying desire to stay out of the house and to hang out with friends, not necessarily religion. In the Wilkesbarre apartment the men were given license to think about what might be, instead of what actually was. And besides, one said later, the pizza was usually free.

CHAPTER 4

"GOD REWARDS THOSE WHO FIGHT"

God has placed those who struggle with their goods and their persons on a higher level than those who stay at home. God has promised to reward all who believe but He rewards those who fight.

—*The Koran IV,* 95

A POPULAR JOKE IN YEMEN goes like this: God decides to return to earth and have an up-close look at how His creation is faring. He lands, first, in the United States. He tours Times Square and then alights on the Hollywood Hills. He throws His hands up in disgust. "This is not at all what I had in mind," He says. He decides to take a look at Europe, hoping for a happier result. Instead, He is again dismayed by what He sees. The pollution makes him cough. No one is in church. Scantily clad women on billboards are selling everything from beer to underwear. Then God goes to Yemen. He looks around, nods His head, and smiles broadly. "This is perfect," He said. "This is exactly the way I left it." Yemenis love to tell foreigners this joke.

Arriving in the old city of Sana'a, Yemen's 2,500-year-old capital, is like time travel. Just steps from the entrance of the old city, men are making sesame oil. A large mortar and pestle takes up the space of an entire room. A single camel circles the oversized big bowl, time and again, in slow, rhythmic steps. He is attached to the pestle, which grinds the sesame seeds to a pulp. Eventually, oil is emptied into gas can–like jugs stacked up for sale in the market. The old city is a maze of multistory houses that rise like eruptions of mud brick from the narrow cobbled streets. The houses look as though they are made of gingerbread: tall, boxy, baked-brick structures decorated with white lye paint that makes them look as though they have been painted with powdered-sugar frosting. There are scarcely any women in sight. When they do appear, they are generally students of the University of Sana'a on their way to class. They are fully covered. Long, shapeless abayas are worn over their clothes. A hijab on their heads allows only their eyes to show.

In Islam, Muslim women are required to cover themselves whenever they are outside their homes or in the presence of men to whom they are not related. Most people refer to the hijab as the headcovering Muslim women wear. Actually, it is more than a headscarf. Hijab refers to an entire way of dressing, behaving, and believing.

The word hijab comes from the Arabic root *h-j-b*, which means to hide from view or to conceal. The proper concealment for women covers the entire body, though the face and hands can be exposed. The clothing has to be long and loose-fitting so the shape of the woman can't be revealed. The headscarf must cover all of a woman's hair and be long enough to cover her ears, neck, and chest. The practice of hijab isn't mandated in the Koran. Instead, it comes from one of the hadiths, or traditions of Mohammed, and the practice is not meant to be oppressive. It is intended as protection, so women are not subjected to men's prying eyes or are able to tempt men in any way.

The men of Sana'a are dressed alike: sandals, white robes in various states of cleanliness, and Western-style suit blazers with the designer label still showing on the left sleeve above the cuff. It seems no one ever told them that those labels were meant to be removed. The uniform also includes a *jambiya*, a curved dagger worn from an ornate gold embroidered belt. For the Yemeni man, the jambiya is a natural accessory, like a watch might be in the West. The dagger is a visual reminder of Yemen's tribal culture. It has always been a country on the precipice of violence. Look up, and it seems that every hill has a fortress on its peak. Outside the main towns, the government has only a tenuous control. The tribes are largely autonomous and each possesses an enormous cache of weapons. There are some sixty million weapons in Yemen, according to government figures. That means in the countryside, there are three weapons for every man, woman, and child. As if to underscore the point, hand grenades are laid out alongside fresh produce in Sana'a's markets.

Roughly 40 percent of all Yemeni men are unemployed. So they spend most of their time lying on street corners, or sitting on stoops, cheeks bulging with laced *khat*. (It contains amphetamine-like substances.) Chewing khat is an important social activity, like drinking coffee in a café might be in Paris. Many homes have a special hot and stuffy room, called the *mafraj*, set aside just for chewing. Khat is an industry in Yemen. The average Yemeni spends a third of his income on the drug and can spend hours socializing with a golf-ball-sized wad of the branches stewing in his cheek. Because of this, there is a lot that doesn't get done in Yemen. The drug has such a following that it is often grown and supplied by criminal gangs. About three-quarters of Yemen's fertile land is used to grow khat. There isn't much fertile soil. So khat is elbowing out cash crops like tea and coffee.

Violence and khat dens aside, there is something unendingly charming about the Old City. Young boys who have picked up smatterings of English wait just inside the gates for tourists, who are few and far between these days. (Yemen is on the State Department's watch list.) The boys take the tourists to a museum of Yemeni art, past artisans who forge metal and wood locks and keys by hand or hammer dagger blades into shape. Yemen used to be the center of the world's spice trade. It controlled the frankincense route that ran from the Indian Ocean through Arabia and the Middle East to the Mediterranean. Frankincense and myrrh were both the most desirable and expensive incense materials in the Middle East at the time. They were used in temples, for rituals, mummification ceremonies, public festivals, and even for medicinal purposes. Up until the fifth century B.C., Yemen was the center for this kind of trade. Just as Lackawanna was synonomous with steel, Yemen was inextricably linked to the spice trade. Then alternate routes and alternate sources flourished.

Today, men sit in stalls at the markets, tending mounds of bright yellow saffron or pungent anise. Meat kabobs sizzle on makeshift grills. Old men throw rounds of dough into clay ovens. There is a certain Middle Eastern–otherworldly magic to the place. The big, open square in front of the Martyrs' Mosque is where the magic fades and Yemen poverty is on full display. The dispossessed lie on cardboard boxes flanked by gas cans filled with water. *Dabdabs*, minivans bursting with passengers, weave in and out of traffic, black smoke spewing from their tailpipes. The place has the sweet-and-sour smell of oil mixed with urine. The Martyrs' Mosque neighborhood is a reminder of how limited the future is. Because nearly half the population lives in poverty, it is no wonder men chose to leave. Certainly, a steel mill in Upstate New York at the turn of the twentieth century seemed to offer more prospects for the future than a life of khat chewing. Wandering the alleys of Yemen one can understand what drove family men halfway around the world to find work. And at the same time, one can understand what always beckons them back, why every couple of years families find the money for a visit.

Yemen is perhaps the least-known region in Arabia because it is so backward and difficult to visit. While it is said that Noah launched his ark from Yemen, it hasn't attracted many visitors. For centuries, control of Yemen was handed back and forth between expansionist powers—Abyssians, Persians, Egyptians, Portuguese, Ottomans—before the British arrived in the 1850s. The British never controlled much more than the area of southern Yemen around the port city of Aden (where most of Yemen's oil is found today). Central and northern Yemen was the land of local imams. When the British withdrew from South Yemen in 1967, its leadership turned to the Soviet Union, Cuba, and China for aid. In 1970, southern Yemen became the Arab world's first Communist state. The country was finally reunified early in 1990.

Many Yemenis who had traveled overseas to find their fortunes—many Lackawanna families from the First Ward—wanted to return to South Yemen after its reunification. There was a widespread belief that Sana'a, the nation's new capital, would experience a renaissance of sorts. Certainly, the end of the internal squabbles that had hobbled Yemen to that point would allow the nation to take its rightful place at the crossroads of Africa and the Middle East. But just as fathers in Lackawanna started making plans to bring their families back to Yemen, the first Gulf War broke out, and Yemen's fortunes faltered.

Yemen made the fateful decision of refusing to support the United Nations' sanctions against Iraq. Gulf neighbors were furious. Saudi Arabia expelled more than one million Yemeni emigrant workers and cut off aid to Yemen. The blow sent

Yemen's economy reeling. Making matters worse was the suspicion with which Americans came to view the country: it was seen as a breeding ground for terrorists in addition to being a Saddam Hussein apologist. The Yemeni government paid dearly for an enormous political miscalculation.

In Yemen, the roots of jihad go back as far as the seventh century when the Prophet Mohammed is said to have declared, "Allah, give me your fighters from behind me," and Mohammed's back was supposedly turned quite purposefully on Yemen. Modern history has managed to solidify this Yemeni sense of jihadist destiny. When the Soviets invaded Afghanistan, it was the Yemenis who emerged as the fiercest of the so-called Afghan-Arab fighters. Afghanistan's mountains were little different than the terrain the Yemenis had navigated their whole lives. While Saudi Arabia and America may have given money and arms to the mujahideen in Afghanistan, Yemen sacrificed its young. After the Soviets skulked out of Afghanistan, there were a raft of jihadists—now with combat training and a renewed religious fervor—with no war to fight and nowhere to go. Certainly the House of Saud was not eager to have these revolutionaries return to their country. Leaders of most other Arab countries shared their concern. North Yemen was the exception. It not only welcomed back the squads of young men who went to fight, it opened its borders to all comers. This is one of the reasons why today Yemen is seen as the terrorist capital of the world and why, for young men seeking adventure, the place holds an uncommon allure.

THE ISLAM PRACTICED in Lackawanna was more earnest than erudite. The elders of Lackawanna's Yemeni community were able to provide their offspring with only the generalities, not the concrete answers or unassailable truths about how Islam applied to their lives. Kamel Derwish offered an alternative and an authenticity they hadn't seen before. He added a heroic narrative to their understanding of Islam because he had been tested and was victorious in the battle against the infidels. The young Muslims of Lackawanna couldn't help feeling they ought to be part of that, too.

Derwish taught them how to reflect on the greatness of Allah and showed how to perform the daily supplications called *salat*. Derwish told them that true Muslims prayed at the mosque five times a day. He taught them how to wash properly before prayers. They spoke about what was *haram*, or forbidden, whether it was a girl in a short skirt or a bottle of beer. Islam isn't like Catholicism in that it lays out a simple outline of rules for behavior, such as the Ten Commandments. Instead, the Koran claims to be a reminder of things people already know intuitively. The Koran introduces topics with queries like "Hast thou not seen?" or "Have you not considered?" In Islam, the word of God is not so much thundering as it is beckoning. It encourages believers to test old Arab insights and traditions. Reciting the Koran is supposed to make Muslims more aware of their history. It does not provide an objective view of salvation. Muslims' prayers and study are supposed to be part of an effort to create something internally, to fight the evil within themselves. For many young men in Lackawanna, Derwish offered a way to do just that. He could help them erase their transgressions. He could remedy their ethnic confusion. He could show them how to be good Muslims in a Western world that seemed intent on tempting them and diverting them from God. What's more, Derwish didn't do this in a heavy-handed way. His touch was lighter.

Derwish and the men played a game they called "Spin the Bottle." The men would sit in a circle and spin an empty soft drink liter bottle. Players would then talk about the good and bad qualities of the person the bottle pointed to. This allowed Derwish to put the men's sins and shortcomings on display in a nonthreatening way. And because the assessments were made aloud, in front of the group, they carried more weight, and there was an incentive for the young men to change and show their friends they were trying to correct their faults.

In other sessions, Derwish had the men analyze passages of the Koran. He kept asking for their opinions about the wars in Bosnia and Chechnya. He asked telling questions, and was careful not to answer them: Why did it take America so long to act to save the Muslims in Bosnia? The young men eagerly joined in the conversation.

"Derwish joked around a lot, he was really friendly to everyone and everyone liked him," al-Bakri said later. "He was really easy to talk to. He didn't push the Islam talk on us. We'd be talking about Islam one minute and then challenging someone to some wrestling match the next. It wasn't, most of the time, this really politically charged thing. It was more easygoing than that."

For Yassein Taher, Derwish was the man who could help him make the transition to responsible adulthood. Derwish told Taher and the others who began to gather every evening in the apartment that if they had faith enough, Allah would become their invisible but constant companion. Allah could help them rise above the depression of the First Ward and the listlessness they felt.

Sahim Alwan, whose work at the Iroquois Job Corps meant that he tended to miss a lot of the evening meetings, came to the gatherings with a different mindset. He spoke Arabic. He understood the Koran. And he and Derwish often tangled over

Koranic interpretation. The other young men tended to look on when this happened. They didn't speak Arabic as well as Alwan did, and, while they were loathe to admit it, they were in no position to enter the discussion. What they did know was Alwan and perhaps Goba were the only ones among them who could question Derwish. And that made them slightly uncomfortable. In a sense, they preferred to have Derwish simply lay the information out before them, they preferred to be passive. It took less energy.

Though Derwish didn't speak much English, the force of his personality managed to keep bringing the young men of Lackawanna back to the apartment, night after night. They felt a vague pull of obligation. They felt guilty when they skipped a session.

Derwish, for his part, made Goba's apartment his pulpit, and it was from there that he spoke to groups of young men.

Occasionally, looking back on it, Derwish may have touched on those subjects people would come to recognize now as precursors to Islamic extremism, but people who attended the sessions said it was part of the flow of a wide-ranging conversation. Derwish took aim at Saudi Arabia, complaining about U.S. troops stationed there. He thought that it was an abomination that the American boys and girls sat in classrooms together at the local mosque school. He talked about a Muslim's duty to train for jihad. He told the young men that if they were not going to fight for their Muslim brothers themselves, the Koran instructed them to find those who would. He spoke with purpose, and in a town where aimlessness was the norm, that in itself made him unusual. To the young, unformed minds around him, Derwish appeared completely comfortable with himself and it appeared Islam was the reason. It presented a world where there were easily identified codes of right and wrong. Derwish was offering the men in the Wilkesbarre apartment a straight path, if only they had sense enough to take advantage of it.

Men at the evening meetings learned about an Egyptian named Sayyid Qutb. Radical movements, it seems, often start with a book. And Qutb's best-known work was a book called *Milestones*. It was a template for young radicals like Derwish. It taught them to cling to their Islamic identities to fortify themselves against encroaching Western culture, something that Qutb found evil. A former Ministry of Education official in the 1940s, Qutb was one of many young men in Egypt radicalized by the British occupation. He saw a great divide between Islam and the East, on one hand, and Christianity and the West, on the other. His distaste for the West only grew stronger after he received a government scholarship to study in America in 1948. He attended the Wilson Teachers College in Washington, DC, and the Colorado State College of Education in Greeley, Colorado, with a generous stipend from the Egyptian government. He immediately proclaimed America "primitive." He said his time in the United States reminded him of "the ages of jungles and caves." Cocktail party conversation around universities was frivolous and superficial, he reported. Americans were racist. He was aghast when he discovered separate entrances for whites and blacks at church. He was disgusted to discover that a Colorado park segregated Anglos from Hispanics. And, in a football town such as Greeley, he managed to isolate himself by developing a deep and visceral dislike of the game. "The foot does not play any role in the game," he complained. "Instead, each player attempts to take the ball in his hands, run with it or throw it to the goal, while the players on the other team hinder him by any means, including kicking in the stomach, or violently breaking his arms or legs . . ."

It would be safe to say that Qutb disliked everything about America. While it was clear from his writings that the people of Washington, DC, and Colorado did their best to make him feel welcome—they invited him to dine in their homes, and showed him every kindness—the harder the Americans tried to embrace him, the more he resented it. He disliked Americans' informality. He complained about the food. He found the college dancers scandalous. He resented the way Americans clapped their hands in time to music. In particular, Qutb seemed obsessed by the sexuality of women in the United States. America, as he saw it, in these golden years after the Second World War, was a bastion of sexual promiscuity. Women dressed provocatively, showing off their bosoms and wearing too much makeup in blatant efforts to tempt men. He hated television. He saw movies that only confirmed his belief that the United States was a spiritual wasteland.

Qutb returned to Cairo in the summer of 1950, convinced that America represented all that was wrong in the world. His books *The Shade of the Quran* and *Milestones* (*Ma'alim fi al-Tariq*), published nearly twenty years later, would become the lens through which Arab and Muslim readers saw the West, too. His words helped radicalize not just impressionable Muslims like Kamel Derwish but, most notably, Osama bin Laden.

Qutb preached that Muslims had to take their destiny into their own hands. They could reclaim the prominence of a bygone era by returning to Islam's unpolluted roots, to a time when God had the final word. Religion had to be the center of Muslim lives, the basis of their laws, the foundation of their government. Only then, Qutb said, could Muslims hope to return to greatness. His prescription was to reshape society by imposing Islamic values on every facet of life. *Sharia*, or Islamic, law had to be strictly adhered to.

One of the men who stood in the way of Qutb doing just that in Egypt was Gamal Abdul Nasser, the army colonel who sent King Farouk of Egypt packing and then seized control of the government. Nasser wanted a Middle East woven together with threads of pan-Arab socialism. He was convinced it would catapult Egypt from its ragged present to a bright, shining future in which the state would be responsible for the care and well-being of every Egyptian. Qutb, by now a leader in the Muslim Brotherhood, saw himself as a counterforce to Nasser's godless vision.

The Muslim Brotherhood had a history. It had not only provided a sustained resistance to the British occupation but at the same time was effective at community outreach. It created its own hospitals, factories, schools, and welfare system. Qutb and the fundamentalists who made up the Muslim Brotherhood eventually tried to assassinate Nasser in the fall of 1954, thinking they would stage an Islamic coup to return Egypt to its correct path. Instead, they bungled the killing. The Muslim Brotherhood leadership, including Qutb, was jailed. It was during his stint in prison that Qutb wrote his jihadist manifesto *Milestones* (*Ma'alim fi al-Tariq*). It was a galvanizing tract, first circulating underground and then finally getting published in 1964, though it was immediately banned. It was the Islamic world's own manifesto, in the likeness of Lenin's *What is to Be Done?*

"Mankind today is on the brink of a precipice," Qutb said at the opening of the book, revisiting his themes of materialism and absence of moral value. "At this crucial and bewildering juncture, the turn of Islam and the Muslim community has arrived."

Those kinds of fighting words led to Qutb's death. Nasser hanged him in 1966. "Thank God," Qutb said when his death sentence was announced. "I performed jihad for fifteen years until I earned this martyrdom."

The young men of Lackawanna who visited the apartment barely understood who Qutb was. They had never heard of him until Derwish introduced him. For Derwish, Qutb was an important component in his bid to shift their attitudes against America and to bring them to jihad. But they were completely unaware of it.

––––

THE WORD "JIHAD" comes from an Arabic root *j-h-d*, the basic meaning of which is striving or effort. In classical texts, its meaning is that of a struggle or a fight. It has been interpreted in a number of ways, including everything from trying to be a better person and helpful son or daughter to being involved in armed struggle. In the Koran, the word appears many times. In its early chapters, when the prophet led a minority group struggling against the pagan oligarchy, the connotation of the word was more about moral striving. In later chapters of the Koran, set in Medina, where the prophet headed the state and commanded its army, it had an unequivocal military meaning. According to Islamic law, it is lawful to wage war against four types of enemies: infidels, apostates, rebels, and bandits. In the terminology of jihad, brothers were meant to defeat the "near enemy"—the secularists in Muslim society—and then move on to the "distant enemy," namely the West. That's why for so long the primary targets of jihad were closer to home: Nasser's secular regime and the House of Saud, just to name two. America would appear in the crosshairs once jihadists felt their own region was in order.

For many Muslims, it wasn't what the United States represented—secularism, democracy, the mixing of the sexes, materialism—that rankled them. It was also a fundamental disagreement over its policies, most notably Israel. The Six-Day

War, in 1967, was a psychological turning point for many Muslims. Egypt's Nasser had demanded that UN peacekeepers leave the Sinai Peninsula, and then he blocked the Strait of Tiran to Israeli shipping. Israel responded with a preemptive attack that wiped out the Egyptian Air Force in two hours. Jordanian, Iraqi, and Syrian air defenses perished the same afternoon. In a matter of days, Israelis took control of the Sinai, Jerusalem, the West Bank, and the Golan Heights. The war humiliated Muslims. Islamic fundamentalists claimed it was their own fault. Muslims had turned their back on God, and God had responded in kind. A return to Islam in its purest form was the only solution, they said.

Muslims came to blame the United States, which backed the Israeli action, for their humiliation. They objected to Washington's unflinching support for conservative Sunni regimes across the Middle East. They groused about Saudi Arabia's unholy alliance with the States, begun on board the USS *Murphy* between Franklin Delano Roosevelt and King Saud, more than sixty years earlier, when the two men had agreed they could help each other: America could guarantee Saudi rule against all threats, and, in return, Americans could be assured of a stable supply of oil, developed and pumped by American companies. And there seemed, for a long time, little the man on the Arab street could do against such powerful forces. The tide began to turn in the 1970s.

Nasser died of a sudden heart attack in 1970, and Anwar al-Sadat, seeking to solidify his position among Muslim fundamentalists, cast himself as the "Believer President" and the "first man of Islam." He offered the Muslim Brotherhood and the fundamentalists who aligned themselves with them a deal: so long as they renounced violence and supported Sadat against those who supported Nasser, they could continue to preach and gather followers. He released Islamists from prison without realizing that they would soon turn on him as well.

Iran's 1978 revolution further emboldened the fundamentalist movement. When students helped topple the American-backed Shah of Iran, Mohammad Reza Pahlavi, it suggested that the United States' influence in the Middle East could be derailed with the right combination of grassroots support and religious faith. The Islamic hardliners who replaced the Shah were quick to give God credit for the win. Three years later, Islamists assassinated Sadat, who had recognized the state of Israel in 1977, becoming the first Arab leader to do so, as he presided over a military parade. His successor, Hosni Mubarak, cracked down on Islamists by jailing and torturing thousands of them. Those who managed to escape fled abroad. Many found solace in Afghanistan, which the Soviet Red Army had been occupying since its 1979 invasion. The Mubarak crackdown and the Soviet invasion provided Islamic fundamentalism with the boost it needed. Thousands who were leaning toward a purer form of Islam suddenly found themselves faced with a textbook opportunity for jihad—infidels had descended on Afghanistan and their Muslim brothers needed their help. If they joined the fight, the voices from the mosques told them, they would return to the roots of their faith. Arabs would rise again. God would return to their side.

IN LATE 2000, Kamel Derwish's tactics changed. He began criticizing the young men in Lackawanna's Yemeni community. He said they were bad Muslims. Yassein Taher remembered later that many of those goading conversations took place at a local BJ's Wholesale Club store. Derwish would chide him about his marriage to Nicole, and Noah's birth out of wedlock. He chastised Taher for drinking alcohol, going to bars, and sleeping with women who were not his wife. "You're going to have problems on Judgment Day," he told him as they strolled the aisles of bulk-buy paper towels and oversized cases of soft drinks. "You are the man in your family and you are responsible for your family. You are responsible for their faith."

In the same way, Derwish would pull al-Bakri aside and ask him about the transgressions of his life. Looking back on it, it was probably easier to convince al-Bakri that Islam was the answer to all his problems. He was young. He was seeking a simple solution that day-to-day life in Lackawanna hadn't provided. Alwan was a harder case. He had a steady job and was, in many respects, a mentor in his own right. He didn't need Derwish telling him right from wrong. He already recognized those distinctions.

In the end, however, what Derwish created was an uncompromising religious atmosphere among those who began to follow him in Lackawanna. And it had ripple effects: the men suddenly became harshly critical of their wives' American habits. People in Lackawanna said later that Derwish worked on making the young men in the First Ward feel ashamed for being "too American." He suggested they search for something that might cleanse them of that egregious flaw, something that would allow them to sacrifice and make amends for all they had done. "Your success with the help of God in guiding one man to the righteous path is better than possessing everything under the Sun," Derwish said, quoting the Koran. Later, while walking the aisle of BJ's, he offered more detail. He told Taher and the others to look at particular Web sites. "God has placed those who struggle with their goods and their persons on a higher level than those who stay at home," he told Taher one afternoon, quoting the Koran. "God has promised to reward all who believe, but He distinguishes those who fight."

Taher gave him a long look. In the back of his mind he could imagine himself in heroic situations in Chechnya or Bosnia. Anything, it seemed, would be better than where he was now: poor, unemployed, and without many prospects in Lackawanna.

———

THE JOINT TERRORISM TASK FORCE in Buffalo had no idea any of this was going on. While Ed Needham had been following leads about money transfers from individuals in Lackawanna to terror-linked groups in the Middle East, he was unware that the seeds of jihad were being planted just miles from his office. The men on Needham's radar were there for other crimes—cigarette smuggling, drug dealing, and credit card fraud—not for anything as ideologically pure or spiritually stimulating as jihad.

Needham and the Buffalo FBI didn't even know who Derwish was, much less what he was planning for the young men of Lackawanna. Had the FBI driven by the apartment on Wilkes-barre Avenue at night and peered into its windows, they would have seen a dozen men laughing and eating pizza. It was hardly something that merited further inspection.

CHAPTER 5

OF MULLAHS AND MADRASSAS

NO ONE IS QUITE SURE who brought up the subject of *madrassas*, or Islamic universities, during one of the evening study sessions on Wilkesbarre. It may have come up organically, just listening to Derwish hint at his travels around the Middle East. It may have been part of the discussion after Derwish suggested the men explore particular Web sites as part of their religious instruction. Or it could have been motivated by wanting to seem as religious as Derwish. In an evening gathering of young men, it was natural that competition would develop. Typically, the members of the group talked up their Islamic ambitions with bold statements intended to win Derwish's approval. Jaber Elbaneh and Goba, in particular, tended to compete for Derwish's attention. Some members of the group recall that madrassas were discussed in the fall of 2000; the subject came up in the context of how men of faith could study and get closer to God. In a shadowy, ungraspable way everyone in the room claimed to have thought about going to Yemen or Pakistan to improve their relationship with Allah. Then, Derwish asked whether any of them had ever seriously looked into the mechanics of going to Pakistan to attend a *madrasa*. It wasn't expensive, he explained, and it would do their souls good. Answers dripping with bravado rang out. What good Muslim wouldn't have looked into going? From there, the conversation naturally flowed once more toward the importance of jihad—madrassa teaching on steroids.

The madrassa's purpose is to spread Islam. The common misperception is that these schools are first and foremost terrorist training grounds. In fact, the religious schools have become a necessity in Pakistan, whose government spends just 1.8 percent of its Gross Domestic Product (GDP) on public schools. The result: 42 percent of the Pakistani population is literate (compared with 65 percent in India), and what few government schools do exist either don't have buildings or books or, in the case of nearly three-quarters of them, even electricity. Parents without means who want to improve their children's prospects have no choice but to place them in the madrassa system. The children might end up with a rigidly traditional education, but at least it is something. The poor in Pakistan will tell you that since the Pakistani government has failed to step up, they have had to look elsewhere for educational solutions. Islam provides many of them. And while parents know a small percentage of Pakistan's madrassas advocate violent jihad and even provide covert military training, it is the price many Pakistani parents are willing to pay in hopes of having children who might escape the most awful conditions of poverty.

Most madrassas are benign. They focus on how to wash correctly before prayers and the proper length of a beard and the teachings in the Koran—a more intensive version of what Derwish had started to instruct the young men of Lackawanna. Most madrassas don't discuss opposing non-Muslims in the West—which is the focus of global jihadists—or act as recruitment centers for al-Qaeda. Most al-Qaeda operatives aren't particularly religious, so madrassas, as a general rule, are not necessarily a good place to hunt for jihadists. And certainly those who turn to violence tend to be the poorer students, the ones who have just a perfunctory grasp of Islamic law. Osama bin Laden, for example, is considered deeply unorthodox. His followers routinely contest the authority of venerable clerics and seminaries, and he issues his own legal opinions or *fatwas* when he has neither the learning nor clerical authority to do so. So, the assumption that madrassas and Osama bin Laden work in concert is vastly exaggerated. Many of these schools are perfectly innocent.

Madrassa, in Arabic, literally means "places of study," and traditionally the madrassas have been a cornerstone of education in Islam involving the study and memorization of the Koran. They were a training ground to show students the way to live as Allah had intended. All this was done, historically, in an environment of general tolerance toward other religions. Allah was the same God that Christians and Jews recognized, so the feeling was that any differences were not fundamental. The tenor at the madrassas began to change, however, soon after the Soviet invasion of Afghanistan. That is when the United States, Saudi Arabia, and Pakistan began using the schools as a place to channel men displaced by the Soviet occupation. More than three million Afghanis fled to Pakistan. With the Pakistan school system unable to handle its own youth, the Islamic schools seemed like a good solution for the refugees. They provided free room and board and paid a monthly stipend to pupils so they could help support their families. The schools kept the Afghans occupied and offered the added benefit of being able to train reinforcements to fight the Soviets back home. It wasn't difficult to stir up these men. They were angry and nationalistic, and they saw the battle to oust the Soviets from their country not only as a national responsibility, but also as a religious duty. As such, the program was very effective. Mujahideen streamed across the border from the madrassas, driving toward the frontlines—and new students were constantly enrolling in schools in Pakistan.

No one thought to ask about what would happen next, or where the madrassa graduates would go once the Soviet occupation of Afghanistan ended. By the time the Soviets pulled out of Kabul in 1989, there were several thousand madrassas in Pakistan and tens of thousands of school boys who had graduated from its program. Nearly an entire generation came of age in a peculiar all-male world where the only concern was the Koran, sharia law, and the glorification of jihad. Many graduates ended up as key members of the Taliban regime and, as a consequence, when the Taliban army required reinforcements during the civil war that followed the Soviet pull-out, many madrassas cancelled classes and bussed their students across the border to fight. Not even the mullahs know how many madrassas Pakistan still has today. The government's latest guess is possibly more than twenty-seven thousand.

Taliban leaders still use madrassas in the border regions of Pakistan as meeting places and recruitment centers for soldiers. Pakistani security forces raided a madrasa in Karachi in September 2003 and brought in more than a dozen Indonesian and Malaysian students linked to al-Qaeda, including Rusman Gunawan, younger brother of the notorious al-Qaeda lieutenant Hambali. Gunawan remains in custody without charges under Pakistan's antiterror laws. More recently, thousands of young Afghan men have come to the Chaman district of Pakistan, directly across the border from the Taliban's stronghold in Kandahar. The suspicion is that they are attending madrassas while they await orders to join the fight against NATO and American forces there.

The turn of events shouldn't come as a surprise. Because so much of the madrassa curriculum is myopic, concentrating only on Koranic study, graduates leave knowing how to do principally two things: pray and fight. They don't learn history or math or computers, so they have no real-world skills. They are malcontents waiting to happen. But from half a world away, in Lackawanna, the idea of going to a madrasa sounded hugely romantic. It had a heroic ring. As young men in western New York sat on cushions on the floor they wondered who among them would be brave enough to become a recruit—to not just *talk* about being a good Muslim but actually *become* one.

When Taher came back from a Ramadan 2000 meeting, he brought up the idea of attending a madrasa with his wife, Nicole. As she prepared dinner, he tested out the notion of going away to become a better Muslim. "Maybe I should go to a madrasa in Pakistan," he told her, without looking up for a reaction. He kept an eye to the floor as he wrestled playfully with his son, Noah. Recently, the house had been eerily quiet. There had been a television there at one time, but Taher had come home one evening from prayers and forbidden it. There would be no music or pictures hanging on the walls, he declared on another occasion. He found them, he said, un-Islamic. Nicole, trying to be supportive, had allowed some of these changes to go on, though she grumbled about Taher's growing fundamentalism. This time, though, she was blunt. "You don't need to go to Pakistan," she told him matter-of-factly from the kitchen. "You can do that stuff right here. We need you here." Her tone did not leave a door open for discussion. Taher wasn't spoiling for a fight, so he kept silent. Nicole, for her part, thought the subject was closed.

THE ROAD TO SITE TOWN in western Karachi runs
through a succession of low-slung buildings known as *katchiabaadis*. They are temporary houses, cobbled together with
whatever residents might find that provides a semblance of shelter. They are the human equivalent of birds' nests, though instead of yarn or plastic straws and bits of paper, the homes are
messy piles of corrugated iron, cinder block, wood, and burlap.
In the summertime when the skies open up and pour buckets of
rain on the earth below, this part of the city tends to submerge.
The katchiabaadis literally droop, and everything—cars, buildings, people—goes dark with dampness and mud. Colorfully
covered motorcycle cabs buzz along the streets kicking up
rooster tails of water. Humidity adds to the oppressiveness. The
air is so moist that it actually seems to have weight. It is like
breathing through wet cotton. Half a million people live in Site
Town, ninety-nine percent of them are Muslim, and all of them
are poor.

The Jamia Binoria International madrasa sits like an oasis of
cleanliness amid the squalor. It is a twelve-acre complex of buildings secured behind solid metal gates and heavily armed guards
in the middle of Site Town. It is unclear whether the protection
is to keep the students in or the intruders out. To get to the
main office, one must go through a seemingly endless succession
of gates. Green grave flags flutter in the breeze around the campus. Wet clothes hang draped on lines from the rooftops and ve-
randas of concrete Mughal-looking dormitory blocks. The
school office sits on one of the upper floors. The leadership sit
on cushions, in a row, along the wall. They all have beards, skull-
caps, and clean white robes. And they all have white, push-
button phone receivers to their ears. They look as if they could

be busy running a call center for a large Fortune 500 corporation. Each bearded leader is stationed behind a low-slung table
where papers shuffle from surface to surface and small Pakistani
flags stand at attention on the desks.

Security cameras scan rooms from corner to corner, panning
from above all the doorways in the school's dozens of classrooms. Monitors show small, flickering black-and-white images
of what is going on throughout the campus. Every classroom is
equipped with a speakerphone so the leaders are able to contact
teachers and give direction from their remote perch. There is
something very Big Brother about it all. The Mufti were everywhere, always watching.

Jamia Binoria boasts that it has the largest contingent of foreign students of any madrassa in Pakistan. It claims to have students from the United States, France, the United Kingdom,
Philippines, Bangladesh, Canada, Malaysia, Thailand, China,
and Mozambique. Some twenty-three teachers provide instruction to as many as seven hundred pupils. "Special care is taken of
these students," the university brochure reads. "These students
are not used to hardship and giving sacrifice like the Pakistani
students. It is the teaching of Islam that people are to be treated
according to their temperament and status. Since these students
do not have much time, the duration of their course is cut to six
years."

Women have their own seminary. "It is imperative to equip
females today with the religious education because the first
school for a child is the lap of the mother," the brochure says.
"The female students who are getting religious education are not
only taught how to deal with the religious issues but they are
made aware of their responsibilities. The female students, thus,
prove themselves to be better mothers and better wives. They are
mentally trained not to follow the so-called modern ladies, but

to emulate herself (sic) according to the female companions in the time of the Holy Prophet."

For the equivalent of fifty dollars a month, the school provides special food, air-conditioned rooms, and a traditional Islamic education for their foreign charges. For the most part, Jamia Binoria is considered a moderate Sunni madrasa, though it espouses an extreme Wahabi and Deobandi school of thought, emphasizing strict Islamic or sharia law. It is one of the leading organizations in Pakistan that operates religious schools and has ten thousand students in nineteen branches, seventeen of which operate in Karachi alone. The other two schools are in Sindh. The school boasts about its department of fatwa where dozens of Islamic jurists are on call around the clock to provide religious guidance. People may ask for a religious ruling on any issue related to sharia law either by calling directly or sending an email. They call it their "online fatwa service." Those who graduate from this department, after two years of additional study, are given the equivalent to a Ph.D.

Terrorism experts and Pakistani intelligence officials say, privately, that the school has a connection to Osama bin Laden. Shortly before the 9/11 attacks, bin Laden addressed the Jamia Binoria student body and talked about the importance of jihad. The school's most famous graduate is Maulana Massod Azhar, the president of Jaish-e-Mohammed, or the Army of Mohammed, an offshoot of the Harkat-ul-Mujaheddin, a Pakistani organization that trains Muslims to fight against Indian forces in the disputed border regions of Kashmir. Azhar began his career as a journalist, editing the Harkat-ul-Mujaheddin's journal, and then went on to try to unify some of the major Islamic terrorist groups operating in Jammu and Kashmir in India under the banner of Harkat-ul-Ansar. The Indian police arrested him in 1994 for fomenting Islamic separatism in Kashmir but had to release him six years later when five extremists hijacked Indian Airlines Flight 814 from Katmandu to Kandahar on Christmas Eve in 1999. The hijackers killed one passenger and then eventually released the hostages in exchange for three Muslim prisoners, one of whom was Azhar.

The Jaish-e-Mohammed is still linked to Jamia Binoria today. The JeM was "banned" by the Pakistani government after its members were connected to suicide attacks in India, so today it is thought to be funded by Pakistani expatriates in Britain. The ban, intelligence officials say, has been toothless. Officials at the school deny any connection to "the sheik." The only problem is, this is something they volunteer, quickly, before anyone asks. They don't deny that Osama bin Laden addressed the students, only that the school has a link to him.

———

ALI AND MAHMOOD KHAN grew up in Atlanta, Georgia, and in the fall of 2006 have been at the Jamia Binoria for, according to fourteen-year-old Ali, "23 months, 3 weeks, and two days." The Khan father drives a cab, and their mother is a housewife. Both boys can't wait to go home. Ali, the eldest, is a good looking, lanky six-foot-tall teenager with loose limbs and an easy smile. His brother, only a year younger, is tiny by comparison. He looks like a ten-year-old. He is thirteen. "He stole all my milk," he says, smiling and hitching a thumb toward his brother. It is clear the two boys have found solidarity in traveling to such a far-off place to study the Koran. They used to fight all the time, one says, now they never do. Both have been to Mecca for the Haj.

"I thought Pakistan was going to be like Tampa Bay," Ali says. "I knew it would be hot, but I was thinking beaches and water. This place is nothing like Tampa Bay."

His younger brother scrunches up his face. "I figured it would be like Saudi, with lots of sand. It isn't really like that, either. But it is a lot more like Saudi Arabia than it is Tampa Bay."

The Khan boys' school day begins at 4 a.m. They wake up on thin mattresses on the floor of a room they share with a handful of other foreign students. The local students bully them, they say, because comparatively their living conditions are so good. Most Pakistani students sleep on the floor in a room they will share with dozens of other students. The Khans' air-conditioning is also something the Pakistani students do without. "A lot of people visit us in our rooms because of our air-conditioning," Ali says. After morning prayer, they have tea and bread for breakfast and then go to class. They spend most of the day reciting the Koran, chewing away at its 6,666 verses. For the average student, it takes about five years to memorize the Koran. Neither of the Khan boys speaks Arabic so, according to Ali Khan, "it is a little like asking a Russian guy to memorize something in Chinese." They now know the Arabic alphabet so they can sound out the words, but for them it is like learning a song by heart without ever actually understanding its meaning. It didn't occur to either of them that not understanding much of what they were reciting might take something away from the exercise of learning the Koran by heart.

"We didn't really have a choice on whether we wanted to come here," Ali says. "Whatever your dad tells you to do, you have to do. You have to respect your parents. If my dad wants me to go somewhere and never come back, I have to go there. If he wants me to marry a girl, I have to marry a girl. That's the way it works."

The Khan parents, the boys said, had always been very religious. Their father wore a prayer cap and *shalwar kemeez* at home. ("He isn't allowed to wear that stuff when he is driving a cab, they won't let him," Mahmood adds helpfully.) Their mother wears a burka, a covering that even conceals a woman's eyes, when she goes to do marketing in their Atlanta neighborhood.

The two brothers say they miss a lot about the United States: hot wings, eating anytime they want, and movies. The last two movies they saw before they left were *Mission Impossible* and the *Fast and the Furious*. They talked about both films with wistful reverence. Under their breath, they revealed that they had sneaked out of the madrasa a few weeks earlier, to celebrate Mahmood's birthday. They decided to go see an American movie. Once they had slipped outside the gates the only film they could find was *The Chronicles of Narnia*. They didn't know it was a Christian allegory or see any irony in the choice. All they said was that they wished they had found *The Fast and the Furious IV* instead.

Ejazullah, nineteen, is from Vancouver. A sweet boy with an easy way about him, he says he had come to Jamia Binoria to interpret the Koran and eventually spread Islam back in Canada. He says his family is also very religious. His mother was a manager at the National Bank of Canada, and his father had his own silk-screening business before they decided that they would be better off in a Muslim country. They moved to Pakistan to be closer to their son and to what they consider a purer way of life.

"My family all had an Islamic revival at about the same time," Ejazullah declares, with the cadence of an inner city kid. People have misunderstood madrassas, he said, though he had given up trying to explain why violence and madrassas did not go hand-in-hand. "If someone is banging on me that this is a bad place, I could give them every proof in the world and they still wouldn't believe me," he said. "If someone wants to be stubborn about a chicken having four legs you will never be able to convince them that a chicken has two legs." The four-legged chicken allusion, he admitted later, was something he had picked up in class at the madrasa.

He says that students who go to madrassas aren't violent because of their Islamic education. "The police and the psychologists will tell you they had a bad childhood, it is the parents' fault. There are a lot of reasons why a person would go to the extreme of violence. It is not Islam, they don't teach that in Islam. In Islam, Allah says if you kill one person it is as if you have killed all of humanity. What about the Texas Chainsaw Massacre and all that kind of stuff? They didn't come out of Islam."

Ismail, twenty-three, looks like a Muslim Elvis. He is dressed completely in black and wears dark wraparound sunglasses that he declines to remove. He has come to Jamia Binoria to learn the basics: reading the Koran, learning Urdu. "There are a lot of stereotypes about this religion," he says. "America and the media just see terrorism. You have to come here to find out for yourself what it is like."

The conventional wisdom is that those who join jihadi groups are poor and uneducated and come from the ranks of second-tier Islamic schools like Jamia Binoria. In fact, now they are more likely to be middle class and university educated.

Their average age is twenty six, most of them are married, and many have children. Recently, Islamic jihad has become a largely bourgeois enterprise. All the July 2005 British Muslim bombers attended universities; one drove a Mercedes.

The leaders of Jamia Binoria say they haven't seen any indication that their madrasa is breeding terrorists. Mufti Mohammed Naeem is a bearlike man with a long, graying beard and thick eyeglasses. He says madrassas are misunderstood. "We only teach Islam," he said. "We don't teach math or science, just Islam. We are teaching students to spread Allah's word. We have had tens of thousands of students enrolled in Jamia Binoria and none of our former or currently enrolled foreign students have anything to do with terrorist-related activities. We are moderate here."

It is hard not to notice that he equivocates and says "foreign students," stopping short of ruling out the jihadisation of any Jamia Binoria student. And while the school professes to be moderate in its teachings, saying so brings up a very basic question: What is a moderate Muslim? Someone who is not very serious about his religion? Or is it someone who is very serious about religion, but not very political about it? That would be the question that would tug at the hearts of the young men in Lackawanna. Eventually, Derwish would convince them that to be a good Muslim one had to be intensely political.

ABDUL KARIM would have been deemed a good, intensely political Muslim. He grew up in the slums of Moosa Colony in Karachi. Moosa is a largely Bangladeshi shanty town with narrow alleyways and open-air markets. The place is wet and smelly and full of flies. It is a south Asian slum out of central casting. Inhabitants look grim and tired. The meat on tables in the street smells of rot. And no one seems to be buying anything. For that reason, there is an underlying futility in the market's very existence. Karim, sixteen, was a Bangladeshi madrasa student who sold popadoms on the street. The second of five brothers, Karim was enrolled at the Jamia Khalilia madrasa in Moosa Colony, but his teachers said that in the two years he studied there he had done nothing to impress them. He was stubborn and not particularly interested in what the imam had to teach. He had the tendency to avoid schoolwork, and his first inclination when confronted with his poor work habits was to run away. He was truant from the madrasa more often than not. His father's reaction to his second son skipping school, apparently, was swift and predictable: he would beat him and drag him back to the madrasa, his neighbors in Moosa said. Then, on a July day, Karim disappeared. There were no calls. No excuses. After several days, he managed to get a message to his family that he was in Lahore.

July 14 began like any other day for Karim. He said his morning prayers and washed himself. Then he carefully pulled on some ragged clothes and smudged dirt on his face. He boarded a bus bound for Gulshan-e-Igbal town, a large residential neighborhood in western Karachi. He had a date with destiny. This bus was taking Karim all the way to Paradise. No one on the bus was likely to have noticed the teenager. Nothing about him was particularly remarkable. Even Karim's parents didn't realize that he had come under the spell of a visiting cleric at the madrasa, a man who had a remedy for Karim's lackluster academic performance, something that would prove that he was a better Muslim than any of his classmates could ever be.

Allama Hasan Turabi, the leader of Islami Tehrik, the main Shiite political party in Pakistan, was just stepping out of his car outside his home in Gulshan-e-Igbal when a young boy, a beggar, called out his name, hand extended. Turabi paused. He should have known better. Only three months earlier, a cart of oranges outside his home had been rigged with explosives. Two of his bodyguards and his son, Murtaza, died in the blast. Turabi claimed the United States was responsible for the attack. He couldn't believe it could be a Muslim force. He had spent so much of his time trying to unite Sunni and Shiite Muslims in Pakistan, he was sure he was loved by all of them. But, that day, Turabi's mind must have been on other things. So he paused and waited for the boy to approach him. Karim was wearing 2.5 kilograms of explosives in a special suicide-bomber jacket.

He took Turabi's hand and pulled the cord. There was nothing left of either of them when the smoke cleared. The blast was so ferocious, body parts were stuck to the second story of Turabi's house.

They found the suicide video days later in the apartment of a man known to train Pakistani suicide bombers. The message was stark. "After accomplishing my mission, I will go to Paradise," Karim told the camera. He waved a gun as he spoke. The camera caught a glimpse of the grenades strapped to his body. He had a bandana over his head. He asked his family to pray for him and told them that he would bring them to heaven with him. "No one is making me do this," he said. "This is an act of God." He called on his brother to follow in his martyrdom footsteps.

Days later, the Pakistani police arrested Mohammad Ashraf Qureshi in a predawn raid. "He has been targeting boys in madrassas, brainwashing them and turning them into suicide bombers," a senior police official said.

Karim's neighbors said he seemed like a nice enough boy, but he stood no chance against older men who came to indoctrinate poor teenagers like him on the virtues of jihad. "They tell them that they will go to Paradise if they die in Allah's way," said one neighbor who was too frightened to be further identified. "He was poor, and he found it easier to live in Paradise than in Moosa Colony. Who wouldn't?"

CHAPTER 6

THE CLOSER

JUMA AL-DOSARI was not an obvious choice for the role of the new imam at the Islamic Center in Bloomington, Indiana. He was young, and he didn't speak English well, but there was something about his demeanor that appealed to the leaders of the place. Just five-foot-five with a wispy beard, he was warm and made eye contact. He was energetic about his faith. And he was able to recite the entire Koran from memory, something that was in great demand during Ramadan when Muslims were supposed to recite the holy book in its entirety. The mosque elders also wanted to get more of the students from the university—Arabs, Africans, and Asians—to come to prayers regularly. The leaders remedied al-Dosari's language problem by having all his sermons translated.

Looking back on it, the mosque leaders should have realized there was something a bit odd about their new employee. While al-Dosari was gentle and some said almost sufilike, he was cagey about his background. He openly supported the Taliban and talked about the importance of Muslims standing up for other Muslims in battles around the world. But his comments, in the fall of 2000, were not of the kind that set off alarm bells. That would happen later.

In the spring of 2001, al-Dosari decided to do a national tour of sorts, visiting various Muslim communities and acting as guest speaker at local mosques. His first stop: Detroit, one of the country's largest Muslim communities. He stayed with friends there, and then he caught a bus to Dayton, Ohio, according to an FBI reconstruction of his movements. Al-Dosari made several unsuccessful attempts to enter Canada, and then returned to Bloomington only to catch a flight to Denver a short time later. It was when he was in Colorado that he received a phone call from a friend in upstate New York. That friend was Kamel Derwish. The FBI would later claim that the two had met on the battlefields of Bosnia and Chechnya where they had fought together as mujahideen in the 1990s. Al-Dosari would say the FBI had the wrong man. He never fought in Bosnia. He had merely gone to Bosnia in the 1990s to find a blonde, Muslim wife. He barely knew Derwish. The only reason he had come to Lackawanna, he said, was because Derwish said he could find a job or a Muslim wife there. Later, al-Dosari would say that it would be crazy for him to suddenly arrive in a strange place and expect to recruit a bunch of people in a mosque with a fiery speech about jihad. To this day, he denies he ever came to Lackawanna to recruit for al-Qaeda.

Whatever the reason, the phone call from Derwish was enough to prompt al-Dosari to fly back to Indiana and then get on a bus to Buffalo the very next day. Derwish picked him up at the station on Main Street and brought him to Lackawanna. He was the man the Lackawanna Six would later tell the FBI was "the Closer."

ASIDE FROM THE KORAN, the most widely read book in the terrorist world might well be a multivolume manual known as *Encyclopedia of Jihad*. It was written by a man named

Ali Abdelsoud Mohammed and co-authored and inspired, in some ways, by the U.S. Army. Mohammed was a martial arts expert, linguist, and former major in the Egyptian army who spoke flawless English, French, and Hebrew, as well as his native Arabic. In the early 1990s, he came to America as an interpreter for Ayman al-Zawahiri, the man who would emerge as al-Qaeda's second in command, who was on a short speaking tour of mosques in the United States. Al-Zawahiri immediately recognized Ali Mohammed's linguistic gifts and suggested he use them to more advantage: he ought to crack into the American intelligence services. Mohammed's first attempt to do so was anything but subtle. He simply presented himself to the CIA station chief in Cairo and offered his services. CIA operatives assumed he was a spy for Egyptian intelligence, but even so he managed to be signed as a junior intelligence officer for the United States in Hamburg, Germany.

Mohammed did little to hide his real intentions. He went on assignment to a Hezbollah mosque, marched up to the imam in charge, and told him that he was an American spy who was supposed to infiltrate the congregation. Unfortunately for Mohammed, an American spy had already infiltrated the mosque, heard his declaration, and reported him to his superiors. Mohammed's CIA career came to an abrupt end. Yet, by the time Mohammed was put on a watch list to be denied a visa for the United States, he was already in America creating a new life, this time in the U.S. Army. He married a California woman he had met on the airplane from Germany, became a citizen, and managed to get posted at the John F. Kennedy Special Warfare Center and School at Fort Bragg, North Carolina where he became a supply sergeant. His superiors had nothing but good words for him and were very supportive of his Muslim faith in that overly accommodating way people can have when they don't completely understand something. Mohammed still prayed five times a day and prepared his food in an Islamic way. The army encouraged him to start pursuing a doctorate in Islamic studies, and even asked him to teach a class on Middle Eastern politics and culture to help his fellow soldiers. He seemed like the perfect conscript. What no one realized was that Mohammed was quietly following through on al-Zawahiri's directive. Mohammed started sneaking maps and training manuals off the base and copying them at a local Kinko's. Those manuals would later become the basis for the *Encyclopedia of Jihad*—a terrorists' guide for everything from hand-to-hand combat to satellite surveillance. Even today, it is thought to be the al-Qaeda playbook.

The *Encyclopedia of Jihad* has eleven chapters and runs to several thousand pages. Key topics include making explosives; use of pistols, grenades, and mines; acts of sabotage; secure communication; brainwashing; reconnaissance; infiltration; the history and design of tanks; how to read maps; and the use of various weapons from artillery to machine guns. Originally, there had been only two dozen complete copies of the encyclopedia. Trainees in the camps were required to copy instructions from the text by dictation. The individual volumes bore an admonition not unlike those guests read in luxury hotels when they are tempted to steal the plush bathrobes. "In the name of God, the merciful, the compassionate, this is the property of the guesthouse," the inscription reads. "Please do not remove without permission!"

After 2001, when most of the al-Qaeda camps in Afghanistan had been destroyed by American bombing, al-Qaeda put the encyclopedia on the Internet, suddenly making available thousands of illustrated pages on bomb-building and how to organize terrorist cells—in Arabic—for everyone to read. An updated version included more instructions from the Arab mujahideen, adding tips they learned while fighting the Soviets in Afghanistan. Now it is impossible to determine who is responsible for ongoing revisions. There are some bits borrowed from Hamas, others from Algerian Islamists and insurgents in Iraq.

The encyclopedia is a very straightforward recourse for terrorist wannabes. It lays out how to select cars in a motorcade that are vulnerable to attack or how to shoot targets from the back of motorcycles. (The rider is to duck down when the angle is right; the shooter is sitting behind him with the firearm.) In the area of recruitment, the manual suggests filling the ranks with immigrants, the poor, fugitives, students, and gamblers. The usual incentives—money, love of adventure, and idealism—are still the best lures to bring in new followers, it says. The candidates are supposed to feel "constant security" when with the recruiter, and the recruiter is supposed to take on the role of a friend who admonishes and corrects behavior but does so "without cruelty." "Care about his family and ask about them often," the manual instructs. The best method of filling ranks is something called systematic recruiting, it says. It suggests hammering on a recruit's weak points and then evangelizing and essentially reprogramming him. "In recruiting, you must exploit the emotional angles," it reads. "Activate and encourage activity among social formations."

When it comes to recruitment, the *Encyclopedia of Jihad* leaves little to chance. The process is very precise. Recruiters are supposed to vet candidates in every detail, essentially opening up dossiers on their charges. The files are supposed to include an exhaustive physical description "from head to toe" of the candidate, a description of their habits and manners, an exhaustive investigation of their neighborhoods and travel history, "his life regimen and his reputation around town," his occupation and qualifications, income and financial resources, the roads he takes to go to work, the time he wakes up, the best times for covert searches and an inspection of his house.

None of this would have been very difficult for Derwish to do in Lackawanna. Nearly all the men he saw as candidates for his new, small army lived within a stone's throw of his apartment at Goba's house. Derwish seemed to be following the manual to the letter. He criticized the men about their half-hearted dedication to Islam; he befriended them, and he prepared them for their next step as religious warriors. Taher would say later that Derwish told stories about Afghanistan that made it sound like the land of milk and honey—the very place where lost men could be found.

———

IN THE SPRING OF 2001, Derwish introduced Juma al-Dosari to the Lackawanna congregation as an imam from Indiana. He was an old friend, he told the mosque elders, offering him up as a guest lecturer. As he expected, it didn't take much convincing to get the elders to agree. By this time, Derwish had melted into the First Ward community, establishing himself as a force for good. Many of the young men from the First Ward who were getting into trouble now seemed to have found a straighter path. They were becoming more religious, more responsible. And that all seemed to grow out of Derwish's mentoring and the time he took with them after evening prayers. Perhaps in the back of their minds, the leaders of the congregation thought the visiting imam could provide more of the same. So they welcomed the small bearded man in the white flowing robe and headdress as one of their own. They never anticipated what would happen next.

Al-Dosari began his talk, and it took some minutes for the congregation to realize that his entire discussion would be in Arabic, a language few of them understood. There was shuffling around the room as the younger men sought out the elders. The room was full of second- and third-generation Yemenis who hardly had an occasion to use their mother tongue. They understood only a smattering of what al-Dosari said. In order to follow his words more closely they had to cluster and bunch around the makeshift interpreters. A low murmuring rose up in the hall as al-Dosari spoke, and his words were quietly translated and whispered to the assembly. One could also hear, as al-Dosari began to talk about the responsibility of Muslims and the need to fight side-by-side with the oppressed, an uncomfortable shifting of limbs and rising nervousness. And as he admonished the group for leaving their Muslim brothers to fight by themselves in Kosovo, Chechnya, and Kashmir, a sense of collective guilt permeated the room. "You need to wake up, people are dying and you are doing nothing to stop it," one younger member of the congregation recalled him saying.

The leaders of the mosque were shocked. This was not the kind of sermon they permitted in the mosque, and they said later that they had no idea that the visiting imam would give such a speech. They saw him making *fitna*—a term for stirring up trouble that is set out in the Koran. If he was going to do that sort of thing, the elders said, he should do so in his own mosque. The Islamic Center in Lackawanna wasn't political, they told him, it was a place of worship. They asked him to leave the mosque. He was not welcome to preach there again. But when al-Dosari and Derwish left that evening, they hardly seemed chastised. Instead, they seemed oddly cheerful, like they had ignited something that needed lighting. Al-Dosari, for his part, said later that the speech might have been considered fiery by some standards, but it was really about the unjust ways of some of the Arab governments. He didn't talk about violence or American policy. His words were blown out of proportion.

As far as Derwish was concerned, however, al-Dosari's speech was precisely what he had hoped for. The words had intrigued the handful of the young men who had been in the Wilkesbarre Avenue apartment. They could hardly wait for the prayer service to finish so they could hurry over to Derwish's apartment and talk with the newcomer. They sat cross-legged on the floor and listened to the man Derwish presented as an expert on Islam tell tales about soldiering in Bosnia and Chechnya. He talked about Islam and what it had brought into his life; he spoke in such a heartfelt way it was as if they were eavesdropping on the whisperings of his soul. He told the assembled that Derwish had told him all about them, and he had bad news. He didn't think making a pilgrimage to Mecca would be enough to save their souls. They must also train for jihad. He was like a doctor providing a second opinion, but in this case his diagnosis was about their relationship with God. Taher and al-Bakri listened to Juma al-Dosari with rapt attention. Here was yet another learned Muslim telling them what they already felt to be true: if they wanted to be good Muslims they needed to do more. They needed to be men of action. Salim Alwan wasn't there that evening. Had he been, he might have injected his usual skepticism into the conversation. Instead, he had to work, and al-Dosari and Derwish were able to cast their spell.

Days later, Derwish and five men from the Wilkesbarre study sessions—Mukhtar al-Bakri, Yassein Taher, Yahya Goba, Shafel Mosed, Jaber Elbaneh, and Faysal Galab—had decided to take their faith to the next level. They would go to Afghanistan and train for jihad. In mid-April 2001, Derwish left Lackawanna and took his family to Yemen. He said he wouldn't be gone long and that while he was gone he would make the final arrangements for the others to meet him in Pakistan.

Sahim Alwan ended up driving Derwish to the airport. Derwish asked him if he wanted to join the others and travel to Afghanistan. Alwan said he would think about it. The next day, he told Goba he wanted to be included.

With that, Salim Alwan, Job Corps worker and father of three, became a last-minute addition to the trip. While he didn't want to be left out, he had a niggling feeling his decision was a mistake.

Goba quickly assumed the management role in the process. He held onto money and made travel arrangements. The five younger men started pulling together cash from relatives and friends, saying they were going to go study in Pakistan under the auspices of a group called Tablighi Jama'at. Tablighi Jama'at often comes up as a cover story for jihadists traveling to the Middle East. It is a well-known Islamic religious organization that seeks to spread the word of Allah, one believer at a time. The six told their families the journey would require them to be gone for three or four months.

The money for the trip came in that way money does when young people set their minds to something. Things were sold and the one thousand dollars needed for airfare came in fists of small bills, dribbling in over the course of weeks. Derwish, ever accommodating and wanting to help them become better Muslims, offered to provide some short-term loans for the trip. Once they were in Pakistan, he said, their expenses would be picked up. For the six, on offer was the adventure of a lifetime. Their bodies took over, and their brains dissolved themselves in adrenaline.

YASSEIN TAHER knew he was going to have trouble convincing his wife that he needed to go to Pakistan. The other men in the group either weren't married or, like Alwan, had more traditional wives who did not question decisions their husbands made. Nicole was, at heart, a down-to-earth Buffalo girl. While she had converted to Islam for Yassein, he knew she had done so to please him. She didn't think it was such a sacrifice to move from Catholicism to Islam. It was so important to Yassein, it seemed a small compromise to make for marital bliss. She didn't complain when they moved into the basement apartment of his mother's house, either. It was a traditional thing to do, and she did it because Yassein was so adamant about the arrangement. The conversion to Islam didn't fundamentally change who Nicole was, however. And she had already been complaining to Yassein about the amount of time he was spending in the Wilkesbarre apartment with Goba and his friends. She didn't feel he was pulling his weight around the house. He was leaving her to do all the rearing of Noah. So when Yassein raised the prospect, once again, of traveling to Pakistan to spread Islam, Nicole reiterated her refusal.

"No," she said firmly. "I don't want you to go."

Yassein started to protest. She hardly gave him time to start. "There are a lot of people spreading Islam in Pakistan, you don't need to go," she said firmly. "They need people to do it here, too. You can just stay here and do it."

The two began to argue. Yassein was upset that she wasn't a more dutiful Muslim wife. The other men who were going had wives who supported their decisions, he told her. And she was always giving him a hard time. He had made his decision, he said; he was going.

The two fought about the trip right up until the time Taher left that spring. Nicole was so angry she moved out of the basement apartment and found her own place, with Noah, south of Buffalo in Hamburg.

Taher shrugged off her intransigence and joined his friends for a shopping expedition at Galyan's Sporting Goods in Cheektowaga. They bought books, diarrhea medication, hiking boots, and flashlights. Elbaneh said he would put it all on his credit card and laughed. He declared he had no intention of returning home, so there would be no bill to pay. By the time he left for Afghanistan, he had racked up $145,000 in credit card debt.

FBI INVESTIGATORS said they had compiled a compelling narrative of Juma al-Dosari's life: He first joined with al-Qaeda at the age of sixteen, training at the Al Sadik training camp in Afghanistan. Six years later, they said, he surfaced in Zenica, Bosnia, where he spent time with the Muslim jihadi group known as *Kateebat*. A year later, al-Dosari appeared in the United Arab Emirates, and stayed with a friend who was planning to fight in the Chechen war. Together, the two traveled to Baku, Azerbaijan, a jumping-off point for fighters bound for the struggle against the Soviets in Chechnya. Al-Dosari was amassing what the FBI saw as quite a terrorist biography.

In mid-1996, al-Dosari was driving two companions through Saudi Arabia to Kuwait when he was arrested in connection with the Khobar Tower bombing. He was released by Kuwaiti authorities eleven days later and then was rearrested by the Saudis, again on suspicion of being an accessory in the Khobar bombing. This time, they held him for seven months. (In June 2001, U.S. authorities indicted thirteen Saudis and a Lebanese man for the bombing, which, the indictment said, was carried out by Hezbollah under orders from the government of Iran.) After his release from prison, the Ghaith Ibn Nassim Mosque in Damman, Saudi Arabia, hired al-Dosari as their new imam. Later that year, he was arrested again by the Saudis, but it is unclear why. The FBI said his passport had been revoked for five years, but in December of that year, he was granted dual Saudi-Bahrani citizenship, which allowed him to continue his travels with a new passport.

Al-Dosari came to America by chance. He met a man in Damman who had lived with relatives in Terre Haute, Indiana, and he told al-Dosari there was a job at the mosque next to the University of Indiana campus for which he'd be perfect. He was young. He was energetic. The man offered to make the introduction. In spite of his checkered past, al-Dosari got a five-year U.S. tourist visa and flew to Indianapolis and spent two months in the States. He didn't officially get the job in Bloomington until the fall of 2000. But in the spring of 2001, the FBI knew none of this. It was all put together after the fact and, as far as al-Dosari was concerned, was an elaborate FBI fabrication that parts company with the truth.

Al-Dosari maintains there was an innocent explanation for all of this, and that the FBI created its own narrative to make him look like something he was not. His trip to Afghanistan at the age of sixteen, he said, was not to train with al-Qaeda. Instead, he was part of a Saudi-sponsored field trip that, basically, had teenagers taking long weekends in Afghanistan soon after the Soviets had been routed. He said he shot an AK–47, but "half of the population of Saudi Arabia has shot the AK–47, does that make them all terrorists?" His trip to Bosnia was to find a blonde, Muslim wife, he said. At the time, he was grossly overweight, 260 pounds, even though he stood only five feet five inches tall, and he was, he said, in no condition to fight. He had stomach stapling surgery a short time later in Saudi Arabia.

Shortly after the Khobar Towers bombing, the Saudi jails were full of suspects, al-Dosari said. According to Saudi investigators at the time, Shias blew up the towers. There was a big difference, he said, between al-Qaeda and the Shias. "I'm not trying to defend al-Qaeda," he said. "They did other explosions. I just don't want this to be confused with al-Qaeda."

———

THE *ENCYCLOPEDIA OF JIHAD* gives precise instructions for new recruits. Use only nicknames, it counsels, never reveal your real name. Don't use alcoholic drinks "because they are weak points and a crime in the organizational legal system." "Train yourself not to get too stimulated or excited, no matter what the circumstances are, and don't get involved in people's daily affairs," it continues. "Don't show animosity toward anyone and try to win the biggest number of friends. Do not be talkative and speak too much for no reason. Remember the Prophet Mohammed said, 'To achieve your needs use secrecy.'" There were twenty-one points to remember in all, including not getting used to a daily routine when doing secret work, and the importance of revealing things only on a need-to-know basis. "If one of the members confessed with everything he knows, the danger would be limited. If he knows everything, he would uncover everything. The issue of knowledge is not a matter of trust or no trust, it is a matter of knowing only what is needed and nothing more," it reads. "When you leave the office, look in your pockets for any secret papers and leave them in a safe place in the office."

It is unclear whether the Lackawanna Six had committed all these rules to memory when the first wave left western New York—Mosed, Taher, and Galab—boarded Pakistan Airlines Flight 712 for Lahore on April 28, 2001. But they had already decided on aliases. Taher's was *Abu Noah*, father of Noah. Two weeks later, Goba, al-Bakri, Elbaneh, and Alwan were on a similar flight to Karachi. Their adventure had officially begun.

CHAPTER 7

"TAKE YOUR SOULS
IN YOUR HANDS"

R UDYARD KIPLING set the first short story he ever
wrote in the Old City of Lahore, in Pakistan. His story
"The Gate of the Hundred Sorrows," about a half-caste opium
addict living in an opium den near Lahore's Walled City, in Pun-
jab, was written when everything in South Asia was still new and
fresh to Kipling. He said later that the story of Gabral Misquitta,
an addict's chronicle six weeks before his death, was inspired by
late-night rambles down the unlit alleys of the old city. This was
the very jumble of brick and stone where Taher, Mosed, and
Galab wandered when they arrived in Lahore in April 2001.

The Sahara Hotel sits amid the dust and confusion of the alleys at the base of the Lahore Fort. The Lahore Fort, or Shahi
Qila, is a succession of stately palaces, halls, and gardens built
by Mughal emperors. It is thought to contain some of Lahore's
most ancient remains. The place has a slightly abandoned feel—
plants are overgrown, walls are crumbling, mosaics are gap-
toothed with tiles missing—which is odd given that it is in the
middle of a teeming Pakistani city.

It must have seemed otherworldly to young men from New
York State. To cross a street they would have had to dodge don-
key carts full of fruit, wave away vendors selling meat kebabs,

and skirt barbers brandishing straight razors from the shade of ramshackle wood and concrete storefronts. The Sahara was set back from the road beside shops selling tires and steel rims and metal bars. Kipling's 1880 Lahore was not too different from the one the young men from Lackawanna encountered. It was "dusty and red hot. You drink there for the liquid, not for the liquor, and the minute you drink it you feel it coming through your shirt," Kipling wrote. The ceiling fans swirling overhead at Kipling's offices at the *Civil and Military Gazette* did nothing but rustle the papers on his desk, he complained. But they were kept "ceaselessly going to prevent suffocation."

The Sahara Hotel is dark and gloomy. Its rooms are filled with damp, sticky air and steam-bath closeness. More of a dank rooming house than a hotel, it has the advantage of being near the Lahore Fort as well as the bus and train stations. The hotel is not a place people come to accidentally. Tourists do not venture into the neighborhood. It is in a part of town where people come only when they have to. It is dirty and smells of rotting food. And beggars, hoping for a quick cash settlement, are known to throw themselves against cars and claim they have been hit. The Sahara doesn't advertise rooms or even erect much of a sign; it is so tucked away you could spend all afternoon looking and never succeed in finding it.

All this is by design. The Sahara was part of a much larger, more complicated operation. It was part of a secret network of jihadi hotels, flop houses for the devout, usually run by men who sympathized with the Islamic cause. The hotel owners didn't fight so they felt compelled to aid those who did.

The jihadi hotel network helped young men find their way to the terrorist training camps in Afghanistan and the border regions of Pakistan. The Sahara, and dozens of hotels like it, served as hubs, holding would-be recruits in place while their minders slipped into Pakistan unnoticed and took their charges out again. The hotels were funded by al-Qaeda and other fundamentalist Islamic organizations. For that reason, room rates were either nonexistent or dirt cheap. The hotel managers would ask for the barest of identification. They would stack the young men like cordwood in the small, airless rooms, sleeping sometimes a dozen in a room that would have been cramped for a frugal couple on holiday. The hotel owners coordinated the flow of aspiring warriors. They would receive reports from across the border about vacancies at the camps or the need for particular recruits and provide what was needed. They arranged transportation so that the comings and goings of their guests were clandestine. This air of mystery only added to the Lackawanna boys' excitement. Dervish had given the young men a contact number to call when they arrived in Lahore. The contact had a single name, Marhajin. He was furtive on the phone. "Call back in a couple of days," he told them. "I will have everything set up by then." Taher called Nicole from a pay phone and told her not to worry: he had arrived safely in Pakistan.

Marhajin showed up two days later and gave the men tickets to fly to Quetta. All three tickets were booked under the name "Khan." The trio gave him fifty dollars. Marhajin instructed the men to take a cab to the Lahore airport. Once they arrived in Quetta, another contact would meet them there. It was all very James Bond-ish with code names and contacts and leaps of faith that someone would actually be there, when they arrived in one city, to direct them to the next.

Mukhtar al-Bakri, Sahim Alwan, Jaber Elbaneh, and Yahya Goba made up the second wave of Lackawanna travelers. They arrived just a week later at their own jihadi drop off, the Hotel Faran, near the Karachi airport. Given the choice between the Sahara and the Faran, one would have preferred to stay at the

Faran. From the outside, at least, it looked more like a tradi-tional hotel than its counterpart in Lahore. Four stories tall with small square windows, it was announced by a giant green neon sign on the roof and a single palm tree by its glass front doors. The tree was decorated with tiny Christmas lights year-round. The lobby, though, was poorly appointed and deserted. Rooms were not available for inspection. No vacancies were advertised. The front desk never asked about room preferences, smoking or nonsmoking. This was a place where guests were there for one purpose and, for that reason, tended to stay to themselves, up-stairs in the rooms, exchanging only minimal items of informa-tion that, if they followed the instructions of the *Encyclopedia of Jihad*, were false anyway. The four men from Lackawanna checked into the Hotel Faran on May 14, 2001, awaiting an es-cort to northern Pakistan and finally into Afghanistan. What they couldn't have known was that less than two weeks earlier, the Faran had hosted another rather infamous guest: Zacarias Moussaoui, the so-called twentieth 9/11 hijacker had stayed there for a week starting on May 2, 2001.

Karachi must have unfolded before them like a movie set. It is a city swarming with people. Streets are clogged with colorful buses, rattling motorcycle rickshaws, and families traveling with heaps of baggage tied to car rooftops. At every stoplight, young men hawk small songbirds beneath fragile red netting. The birds are trained to go, deceptively, with whomever purchases them streetside and then return, like homing pigeons, to their real masters at dusk. The scene must have been an intoxicating mixture of daunting and romantic. As the Lackawanna men lay on the floor of their hotel room among other young men all de-termined to become Muslim fighters, breathing in the sweet-and-sour smell of the bodies all around them, their hometown must have seemed very far away indeed.

Within days of the Lackawanna men's arrival in Karachi, Derwish himself appeared at the Hotel Faran, swinging open the door of the hotel room with fanfare and a huge, satisfied smile. There were hugs and back slaps and perhaps some nostalgia because in this place where nothing was familiar, Derwish's bearlike form was something they recognized. Derwish motioned them to sit down. Something very special was going to happen, he told them quietly. If all went according to plan, they were "going to meet the most wanted." Alwan and al-Bakri exchanged looks. They knew precisely what that meant. Derwish revealed the meeting flatly in a voice that made clear that any participation in a conversation about what was about to occur was unnecessary.

Back in the United States, word was filtering around the Bureau that al-Qaeda was planning another suicide mission. The new attack would come on U.S. soil, in major American cities, including New York. The informant told the FBI the attack would involve planes. The agents had reason to trust the veracity of the report. The source was a veteran Iranian agent who had been stationed in Afghanistan in the 1980s. While the informant couldn't go into the details of the plan—he didn't know exactly where or when the attacks would occur—the case officer took down the information. It is unclear whether the brief ever made it off his desk.

———

IN AFGHANISTAN, there are unbroken stretches of desert that run as far as the eye can see. The roads are largely deserted but for pickup trucks mounted with machine guns patrolling the roadways. In the nineteenth century, the British were intent on keeping Afghanistan as a buffer between British India and the armies of the czar. One of the major routes to Afghanistan lay through Balochistan, a vast, remote area run by seventeen major tribes, none of which are particularly fond of foreigners. The Brits spent more than forty years trying to subdue the area, and, in the end, decided that they should declare a truce. In 1876, the British entered into an agreement with the rulers of the larger tribes and princely states. In return for stationing troops along the roads and rail lines of the Afghan border, the British gave the tribes autonomy. The British set up a military cantonment in Quetta and left the rest of Balochistan to its own devices. During Partition in 1947, Balochistan asked for independence. The British refused. When the Balochis tried to declare independence, the Pakistani army moved in and crushed the insurrection. The Balochi were furious. They have yet to forgive.

Today, Balochistan is like America's Wild West. Tribal law rules here. Criminals are judged by their own people, and they accept the verdicts without question because of the loyalty they feel toward their *nawabs* and tribal leaders.

Those accused of crimes, for example, don't prove their innocence with alibis supported by relevant facts. They are more likely to be asked to "walk the fire," an age-old tribal ritual that allows God to separate the innocent from the guilty. The accused must walk barefoot along hot coals for some distance. If his feet don't blister, his accuser must pay him compensation and may never accuse him of the crime again. If the soles of his feet let him down, death or some other penalty could soon follow.

Al-Qaeda and Taliban members cross the Baloch mountain frontiers with impunity today, and some of the most renowned members of the jihadi movement come from these mountains and hills. Ramzi Ahmed Yousef, the man later convicted in the 1993 World Trade Center bombing, was from Balochistan. The area would have been written off long ago were it not so strategically important. It sits astride the oil fields of the Persian Gulf, where Pakistan, Iran, and Afghanistan all come together. Balochistan accounts for nearly all of Pakistan's coastline along the Arabian Sea. It has nearly half the land of Pakistan as a whole.

The capital of Balochistan is Quetta, just a few hours' drive from Kandahar. The air in Quetta is a soup of diesel smoke. The markets are packed with farmers and weavers and artists and butchers, and everywhere there is the tang of the illicit. It was in Quetta twenty years ago that the mujahideen first sold Stinger missiles to Iran. The Iranians consider the outpost so important to its efforts to monitor the insurgency along the Iranian-Balochistan border that they have stationed a diplomat there permanently. Quetta is where the Taliban is openly reassembling under Mullah Omar and his leadership council. Their resurgence against NATO troops is based here, too, amid an odd nostalgia for the jihad against the Russians. In the dusty, open-air markets, lying alongside grenades and rusted weapons, there are tapes and video discs romantically depicting past battles. There are video montages of masked fighters taking on Apache helicopters. Footage of American bombing is woven with images of crying children and Muslim victims. Foreigners have invaded our lands again, the message says. American or Russian, there is no difference.

Taher, Mosed, and Galab—the first group from Lack-awanna—arrived in Quetta in late April 2001. They were immediately whisked off to a guesthouse where they were given Afghani clothing and headscarves. They were told to hand over their passports and any money they had brought with them. Their contact, Abu, told them that the passports would be returned when they crossed into Afghanistan. Derwish told them this was standard procedure.

The border town of Spin Boldek, the last stop before Kandahar, is the Afghan equivalent of a truck stop. It is aggressively dusty. Container trucks cross the border into Afghanistan from here and kick up clouds of sand and dirt as they drive through town. There is the sound of grinding gears and oversized tires trying to find purchase on the roads. This is the kind of town where one stops only long enough to lick a postage stamp. The border guards are busy and distracted. Visitors stop once before the border to get an exit visa from Pakistan, drive forward one hundred feet, and stop again to get an entry stamp from Afghanistan. Taher, Mosed, and Galab were in Spin Boldek only long enough to use the bathroom and grab some roadside food and bottled drinks. Their guide returned their passports and they switched cars. They headed for Kandahar in an old Toyota station wagon.

All told, it took the trio more than a week to travel from Buffalo to Kandahar. They were led, with about a dozen other recruits, into another guesthouse for new arrivals. A black man at the front desk greeted them in broken English.

"Military experience?" he asked the young men.

They shook their heads.

"Police experience?" he continued.

They shook again.

Taher introduced himself. "I am Abu Noah," he said. The man asked for his passport, put it in an envelope, and scrawled his code name across the front. He told the Lackawanna recruits to extract a single set of clothes from their luggage. He handed them camp fatigues. The clothes looked like *shalwar kemeez*, a loose shirt and baggy trousers.

AL-BAKRI, GOBA, ALWAN, AND ELBANEH—the second group—were about a week behind the first wave of Lackawannans. Goba called Derwish at a prearranged contact number with a calling card he had bought at Sam's Club in Buffalo. The second group of Lackawanna recruits, he told him, was ready for the next leg of their trip. Derwish suggested that the men leave in two smaller groups so as not to arouse suspicion. So Goba and al-Bakri flew to Quetta first. They met a contact in a pickup truck at the airport and then went directly to a guesthouse on the outskirts of the city.

When the two Lackawanna men walked the streets of Quetta, the Taliban were everywhere. It would have been hard to tell, except for the border guards' presence, where Pakistan ended and Afghanistan began. It was not just the dun-colored houses set on dun-colored hills that faded into the afternoon light that suggested a blending of two cultures. It went deeper than that. Balochistan's northern border with Afghanistan had for all practical purposes disappeared with the Soviet invasion. Locals said the border between Pakistan and Afghanistan moved fifty miles south when the Soviets came in, and it has never gone back.

The next day, Goba and al-Bakri took separate taxis to the border. Once there, they met two other contacts who instructed them to mount two old motorcycles and go around the border check points. They disappeared into the gravelly dunes and treeless, mud-rock hills of southern Afghanistan, in late May.

Derwish, Elbaneh, and Alwan followed a day later and stayed at the Matafah Guesthouse in Quetta. Alwan asked where the name came from. Derwish explained it was named after one of the men who died in the bombing of the USS *Cole*. Alwan swallowed hard. The next morning the three men slipped across the border in the bed of a pickup truck bound for Kandahar. They said later that this all felt like more than they had bargained for. It felt dangerous and reckless and a little uncomfortable. But they felt they had no alternative but to press on.

———

IT IS HARD TO IMAGINE a bleaker or more rugged place
than the road to Kandahar. Everything, as far as the eye can see,
is the same shade of beige. The new recruits moved out at dusk
with their guides. They drove in silence up into the hills. Derwish sat contentedly in the back of the truck. Alwan and Elbaneh took it all in with some trepidation. The mujahideen who
picked them up looked like holy warriors out of central casting.
Their faces were ruddy and their beards unkempt. Their clothes
were dusty and their hands calloused and rough.

They drove past low, one-story makeshift homes that had a
sad, abandoned look. The hills were sprinkled with scrub and
covered in the kind of small, sharp gravel that always manages
to find its way into a hiking boot. The roads would periodi-
cally fall away without warning: solid under the tires one moment, then vanishing the next. Burned-out Soviet-era military
tanks and armored personnel carriers dotted the hills, sitting
beside the twisted, raw metal of trucks and jeeps that had either been blown up by rocket-propelled grenades or whose
drivers misjudged the roads and had become snarled on the
rocks below. There was something apocalyptic about the whole
scene.

Kandahar City is the homeland to the Pashtuns. The city lies
in a semiarid plain between Iran to the west and Kabul to the
north. The desert highways that traverse Kandahar used to
carry great caravans between India and Persia. It is a flat, dust-
caked city with nothing but buildings of mud-brown brick. The
Taliban have been a fixture here almost as long as anyone can
remember. *Taliban*, which can be translated either as students
of Islam or seekers of knowledge, were to the Pashtun villagers

around Kandahar as local Catholic priests might have been in the Irish countryside. They set up schools, led prayers, and were a part of day-to-day life. They would attend madrassas in Pakistan or Kabul and then return to a village school as a mullah, a giver of knowledge. Before they were associated with sharia law and Osama bin Laden and terrorism, the Taliban were a welcome part of the fabric of this frontier society.

A small motorcade of motorcycles and trucks stopped just outside the center of town. Uniformed men told the new recruits to line up. They stood before two low-slung guesthouses called, they would learn later, the Nibras Guesthouse and the Hassan Guesthouse. The men were told that, again, both houses took their names from the men who martyred themselves in the *Cole* attack. Sahim Alwan and his friends were directed to the older of the two buildings—Nibras—and given instructions. They were not permitted to leave for any reason. They had to stay at Nibras, eat there, drink there, and sleep there.

The operation appeared to be run by Arab Muslims, though the cooks, Alwan noticed, were Afghans. Recruits were forbidden to talk to anyone on staff, but could talk among themselves. There was a boot-camp feeling about the place. Passports, money, and valuables were once again collected, along with anything that might have hinted at identity. The men were told to wait for further instruction. It quickly became clear this was their last stop before entering the camps. Men who appeared to be in charge told the recruits there was an unexpected overflow of volunteers, so the newest group would stay in the guesthouses until there was room for them up at the training facility. Taher said later that the officials at the guesthouse greeted Derwish like he was Norm on *Cheers*. They clearly had met him before.

In one of the guesthouse sitting rooms, Alwan noticed a book ostensibly written by Osama bin Laden. He opened it up and leafed through it. On one page he saw a map of the Middle East and a number of American and British flags dotted along the coastlines. Alwan wasn't sure, but the flags seemed to represent American and British military bases. He skimmed the Arabic text. It focused on the concept of the snake and, as bin Laden saw it, the head of the snake was America. "So if you kill the head, then . . . ." Alwan found himself feeling queasy. Another section focused on how all Muslim governments were hypocritical because they didn't follow the examples of Islam. It was all a little more strident than Alwan had anticipated. He began to rethink the wisdom of being there, although, he told himself, now it was a little late. They had his money. They had his passport. They were in charge.

Whatever frivolous and adventurous atmosphere might have infected the trip to that point evaporated in Kandahar. Over meals at the guesthouse, the recruits would argue over martyrdom missions and interpretations of violence in the Koran. The Lackawanna men were dumbstruck. This was violent talk. The tenor of the conversations had taken a sinister and, to them, unexpected turn. The chatter in the guesthouse was not just about Russians and atrocities in Chechnya, but about America, its support of Israel, and its anti-Arab policies. The men gathered there were ranting, fueled by the fervor of the new revolutionary, who felt he had been called into action by injustice. The camps directed their passion, funneling it toward a common enemy. As the talk continued, it sounded increasingly as if the common enemy was America. The men from Lackawanna found themselves hunkering down.

That evening after prayers, leaders of the guesthouse gathered the men together in a common room for a movie presentation.

Dozens settled on the floor, sitting cross-legged in front of a large television and video recorder. Arabic music flooded the room and slow-motion images of the American destroyer, the USS *Cole*, came into focus. The camera panned the damage from the explosion, the house-sized hole in the hull. There was a montage of news clippings about the attack followed by film clips of the embassy bombings in Tanzania and Kenya. The tape cut to Indonesia and the abuse of Muslims there. Then Lebanon. Then Afghanistan. And, finally, Palestine. For the first time, it dawned on Alwan that this wasn't just a camp for holy warriors fighting the good fight shoulder-to-shoulder with other Muslims. There was a definite anti-American flavor to the proceedings. He wondered if anyone had guessed he was American. His guides had told him to say he was Canadian. The film ended with a video montage of prayer and explosions and the music and words of an Arabic chant of triumph. Alwan wondered what he had gotten himself into.

That began to become clearer two days later, when Osama bin Laden arrived, unexpectedly, at the guesthouse to meet the new arrivals. Bin Laden was standing when Alwan, Derwish, El-baneh, and two Saudi recruits walked in. They met in the guesthouse prayer area. A tall, imposing figure with a full black beard, bin Laden seemed otherworldly in his calmness, as if he were barely breathing. He nodded and smiled at Derwish. Then he shook each recruit's hand and sat down on some cushions on the floor. He nodded shyly in each man's direction. He asked, in Arabic, where they were from. Of course, the question was academic. No one was supposed to reveal their real names or where they came from. They had already been instructed not to provide that kind of information to anyone. One of the bolder men piped up. There was a rumor that something big was going to happen, he said quickly. Bin Laden considered the question quietly and spoke barely audibly. "They're threatening us," he said. "And we're threatening them. But there are brothers willing to carry their souls in their hands."

Alwan would say later that it was in that instant that he realized that he was doomed. The adventure, the game of playing jihadist, suddenly went to a level for which Alwan hadn't prepared. The next day, he took Elbaneh aside and whispered, "This stuff isn't right. Do you want to stay?"

The younger man looked surprised at Alwan's lack of commitment. "I want to be a martyr. I want to die," Elbaneh told him. Alwan looked at him with disbelief.

OSAMA BIN LADEN opened his first training facility in Afghanistan in 1986, modeling it on the camps run by Pakistani intelligence in Balochistan. Bin Laden wanted to teach young Arab jihadists how to use assault weapons, explosives, and detonators. He wanted them to listen to lectures about why they were bound, as Muslims, to fight. Bin Laden called his first camp "al-Ansar" or the Lion's Den. Dozens of other training facilities soon followed.

The *Encyclopedia of Jihad* has specific directions for setting up a camp. If it is military, it should be placed in a friendly location and should have many ways leading to it "for three kilometers." "It should have a secret exit for emergencies and for evacuation if attacked by the enemy. It should also have natural facilities to train for different situations." The camp needed to be equipped with air and land defenses, and guard posts should have alarms and be placed far enough from the camp that the facilities can be evacuated before the enemy reaches them. Each camp was to be equipped with a leadership tent or room, a location to pray, a kitchen, a place for lectures alongside sleeping tents and a water tent. A medical tent and a receiving tent, for visitors, should also be available, the manual says.

Rules for camp security included the necessity of passwords to gain entry, the use of nicknames instead of real ones when addressing members, uniform regulations, the importance of security people to accompany trainees at all times to monitor "their behavior, conversation, and ideas." Movement inside the camp was limited. "The shorter the training regimen, the better it is," the encyclopedia reads. "This happens through knowing the camp's goals and principles. It should not be more than 15 days, all attendees should be carefully documented, and most importantly no one should be allowed out except for the most extreme emergencies."

It was early morning when Taher, Mosed, and Galab climbed into a bus with a dozen other trainees to go to al-Farooq camp. The bus cut across trackless desert for about an hour before it came to a stop at the bottom of a dune. The group was told to gather their things and walk the rest of the way. Taher had brought what he thought he might need: a flashlight, a blanket, and new sneakers. The camp, Derwish had told them earlier, would provide the rest. The facility was announced by a sign that read "Al Farooq" and a green-and-black flag that bore the words "There is only one God and Mohammed is the Prophet." A line of old tires, cut in half like frowns, marked the path the men were supposed to take to the front gate.

More than a week later, Alwan, Elbaneh, al-Bakri, and twenty other men followed. They climbed into another bus and drove into the mountains west of Kandahar. The bus pulled up in front of a sandy hill, and the men were instructed to follow the path of tires to the entrance. The group waited for three days in tents outside the camp before they were permitted to enter.

What followed was a punishing routine. It began with daily prayers at 4 a.m., then exercises, weapons instruction, and lectures on the importance of patience when waging jihad. The curriculum followed the outline set out in the al-Qaeda manual. It began with dry-firing arms like Kalashnikovs and 9mm hand guns, and ended with a primer on basic military tactics. The recruits ate rice, beans, and past. At night, they bundled themselves in rough blankets and slept on the ground, four to five to a tent. Al-Bakri, for one, hated the routine. He had trouble waking up at 4 a.m., and the punishment for those who couldn't adapt to the hours was harsh. Trainers would pour a bucket of cold water on a recruit's groin. Clearly displeased with al-Bakri's progress, the trainers made him stay an extra week for remedial training. Al-Bakri started to think maybe he wasn't cut out to be a zealot.

Yassein Taher was having his own doubts. Things were not exactly as Derwish had advertised. Among other things, it was clear that the Taliban were not preparing to fight infidels. They were fighting the Northern Alliance—other Afghans—and that wasn't true jihad as far as Taher was concerned. The rigors of the camp also set his teeth on edge. It wasn't just the long days and the physical effort required by the exercises, it was the punishments for anything anyone did that might deviate from the schedule. Taher overslept one morning and missed prayer. His commanders punished him by making him carry stacks of bricks up a hill. It wasn't what he had signed up for.

Certainly, there were some exciting parts of the training. The recruits were trained on the mechanics, ballistics, maintenance, and care of a number of guns, most of which Taher had never seen before, much less held in his hand. While the weapon of choice was the Kalishnikov, the recruits also learned about the PK, the M16, the RPG grenade launcher, and the long rifle.

After the first day of Kalishnikov training, one of the trainees was able to get a translated copy of the weapons manual in English for the Lackawanna trainees, since they couldn't speak Arabic. That made it much more interesting for the young men, now that they could follow what was being said. Target practice was done on a shooting range. Recruits generally aimed for tires set up some distance away in the sand or black paper targets they had set up on pieces of wood.

There were lots of rules. Trainees were required to carry their Kalishnikovs at all times, like college football players who are given a ball and told they have to carry it twenty-four hours a day. Most of the time, there were no magazines or bullets to go with them. Ammunition was too scarce. Graduates of the weapons' training unit were then folded into the guard duty lineup. There were generally eight guards on duty at any one time: several at the front gate, another at the mosque, one at the ammunition storage area, another around the trainee tents, and two guards at the back entrance. Everyone standing guard had a loaded weapon. Guards were required to demand passwords before allowing passage. Training included having recruits try to break into the camp to test the guards' vigilance. To say that Taher and most of his friends began questioning the wisdom of their decision to come to Afghanistan just weeks after they arrived would be an understatement. After the trainers passed around a list for people to sign up for suicide missions, the men started gathering at night after prayers trying to find a way to get out. Taher was tired of drinking water from rusted cans, and the food had made him sick. He passed out one afternoon during prayers and threw up in the mosque. He was sent to the camp's infirmary in Kandahar City and woke up to find someone feeding him honey from a spoon. He stayed there for a week, convinced that he had contracted typhoid. When he returned to the camp with tales of better food at the clinic, Mosed responded the way any hungry young man would: he faked a leg injury. He tried to suppress a smile as he was, in turn, packed off into a car and driven in the direction of town. He was sure he was leaving his hundred sorrows behind him. Mosed stayed at the guesthouse for weeks until nearly the whole Lackawanna crew picked up and left Pakistan for good.

CHAPTER 8

SITTING DOWN
WITH THE SHEIKH

M ARC SAGEMAN, a former CIA case officer who served
as a liaison to the Afghan mujahideen in the late 1980s is
now one of America's best-known al-Qaeda specialists. He has
spent years chronicling the life histories of more than four hundred jihadists in order to ferret out patterns and common de-
nominators among them. Nearly all the recruits he interviewed
came from religiously moderate middle-class families. Many of
the men were married, had children, and enjoyed what would be
regarded as relatively stable home lives. While they had some
level of education, most often they were underemployed. In
short, their profile tracked closely with lives and circumstances
of the Lackawanna Six.

The common element wasn't poverty but alienation. The men
were frustrated: socially and religiously isolated, they had become noticeably more religious just before joining a jihad. In
many cases, some sort of personal crisis—the death of a loved
one or change in personal circumstances—helped pull them into
the radicalized camp. The biggest factor motivating those who
answered the call, Sageman found, was the bond of friendship.
Most recruits established a link to the jihadists through friends.
The push rarely came from recruiters like Kamel Derwish.

Instead, men joined up because their friends did. Sageman found that, typically, a group of friends developed an interest in jihad and then gravitated, together and en masse, toward radical clerics who could teach them more about it. They went to a mosque and met someone with jihad experience who helped them contact the right people for training. Almost seventy percent of those who joined jihad did so while away from home, Sageman found. He called them the "elite of their country." They had been sent abroad to study in the better schools in Germany, France, England, and the United States and became violent extremists during their sojourn.

It wasn't so much a question of good kids gone bad. It had more to do with how young men dealt with feeling left out, becoming separated from traditional bonds and culture. The would-be jihadists drifted to the mosques for companionship and found there an all-encompassing explanation for their feelings. The corruption of the West was to blame. They bought into the narrative and, Sageman said, "When you buy into something that seems to explain everything, you can soon be coaxed into doing almost anything."

———

THERE WERE THREE separate training facilities at al-Farooq: Basic, Anti-Aircraft, and Tactics. The Lackawanna men were in the Basic or *Taseesy* section of the camp. Kamel Derwish was in one of the advanced programs. He attended artillery fire and tactics' training while Alwan, Taher, al-Bakri, and the rest of the Lackawanna group labored through more remedial fare. Alwan wasn't the only one who felt that the camp was nothing like what Derwish had advertised. One afternoon, Taher cornered Derwish to discuss how he could leave. Taher said the recruits were not being prepared for real jihad, but were focused on Afghans fighting Afghans—Taliban versus Northern Alliance— and he wanted no part in a civil war. "I want to leave," Taher told Derwish, pointedly. Derwish, ever the negotiator, tried to calm him. Look, the training was only going to take two months, not four as Derwish had originally said. Taher just needed to be patient, he said. The next stop would be Kabul, and Kabul was much nicer than Kandahar. Training here was the hardest part of the trip, Derwish continued. The next phase would be much easier. The Kabul training focused on city warfare and how to make bombs, including suitcase bombs, and how to set them off. Derwish tried to make that sound exciting. Taher seemed unconvinced. Derwish tried another tack. He said he would have a chat with the trainers so they would let up on Taher. He really wanted Taher to stay, he said.

Yassein Taher was temporarily mollified. Derwish always had a way of convincing him to do things. Taher spent the next week in explosives' training and worked with TNT and grenades. The trainees learned about C4, petin, and plastic explosives. Instructors allowed the men to blow up an old Russian tank. There was an afternoon of Molotov cocktail instruction. The trainers broke up the men into groups of four or five to teach them how to use detonators and fuses. Each group was allowed to construct and ignite three TNT devices. It was much more fun than exercising in the heat and carrying bricks up a mountain.

While Derwish had managed to derail Taher's efforts to leave, temporarily, Derwish was unable to convince Sahim Alwan to be patient. Alwan decided he had had enough. He told the leader of the camp that he wanted out. One of his trainers said the only way he could leave was to have a talk with Derwish. Alwan said he wanted to see Derwish immediately. The advanced military training in which Derwish was engaged was going on in another part of the camp, the leader explained patiently, and trainees could only cross into that area on Fridays. Alwan would have to wait until then, the leader told him. Alwan cornered Derwish at the end of the week and told him that he was going home. Derwish listened to Alwan's concerns and then added one of his own. If Alwan left now, he said, leaders in the camp would think he was a spy. Stick it out a little longer, Derwish told him. Alwan reluctantly agreed.

Jihad had seemed theoretical when they had discussed coming to Afghanistan for jihad training in the Wilkesbarre Avenue apartment. It was something they could talk about, with bluster and bravado, without having to make good on their words. But now, as the men found themselves in the hills of southern Afghanistan, slumped at various degrees under the desert heat, the whole idea of becoming a Muslim holy warrior to atone for sins seemed crazy. Alwan, who signed up for the trip in a moment of weakness when Derwish asked him to come along during a ride to the airport, may have understood this more clearly than any of the others.

————

THE *ENCYCLOPEDIA OF JIHAD* had very precise instructions for protecting jihadi leaders from assassination. "There should be three cars that are similar in everything, except for the license plate," the manual begins. "Confirm the trust worthiness [sic] of the escorts and drivers and leak the news that the leader is in one of the three cars. Windows should be tinted and dark and the cars should be kept in a locked garage and entry has to be restricted. The cars should be guarded 24 hours a day. The principal rides in one of the cars and a two-second distance should be kept between the cars.

The speed of the cars should be determined and the recommended distance between the cars is 10 to 15 meters in normal situations."

———

THE SUN WAS SETTING on the camp when the trainers began gathering guns, disarming sentries, and tugging Kalishnikovs from the hands of recruits who were reluctant to give them up. They instructed their charges to cover their faces. There were going to be cameras filming, they said. All we want to see is your eyes.

Then, out of the desert, trailing sand and dust behind them, three four-wheel-drive Land Cruisers and four-door pickups raced up to the camp. Trainers in the hills and on the rooftop of the mosque began firing their weapons in the air as a celebratory greeting. Rocket-propelled grenades flew skyward. For many minutes, the noise of ammunition was deafening. The Lackawanna boys suppressed the urge to take cover and craned their necks to see who had arrived. The guards emerged first. Armed to the teeth, they fanned out around the vehicles. On top of their *shalwar kemeez*, they wore camouflage vests. Their faces were covered, though what caught the eye of the Lackawanna Six was the weaponry they carried. There were Kalishnikov and rocket-propelled grenades. There were long magazines of bullets and handguns. Bin Laden, Alwan whispered under his breath. Then, the sheikh emerged.

Bin Laden is protected by concentric circles of security: there is an outer ring of loyal villagers, a second ring of tribal leaders, and an inner ring of personal aides and bodyguards. It was this last group that emerged from the vehicles that afternoon. Bin Laden's bodyguards, officials say, are thought to include as many as five of his sons. It is said they would rather "martyr" their father than allow him to be taken alive. Alwan recalled seeing one particularly tall guard he assumed was a bin Laden.

Osama Bin Laden swung out of the car, bending almost double to squeeze his frame out of the small door opening. He was trailed by Ayman al-Zawahiri, the man who would emerge as his second in command. Born into a prominent middle-class family in a suburb of Cairo, Zawahiri was a leading organizer of radical Islamic jihadists in Egypt. He had fought, like bin Laden, in the Afghan resistance against the Soviet Union in the 1980s. The Lackawanna Six had never heard of al-Zawahiri and didn't recognize him. But the way he moved around bin Laden suggested he was someone important.

One of the trainers bowed to bin Laden, read a poem in Arabic the six did not understand, and then followed obsequiously in the sheik's wake as he made his way into the mosque. The al-Farooq students filed in after him. What the six didn't realize at the time was that they were witnessing history. Osama bin Laden had arrived at the camp to codify what terror analysts in America had long suspected: al-Qaeda and Zawahiri's Islamic Jihad had merged. As the trainees settled themselves around the mosque floor, bin Laden began to rant against Saudi Arabia, Israel, and the United States. The Saudis should never have allowed the Americans to station troops on their soil. The infidels were too close to Mecca, he continued. A guard behind bin Laden seemed unable to contain himself. "Down, down with Jews," he began to chant, trying to get the group to follow his lead.

Bin Laden talked about the new alliance he and Zawahiri had forged, stressing that Muslim brothers were required to train and fight the infidels as a united front. To that end, bin Laden and Zawahiri were no longer going to have competing organizations, he told the assembly. Instead, they would work as one, hand in glove. All told, the speech lasted about twenty minutes. It was entirely in Arabic. Bin Laden called on his charges to be patient in their battle against Israel and the United States. In the end, those on the side of Allah would triumph, bin Laden said. As if to prove his point, he mentioned that one of his former training camps had been hit by seventy-two American missiles. "Only a couple of chickens and camels died," he chuckled. Then he became somber: "Let the U.S. do it again, and we're going to hurt the Jews." Then he smiled calmly and called on the gathering to pray for forty martyrs who were en route for a very important mission.

While Taher didn't understand everything bin Laden said, he recalled later that bin Laden was hinting that there were forty men prepared to "take their souls in their hands" to carry out suicide bombing missions against the United States and Israel. Taher swallowed hard and exchanged glances with his friends. Alwan, in particular, looked shocked. The men were told to remain in the mosque while Osama bin Laden departed. He and his entourage left al-Farooq camp through the back gate, disappearing in their Toyotacade over the hill and into the desert. The Lackawanna Six were part of a small handful of Americans ever to have seen bin Laden in person. The meetings with the sheikh would come to haunt them.

———

ADDING TO THE SENSE of foreboding for the men from Lackawanna was the palpable sense in the camp that something big was brewing. It wasn't just the rumors of volunteers taking their souls in their hands or the buzz about imminent attacks against the infidels. The camp itself seemed to be on a high state of alert. The trainers and trainees were practicing evacuation drills. Hundreds of recruits would race to the gates at their commanders' signal and then sleep in the mountains until they were told it was safe to return. Derwish said that the leaders were bracing for bomb attacks from the United States.

That just added to Sahim Alwan's unease. It took him ten days to finally talk his way out of the camp. Taher would say later that Alwan was able to convince leaders to release him before the others because he could speak better Arabic than the rest of them. Taher, stumbling along in English, lacked such powers of persuasion. Day after day, he watched Alwan argue with camp leaders, and Taher was pretty sure he knew what it was about. Finally Alwan started favoring an ankle. He said he had hurt it in training.

"You're going home, aren't you?" Taher whispered to Alwan one afternoon.

Alwan nodded. Derwish didn't want anyone to know, so Alwan asked Taher not to tell the others. A car came to the camp once a week. Alwan would take it the next morning to return to the guesthouse and then, he hoped, he would soon be able to fly back home. He'd been gone, by that time, about five weeks. Taher's resolve to leave only strengthened. Alwan was right, Taher thought to himself, it was time for all of them to go.

For all the talk of how nimble al-Qaeda was as an operation, it was actually quite bureaucratic. It even had an employment contract that included vacation days and pay scales. The last page was devoted to a pledge, a 130-word promise meant to extract complete fidelity to bin Laden.

"I pledge by God's creed to become a Muslim soldier to support God's religion, and may God's word be most supreme," it reads. "I pledge to adhere to the holy book and Assuna and commit to the brothers committed with us in this mission so God is my witness. I vow by God's creed to obey those responsible in this mission, in thick and thin, and thereupon may God's word be most supreme. By supporting God's religion, I am a warrior in this mission regardless of my position, as long as the work is existing. I have to preserve the secrecy of the work in al-Qaeda, so God is my witness."

Below the pledge were five blanks for an alias, nationality, date, marital status, and a signature. It was unclear whether one was supposed to fill that all in truthfully.

"DO YOU WANT TO SEE THE SHEIKH?" one of the officials at the guesthouse asked Alwan when he arrived back from the camp.

Alwan shook his head. People usually had an audience with bin Laden when they were going to give a pledge to al-Qaeda, to become a full-fledged member. Alwan had no intention of doing that.

"Don't worry, he's not going to ask you for a pledge," the official said, reading his thoughts. "You're just going to see him. He knows you are going back."

When Alwan entered, Osama bin Laden was sitting on the floor. He stood up and shook Alwan's hand. "How are you doing, how are your brothers? Did you finish the training?"

Alwan shook his head.

"Why are you leaving?"

Alwan felt like he had to make an excuse. He left home very suddenly, he lied, and his family was worried, and he didn't know the training would take so long. "Maybe I'll come back," he offered helpfully.

Bin Laden said nothing for a long moment.

"You came through Pakistan? Do you need to clean your passport?"

Alwan said it was fine.

There was more silence from bin Laden. "How are Muslims there in America?" he asked.

"We have more freedom over there," Alwan offered. "We're free to practice our religion, and it is even better than some Muslim countries."

He gazed down.

"How are the youth?"

"They're good," Alwan said, not sure what the sheikh was getting at.

"What do they think of suicide operations?"

"We don't even think about it." Alwan blurted out. He was stunned by the question. He wanted to change the subject. He knew that wasn't the answer bin Laden wanted to hear.

"They keep saying something big is going to happen, that there are forty martyrs . . ."

Bin Laden was still for a long time, and then he smiled. He didn't answer.

"They told me I can leave tomorrow," Alwan ventured.

"May God make you successful," Osama bin Laden answered.

He stood up. And Alwan walked back into the sunshine. He ate with his guards that afternoon. They prayed together, and then he received his belongings, money, and passport.

"You're going to Karachi first, can you take these with you?" a man at the guesthouse asked Alwan. He was holding a stack of videotapes. Alwan agreed.

He left Kandahar the next day. For the first time in a long time, Sahim Alwan felt free. He dropped the video tapes off in Pakistan and headed home.

ALWAN'S DEPARTURE WAS the final straw for Taher, Mosed, Galab, and al-Bakri. The four felt that if Alwan was able to change his mind about training at al-Farooq, they should be able to as well. Derwish did his best to convince the four that their options were limited. Leaving the camp early would raise all kinds of questions, he told them. People would think that they were spies. It could be dangerous, he warned.

But by this time, clearly, Derwish had lost the power to convince his charges. Finally, he said he would speak with the leaders and try to get the Lackawanna boys on the next truck leaving the camp. If Derwish had hoped to raise his profile among al-Qaeda leaders by bringing a handful of passport-carrying Americans into the fold, the early departure of the group must have been a devastating blow to his credibility. Derwish was disappointed, but it was clear that all but one of them had their minds made up. Derwish had to find solace in the fact that he had successfully recruited one true believer: that was Jaber Elbaneh.

Taher, Mosed, and Galab had nowhere near the send-off Alwan had had. No one asked them if they wanted to see the sheikh. It could have been that, by then, Osama bin Laden knew why the lads were leaving. Or he may have left Kandahar altogether by that time, heading for the caves of Tora Bora. So without delay, Taher, Mosed, and Galab were handed their passports and their money and driven to Quetta. The trio were so eager to get away, they decided to take a bus to Karachi rather than wait for a plane to take them there the next day. Two days later, the three flew out of Karachi to the United States, leaving Derwish, Goba, al-Bakri, and Elbaneh behind. But for the three, they hoped their jihad adventure was over.

ANONYMOUS TIPS ARE a necessary and fundamental part of FBI work, and sorting through them, getting to the bottom of motivations and revenge reports and outright falsehoods, was part of the bread-and-butter of a field agent's work. Domestic surveillance was fraught with rules. It became a cause celebre during the Vietnam War when American intelligence agencies launched spying operations against protestors and civil rights activists. When the effort was exposed in the 1970s, Congress passed the Foreign Intelligence Surveillance Act (FISA) to safeguard against future abuses. FISA was supposed to impose strict limits on intelligence gathering on American soil. The law made it illegal for people gathering intelligence to share their information with those constructing criminal cases. In most instances, the separation was more of a nuisance than a hobbling factor for investigators. For Ed Needham, the wall between intelligence and criminal investigations became a nightmare.

Even today, Needham recalls vividly when his administrative assistant, Lisa, handed him a letter in early June of 2001. He immediately sensed when he opened it that it was important. The handwritten missive, two pages and unsigned, laid out a frightening scenario. "Two terrorists came to Lackawanna . . . for recruiting the Yemenite youth," it began. It gave the names of eight men who had gone to an al-Qaeda camp and four more who were waiting in the wings to follow them to Afghanistan. "I can not give you my name because I fear for my life," the letter ended. The letter wasn't signed. But the details it provided indicated it was from someone in the community and likely someone who had attended at least some of the sessions in the Wilkesbarre Avenue apartment.

Needham started running checks on the names in the letter. Many of the men had criminal records for cigarette smuggling and drug trafficking. He wondered if this could be a poison pen letter sent to cause trouble for a rival drug dealer. Maybe this had nothing to do with terrorism at all. On the face of it, it seemed far-fetched, men from Lackawanna traveling all the way to Afghanistan for jihad.

That said, the letter landed at the JTTF offices in Buffalo at an interesting juncture. It arrived just as intelligence agencies were picking up a lot of chatter that suggested a terrorist attack against America was in the works. The details were sketchy. It was unclear if it would be a strike on America itself or on American soft targets overseas. FBI officials were already investigating al-Qaeda camps and were seeking to track their graduating members. Needham reported his investigation up the chain and opened a case file. June 15, 2001, the day he opened the letter and started the Lackawanna investigation, would be the date he would keep going back to. Years later he would still say, "What would have happened if we never got that letter? Whoever sent it to us is a hero."

CHAPTER 9

"FOR MUSLIMS IN
THIS COUNTRY, IT IS OVER"

THE AMERICAN intelligence community estimates that
about seventy thousand recruits graduated from al-Qaeda
training camps in Afghanistan between 1989 and October 2001.
The numbers are misleading because al-Qaeda wasn't the only
terrorist organization taking advantage of the Taliban's hospital-
ity. Only about three percent of the people who went through
the camps, as the Lackawanna Six did, were recruited into the
actual al-Qaeda organization or were asked to sign on the dotted
line and offer fidelity to bin Laden. None of the Lackawanna Six
signed that pledge. Kamel Derwish told Goba that he had never
signed it because he didn't want to lock himself into being at bin
Laden's beck and call.

Those who did sign were asked to fill out an employment
contract. It began with a mission statement of sorts, defining the
aims of the group. Its goal was to "carry out jihad. Members of
al-Qaeda have gathered together with performing the different
duties of Islam as much as possible," the statement says. The organization's objective was to "support God's religion, establishment of Islamic rule, and the restoration of the Islamic
Caliphate, God willing."

Al-Qaeda was highly selective, and it was considered a high honor among jihadists to be accepted as a full member. Al-Qaeda specifically targeted men who have woken up from "their sleep" and returned to Allah, "regretting and repenting."

Duties, as laid out in the contract, for an al-Qaeda member included "preserving the unity of al-Qaeda" and the speed of Islam to others. "It starts with relatives and friends," the contract instructs. "You may not be able to do this, if your work demands extreme secrecy." In return for this devotion to jihad, al-Qaeda promised to do its part to keep its employees happy. Married members got a week's vacation for every three weeks worked, although al-Qaeda could, at its discretion, deny the vacation time for up to four months. Bachelors were given just five days a month for vacation. For all concerned, vacation travel requests had to be submitted two and a half months before the travel date.

Salaries for married members were 6500 Pakistani rupees ($107). They received 500 rupees ($8) a month for each newborn child. Bachelors made a fraction of what their married counterparts did. They got about $16 a month. Home leave for a bachelor included a roundtrip ticket after a year of membership. "Mujahideen won't get reimbursed if the ticket is not used," the contract reads. "But he has the right to change it to a ticket to perform the pilgrimage." Married members and their families qualified for roundtrip tickets to their country of origin after two years. "Anyone who leaves al-Qaeda without a legitimate excuse does not qualify for vacation or travel expenses," the contract warns primly, as if it protects al-Qaeda against future lawsuits from disgruntled employees who left without benefits.

According to the *Encyclopedia of Jihad*, signing the contract meant that recruits had fulfilled fourteen mandatory qualifications: knowledge of Islam, ideological commitment, maturity, self-sacrifice, discipline, secrecy and concealment of information, good health, patience, unflappability, intelligence and insight, caution and prudence, truthfulness and wisdom, the ability to observe and analyze, and the ability to act.

Most of the Lackawanna Six had an ill-formed or vague longing for the perfect faith—they were searching for something that would provide their aimless lives with direction. They clearly lacked knowledge of Islam, commitment, maturity, discipline, or patience—the qualifications the organization said it sought. What the Lackawanna Six had, which isn't listed but would have trumped most any other requirement, were American passports. That meant they could come and go from America with impunity, and for al-Qaeda, which was planning to strike the United States, a homegrown recruit was priceless. The Lackawanna Six had hoped to gain some respect, some sort of social recognition in return for their training. In the end, the prospect of that respect didn't outweigh the sacrifice of spending three months in the Afghan desert, even if it meant salary and vacation benefits. So they left.

Taher, Mosed, and Galab came back to the United States on June 27, 2001, just a week after Alwan and al-Bakri returned from Karachi. They were stopped at John F. Kennedy Airport. Detained for two hours, their bags were searched and immigration officials questioned them about where they had travelled and what they had been doing overseas. They were pulled aside for a simple reason: based on the letter he'd received months earlier, Ed Needham had put their names into the FBI's watch list. He wanted to know when they came back. Immigration held them for two hours and then released them.

Yahya Goba returned to his apartment on Wilkesbarre on August 2, 2001. Only one of the Lackawanna group did not return home. Jaber Elbaneh. The man who had told Alwan he was ready to martyr himself, if asked, had other plans.

The summer of 2001 was a tense one for the FBI. Rumors were everywhere. The so-called chatter, the message traffic between terrorist groups, had become a cacophony. Clearly something was afoot. It was unclear what it was. In hindsight, of course, the dots connected. On July 5, 2001, Richard Clarke, the national coordinator for counterterrorism, held a meeting with members of the Federal Aviation Administration, the Immigration and Naturalization Service, the FBI, and the Secret Service, among others, and issued a warning. He told them that something spectacular was going to happen. John O'Neill, Needham's old boss, was in Spain that day, addressing the Spanish Police Foundation. O'Neill had met only days earlier with Larry Silverstein, the president of Silverstein Properties, which had just taken over the management of the World Trade Center. Silverstein wanted O'Neill to be his new chief of security. O'Neill was considering the offer. What he didn't know was that two people who would also change his life, Mohammed Atta and Ramzi al-Shibh, also happened to be in Spain. They were at the coastal resort of Salou, going over the final details of the September 11 attacks.

THE LACKAWANNA SIX were among the last men to actually attend al-Farooq. The organization shuttered the training operations in August 2001, leaving little sign of the encampments that once dotted the Pakistan-Afghan border. After the fall of the Taliban, and with the United States on constant lookout for facilities, al-Qaeda largely abandoned its formal training track scheme. Suicide missions were easier to engineer. Driving a car into a convoy required a minimal logistical investment. Terrorist leaders just needed someone who could drive a car and press a button. The mass production of soldiers, the leadership concluded, was no longer required. Even if the Lackawanna Six had wanted to stay at al-Farooq for the entire basic training, they would have found themselves part of an old strategy, not the new one.

————

THE PHONE RANG in Nicole Taher's Hamburg apartment in August 2001. Her husband's sisters were on the line. "Come for coffee, Nicole," they cajoled. "We haven't seen you, we'd love to see you."

Nicole had been busy in her husband's absence. She was working double shifts and managing the difficult schedule and childcare needs of a young son. Driving over to Lackawanna to see her sisters-in-law didn't fit in.

"I've already had breakfast and I really don't want any coffee . . ." she began.

But the Taher girls were persistent. Nicole sighed and said she and Noah would be over in an hour.

Her husband was sitting on the couch when she walked in. She hadn't seen him in months, but there he was sitting in front her, grinning. Nicole couldn't decide how she felt. The man sitting there didn't look like the Yassein she remembered. This one had a long beard and looked disheveled and dirty.

"When was the last time you took a shower?" she asked incredulously.

Yassein just kept grinning at her.

It says a lot about Nicole Taher that she took her absent husband in after he returned from a trip to the Middle East that she had so vehemently opposed. She had been prepared, mentally, for their marriage to be over. And then he surprised her by staging a reunion.

In his absence, Nicole had written Yassein a letter every day. She had no place to send them, she didn't know where he was. Instead, she kept them all in a spiral notebook, awaiting the day when Yassein would return, and she could show it to him.

She made him read them all in one sitting.

———

ALWAN WENT RIGHT BACK to work when he returned from Pakistan. He had a sense that if he just acted as he had before somehow nothing would change, and no one would know what he had done or who he had seen. Then, he returned home one evening after work a week after his return from the Middle East to have his wife waiting at the door with a phone message. "Some man from Allstate called you," she said, handing him the number.

Alwan was confused. He was sure he didn't insure anything with Allstate, so he was perplexed about why one of its insurance agents would be calling him. Maybe it was a sales call, he thought. Maybe they wanted his business. Then he saw a familiar name scrawled in his wife's handwriting. It was an FBI agent he had helped some years earlier with the investigation of a fraud case. Alwan swallowed hard. Did they know?

"Thanks for calling me back, my name is Edward Needham, and I am with the FBI. I would like to meet with you for a cup of coffee, if you have the time," the first phone call between Needham and Sahim Alwan began.

Alwan readily agreed. He had always had an interest in police work. He studied criminal justice at a local community college and at one point, before he landed his Job Corps job, had worked in security for Blue Cross/Blue Shield. He had helped FBI agents with an investigation when he was at Blue

Cross, and he got a vicarious thrill from working with the agents. He even asked them how he might join up and become an agent, too.

Maybe Alwan had become a favorite son in Lackawanna's Yemen community because of his eagerness to please. He was affable and tended to tailor what he did or said to suit the audience immediately before him. If he was with his friends at the mosque, he was particularly devout. If he was at the Iroquois Job Corps building with young men, he was youthful and cool. And if he was with an agent, someone like Ed Needham, he found himself trying to find ways to appeal to him. So when he sat down in a local diner to have coffee with Ed Needham, Alwan was fighting opposing inclinations: part of him wanted to keep his trip to the camps secret, but another part was keen to tell Needham everything he knew.

The waitress set their coffee on the table, and Needham got right to the point. He said he knew that Alwan had just returned from overseas, and part of his responsibility with the JTTF was to determine threats to this country. He read through a list of names from the anonymous letter and, without providing the provenience of the information, said he knew Alwan had been in Pakistan. He wanted to know why.

Alwan smiled and looked relieved. "Oh that," he said, using the cover story that Derwish had concocted. "It was mostly a cultural thing. We went as part of Tablighi Jama'at." He talked about how he had gone to reacquaint himself with Islam, but in the end he came back early because he had to get back to work and he missed his family.

"You can get cheap Lasik surgery there, too," he added, helpfully. "So I was checking into that." He said he had stayed in the Faran Hotel in Karachi for a week but mostly stayed in local mosques because it was cheaper.

"Did you go to Afghanistan?" Needham asked.

Alwan shook his head. "Just Pakistan, doing cultural stuff."

Although it was clear to Needham that Alwan was holding something back—Alwan looked nervous, he couldn't hold eye contact, and he kept shifting his weight—Needham felt his story was broadly plausible. Alwan was a stable family man. He had a job, he had standing in the community. Certainly someone like him was hardly likely to train for jihad in Afghanistan.

Nicole had received a similarly cagey response from Taher when she asked him about what he had done in the Middle East.

He told her about Tablighi Jama'at and spreading Allah's word in Pakistan. He never mentioned going to Afghanistan or the camps.

"Where did you sleep?" she would ask.

"Sometimes I slept under the stars," he told her. In his mind, he wasn't lying.

———

YASSEIN TAHER was so deeply asleep the morning of September 11, 2001, that he had the sense he was recessed into the mattress. There was some commotion outside that roused him, but he was only dimly aware of garbled words as he began to literally drag himself, almost climb out, of sleep. The windows of his mother's clapboard house were wide open, taking advantage of the good sleeping weather, the cool nights, and bright days of western New York's Indian summer. The sky above the husks of the abandoned mills was piercing blue. A gentle breeze rattled the plastic Venetian blinds. Taher was dimly aware of someone telling him to turn on the television. Nicole was up and turned on the set before he had time to stir. Noah rubbing sleep from his eyes and sat in his father's lap as they watched the scene unfold. All the channels were broadcasting the same eerie picture: a slightly grainy image of smoke billowing out of the World Trade Center in New York. The headline banner on the screen was simple: Plane Crashes into World Trade Center in New York City. It was a little after 9 a.m.

"Someone must have accidentally flown a plane into the building," Nicole said, eyes glued to the screen. Taher didn't answer, though he felt his stomach start to sink.

The young couple settled themselves on the end of the bed, legs crossed beneath them and watched as the second plane hit Tower Two of the World Trade Center. Noah was just a toddler, but even he could sense something was very wrong. Then Taher did something that his wife will never forget: he quietly got up and without a word began drawing the shades, letting the string that held up the blinds slip through his fingers and then, almost in a single motion moving to the plastic wand that controlled the levelers, closing them tightly. Later it became clear that Taher was having a panic attack: a riot of atoms was making his head literally buzz. He moved away from the window, and he curled up in a ball on the floor. Nicole was incredulous.

"Are you crazy, what are you doing?" she asked, moving toward the window shades to open them.

"Muslims are going to be targeted now, can't you see?" he started to say from his crouched position.

Nicole gave a roll of her eyes that took her whole head with it. "Don't be ridiculous," she said.

"I am not being ridiculous," he answered firmly, sitting up on the floor. "For Muslims in this country, it is all over."

The rumors in the camp about an attack on America had come to pass, and Yassein Taher and five of his friends were among a handful of people who had known, in advance, that something was going to happen. They didn't know what it would be, of course. But as he watched the images of New York City burning, Yassein Taher was all but certain he was looking at the act of some of those forty martyrs willing to "take their soul into the hands." He had heard the words from the sheik's own lips when he stood in the camp outside Kandahar, and he had done nothing to stop it.

————

THAT SEPTEMBER MORNING, Ed Needham had scheduled his annual physical. There were some agents who fretted about those annual visits, but for Needham it was just another day. He ran. He exercised. And he was as fit now, at forty-five, as he had been at Father Baker High School where he had played football and lacrosse as a teenager. Needham was killing time with paperwork before his doctor's appointment when one of the special agents walked up and stopped before his desk. "A plane just crashed into the World Trade Center," he said evenly.

"My old boss just took a job there a couple of weeks ago," Needham responded, referring to John O'Neill.

A row of televisions were all switched on in the Buffalo headquarters' conference room known as the Buffalo Room—after a stuffed buffalo head that hangs on the wall there. A handful of agents stood around the room, eyes glued to TV screens. There was some talk of a Cessna flying into the tower by accident and speculation as to how that might have happened. The agents started their morning meeting, talking about the cases they were investigating, while keeping an eye on the televisions at the side of the room. When a second plane came roaring into the second tower, the room was momentarily stunned into silence. And then, moving with silent speed, the agents all disappeared, taking up positions around the FBI headquarters in case of attack.

"We looked at each other and knew the world had changed," Needham said later. His immediate thought as he headed down to the first floor of the FBI headquarters on South Elmwood was that this was the work of al-Qaeda. The big attack had happened. The reason for the chatter had finally come to pass.

Needham spent most of the rest of September 11 in a car, listening to the radio, hearing the message traffic from the agents who had set up a perimeter around the FBI building. For Needham, the events took on a special resonance given the work he had just started, digging into the travels of the Lackawanna Six. As Ed Needham listened on the radio and the Tahers watched on their television set ten thousand gallons of jet fuel on the plane had carried did its damage. It softened the steel frame of the tower and then started off a chain reaction of buckling glass and collapsing walls. Needham only heard it, on the radio, as it was happening. Taher and Nicole watched the collapse live on television, gasping when the first tower literally melted from the sky, as if someone had taken an enormous eraser and rubbed it from the Manhattan skyline. Needham found out the next day O'Neill, the man who had set up the bid Laden unit at the FBI, had died in the attack. Bin Laden had gotten him, before he managed to get bin Laden.

———

SAHIM ALWAN had the television set at work tuned to CNN. He listened as experts started to finger al-Qaeda for the attacks. Alwan felt ill. He told his supervisor he would need to go home early. Once outside, he decided he would pick up his children at school. His thoughts mirrored those of Taher: It wasn't safe to be a Muslim right now. He went to the Islamic center in the First Ward to pray. That afternoon, a *Buffalo News* reporter happened to interview him outside the Lackawanna Mosque. Alwan provided a reassuring response. "The Koran says one of the greatest sins in our religion is to commit suicide," he told the reporter. "The Prophet Muhammad says, 'Let he who kills himself know he is in the deepest hellfire.'" Shortly after Alwan gave the newspaper interview, the phone rang on Needham's desk.

"Ed, I know you're busy," Alwan began, "but whatever you need, whatever it is, assistance, just tell me what I can do."

Needham said later that he thought Alwan called to assuage his conscience and to bolster his cover, to look like he had nothing to hide and wanted to help. Alwan had heard in the camp about the martyrs willing to take their souls in their hands. Of course, he didn't know where or when the attack would come, but now that the attack had happened he felt an old sense of responsibility, a culpability by association. He kept all this to himself as he stumbled through a conversation with Needham. Needham told him to keep his eyes and ears open. "Has anyone new come into town?" Needham asked.

Alwan said no one had. He promised Needham he would keep his eyes peeled. While the phone call was meant as a gesture, a reassurance that not all Muslims sided with Osama bin Laden, Alwan had once again told a half truth. In fact, someone not entirely new had just returned to Lackawanna, and Alwan knew it. Juma al-Dosari, the so-called Closer, was back in Lackawanna and staying in the apartment on Wilkesbarre Avenue. He was hanging around some of the young men in the First Ward. There had been talk of another group of travelers going to Afghanistan, but September 11 derailed the trip. Instead, the chain of al-Qaeda camps along the border with Pakistan was evacuated for good.

———

TENSIONS BETWEEN YEMENIS in the First Ward and their neighbors ignited in the days and weeks after the attacks. Muslim parents in the First Ward kept their children inside. Adults stopped going out at night. There was verbal harassment. One Muslim was spit on at a local grocery store. Others were told to go back to their country. Sahim Alwan told the *Buffalo News* that he hadn't felt this kind of fear since the Gulf War when he and a friend were attacked by a group of men outside a Lackawanna restaurant. He said he was scared to stop at red lights. Leaders in the Muslim community suggested parents just keep their children close to home to avoid trouble. A Buffalo councilman, Charley Fisher, an African-American, suggested the city pass a new deli oversight law. He said local delis in Lackawanna and Buffalo might have ties to al-Qaeda and "we shouldn't be giving money to terrorists."

———

AL-DOSARI LEFT LACKAWANNA before the FBI ever found out he had returned. He told the small group of men who continued to haunt the Wilkesbarre apartment that he was leaving to fight with the Taliban. By that time, America had not yet mounted its Afghanistan campaign. The government was still negotiating with the Taliban in hopes of getting Mullah Omar to extradite Osama bin Laden. According to the FBI, al-Dosari flew to Bahrain and then to Iran where he collected three thousand dollars from an associate and crossed the border into Afghanistan. What he did, exactly, after that is unclear. All the FBI will say is that a little more than a month later, al-Dosari was detained by a Pakistani border patrol and eventually turned over to American forces in Afghanistan. He was accused of being "present at Tora Bora," and was sent to Guantanamo Bay (Gitmo) as an enemy combatant.

Al-Dosari maintains he had nothing to do with the recruitment of the Lackawanna Six or that he had any link to al-Qaeda. "I am not an enemy of the United States," he has said since, time and again. Whatever his intentions, both sides agree that his travels came to an abrupt halt in November of 2001. The majority of detainees in Gitmo were captured as they were leaving Afghanistan in late 2001. And certainly, not all of them were aid workers or Islamic workers who happened to be visiting just as war was breaking out. Most of the men held in Guantanamo, like al-Dosari, were arrested by Pakistanis or Afghans who were paid from one thousand to ten thousand dollars for every mujahideen they turned over to the Americans. Flyers dropped over Afghanistan promised "wealth and power beyond your dreams" for finding terror suspects and handing them over. Al-Dosari, for his part, said that he was in Afghanistan working for a Saudi humanitarian organization and had never been to Tora Bora. His arrest was, he assured anyone who would listen, some sort of mistake.

It took a few months for the FBI to figure out that al-Dosari had been the imam who visited Lackawanna in April 2001. A senior FBI official familiar with the investigation into al-Dosari said that there were lots of connections between the young imam and terrorist operations in the Middle East. A number of calls made from "associates" of al-Dosari during his time in the United States have been identified as "hot numbers" by the CIA, suggesting connections to known terrorists. Al-Dosari, they said, deserved to be with "the most dangerous, best-trained, most vicious killers on the face of the earth" at Camp Delta in Guantanamo. Al-Dosari became detainee No. 261. To hear him tell it, his nightmare had just begun.

CHAPTER 10

ON THE HOT SEAT

WHEN HE NEEDED TO THINK, Ed Needham liked to drive through South Buffalo. It wasn't the beauty of the old neighborhood that drew him—although, in his own way, he found it so—it was the familiarity, the comfortable rhythms of a place that held his history. He would get in the car and would drive slowly down Ganson Street, over the rusty lift bridge. He would turn on Hamburg and unconsciously slow when he pulled alongside his childhood home. It looked smaller now. The visits inevitably included a stop at Mazurek's, a bakery like the ones in old Jimmy Stewart movies with displays full of cookies and cakes and where cinnamon buns still sold for fifty cents. Needham always tried to get Mazurek pastries for meetings at the office, if only to find an excuse to go in and breathe the warm, sugary, vanilla tang of the air inside. "It is a real bakery," he would say. "They don't have bakeries like that anymore."

New agents assigned to Needham's task force inevitably got a tour. He liked to take people to the old neighborhood and talk about Jim Boy Smith, "the toughest scooper in the ward." Needham would talk about the old footbridges that ran above the railway tracks, or the epic fights the Irish boys in the neighborhood had, and the cars they drove, and the winters they spent on these windswept streets by the lake.

By the spring of 2002, Needham had had half a dozen conversations with Alwan. Sometimes, they were no more than a quick touching base, other times a cup of coffee at a local diner. The interviews always led to the same place. Alwan claimed that he had gone to Pakistan to learn more about his Muslim roots. This was less about religion, he kept saying, than it was about culture. He wanted to understand his culture. But little details about the trip sometimes changed. Alwan would add a little nugget here or subtract something else there—he felt he needed to keep providing something new for the agent who was buying him coffee and paying so much attention to him. Needham, for his part, had begun to notice tics in Alwan's speech. He tended to end sentences with "and that kind of thing" and "that sort of stuff." Needham suspected those phrases came up when Alwan cornered himself, when he started a story and realized that its end would be incriminating. Alwan was making a classic mistake: he was convinced he was smarter than everyone around him and that he could control the information he provided. He couldn't. The problem with telling the truth slowly, as he clearly was doing, was that one had to keep the story straight. Needham was trained to focus on inconsistencies. The longer he talked to Alwan, the more it seemed that the story, the one he was getting, was only an abridged version of what had actually occurred.

Needham met with Yassein Taher and asked him the same series of questions. Where had he gone? What had he done? Did he visit Afghanistan? Taher was adamant that he had gone on a purely cultural exchange. Needham would say later that he virtually begged Taher to come clean. "You should tell me now while I am asking, and I can help you, and not months from now when we are sitting across the table from each other in a very different situation," he said. Taher wouldn't move from his story.

AS NEEDHAM and the terrorism task force at the Buffalo
Field Office kept digging for information on the case, the legal
landscape kept shifting. Back in May 2001, officers gathering
intelligence were not permitted to reveal what they had found
to agents working the criminal case side. Special Agent David
Britten was working intelligence. A West Point graduate with a
brusque manner, Britten was piecing together the story of the
Lackawanna Six from overseas sources. The FBI was running
names through its databases to find connections with al-Qaeda
or known terrorists. The problem was, because of domestic
surveillance laws, Britten couldn't tell Ed Needham what he
knew. After the 9/11 attacks, the situation improved for the
agents somewhat as it looked like sharing information was permissible. Still, they were doing so cautiously, unclear about
whether that provision of the Patriot Act might be deemed un-
constitutional by the courts. Attorney General John Ashcroft
tried to clarify things by declaring in March 2002 that the two
sides of the investigative house could share information. Two
months later, FISA courts reversed the attorney general's declaration. Investigators in the Lackawanna Six case were working
on the cutting edge of a new law and were trying to stay on the
correct side of it. It made an already complicated situation that
much more so.

AFTER THEIR RETURN from Afghanistan, Alwan, Taher,
Mosed, Galab, and al-Bakri all went back to what seemed like
normal routines: Alwan at the Iroquois Job Corps and Galab
back at the gas station. Taher and Mosed did a lot of hanging

around. Nothing the men did suggested they were up to anything. In some ways, the Lackawanna case was one in which the
FBI was looking for something it hoped it wouldn't find. If the
Lackawanna Six were somehow related to al-Qaeda they represented all their worst post–9/11 fears. The young men could be
the beginning of something that would be nearly impossible to
fight: a vast, invisible army, not uniformed and moving freely—
anywhere in America, armed with downloadable manuals and
dark intentions. Derwish and Elbaneh had not yet returned to
Lackawanna. What the FBI had to find out was whether the
young men's interest in jihad had truly been abandoned on
the gravel desert floor of Afghanistan or if it was bubbling
beneath the surface.

That spring, the Joint Terrorism Task Force investigators were
spending their days looking at the gossamer connections between hard-to-parse Arab names and the six young men from
Lackawanna. The big break came when intelligence officials in
Washington plugged some of Derwish's aliases into their
database. Connections lit up. The trail led directly to al-Qaeda.
He had attended several training camps in Afghanistan in the
1990s when bin Laden had just started training his own army.
He actually fought shoulder-to-shoulder with Muslims in Bosnia
in 1996 and 1997. He had spent time in Yemen and had connections to the men who helped plot the USS *Cole* bombing. He
had become so entwined with the jihadi movement, when he returned to Saudi Arabia the government there jailed him for
extremist activities. The FBI tracked Derwish through advanced
weapons training in the al-Qaeda camps where, it appeared, his
hardened radical beliefs had been hammered into brilliant resolve. It was the first time that law enforcement officials could
unambiguously link the Lackawanna Six to an individual with a
clear attachment to the al-Qaeda network.

The deeper intelligence officials dug, the worse Derwish appeared. They located communications showing Derwish had spoken with Saad bin Laden, Osama's son, and Tawtig bin Attash, one of the *Cole* planners. The more the FBI learned, the more closely Derwish was aligned not only with al-Qaeda, but the organization's operational decisionmakers.

When Britten and Needham finally discussed Derwish, Needham felt his stomach sink. He would later call the Derwish connection the Bureau's "holy shit moment." As soon as Derwish's identity was revealed, the Lackawanna Six were transformed in the eyes of the FBI, and especially to agents in Washington, DC, from naïve young men to potential terrorists. For months, President Bush had been asking FBI Director Robert Mueller whether there were terror cells in America. Now, the FBI chief could finally say he might have found one. He had certainly found a suspicious connection. For a president eager to see evidence that his war on terror was working, the Lackawanna Six provided fodder. FBI agents began swarming into Lackawanna to help with the case.

Needham started working closely with Britten and state police investigator Mike Urbanski who was on loan to the FBI. They formed a task force of some two dozen officers from federal, state, and local agencies. Investigators applied to a special FISA court for warrants to monitor the phone and email traffic of the Lackawanna Six as well as some of their friends. Although the FISA courts were known for being reluctant to approve such warrants, they gave the Lackawanna task force a quick go ahead. Needham and Britten started briefing headquarters in Washington twice a day providing small details of the six's whereabouts and movements.

About this same time, Mukhtar al-Bakri left for his marriage in Bahrain. With the FBI's newfound intelligence on Derwish and the clatter of intelligence that spring, al-Bakri's trip appeared genuinely sinister. Agents began tracking his every movement. For people who might have been looking for hard evidence for what they already believed—that al-Bakri was part of a sleeper cell in America—he seemed to provide plenty of clues. "I started to be convinced that he was in the Middle East to level some attack against American military installations there," Needham recalled. "He was in Saudi Arabia and did a pilgrimage there, and he was in Bahrain, where the U.S. also had forces. The more he moved around, the more it worried me."

Everyone was on high alert. Investigators who only a month earlier weren't sure what to make of the Lackawanna Six, now could see hundreds of sinister connotations. Why were they making so many calls from pay phones? they wondered. Why hadn't Derwish and Elbaneh returned to Lackawanna? Were they involved in some operation? The men and Derwish had been in contact. When Derwish asked, "How are the guys doing?" was this code for activating the cell? Why did they continue to be in touch with him if they weren't a cell? Friends of the Lackawanna Six were talking to Derwish, too. One warned him that the FBI was watching the neighborhood.

With the 2002 Fourth of July holiday approaching, nerves were more on edge than ever. Independence Day, the national birthday, seemed a perfect opportunity for al-Qaeda to attack. When one of the men named in the anonymous letter that had been sent to Ed Needham a year earlier bought propane tanks at a local hardware store, the agents immediately thought they had discovered a bomb plot. In fact, they had discovered a plan for a family barbecue.

It was in that tense environment in July 2002 that al-Bakri sent an email to Kamel Derwish from Saudi Arabia. To this day, everyone is at pains to explain it.

After a succession of community centers and soccer clubs came and went, the Lackawanna Islamic Center, left, emerged as a natural gathering place for young Yemenis in the First Ward. Yahya Goba and Kamel Derwish lived just a short walk from the mosque in a red brick building at 21 Wilkesbarre Avenue, below left. It was here that they held meetings with a handful of young men, mixing talk about Islam with large take-out pizzas.

3

4

Nicole Frick, above and far left, met Yassein Taher, far right, in high school. She was a cheerleader. He was a star soccer prayer. In this picture, his mother is holding their son, Noah. Sahim Alwan, lower photograph, was considered one of the First Ward's success stories. He had a steady job, a devout Muslim wife, and three children. He was one of the few men in the ward who always wore a shirt and tie.

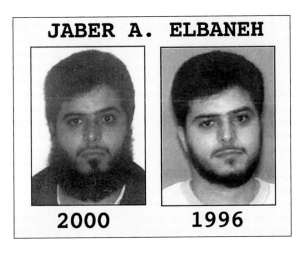

JABER A. ELBANEH

2000　　**1996**

5–11

Jaber Elbaneh, pictured here in a FBI Most Wanted poster, never returned to Lackawanna after he attended the al-Qaeda camp in Kandahar. There is a $5 million bounty on his head. The FBI released the mugshots of the Lackawanna Six soon after their arrest in September 2002. They were immediately dubbed America's first homegrown terrorist cell. From left to right they are: Mukhtar al-Bakri, Yassein Taher, Faysal Galab, Shafal Mosed, Sahim Alwan, and Yahya Goba.

Special Agent in Charge Peter Ahearn, far left, told U.S. Attorney Michael Battle, on the right, that al-Qaeda had come to western New York. Shortly before the September arrests, Ahearn asked Battle if he had any vacation coming up and, if so, to postpone it. "We've got something big coming up."

12

Ed Needham, far right, looked and acted the part of an FBI agent. Deliberate and thoughtful, he ran the Joint Terrorism Task Force in Buffalo. He received an anonymous tip about the Lackawanna Six and opened up the original investigation in the spring of 2001. Below, Lackawanna Mayor John Kuryak assured the people of Lackawanna in a September 2002 news conference with New York Governor Pataki that although al-Qaeda had been discovered in Lackawanna, the citizens were still safe.

13

14

15, 16

The Hotel Faran in Karachi, top, is one of a series of hotels and guesthouses in Pakistan and Afghanistan that help channel jihadists to training camps. Three of the Lackawanna Six passed through Karachi. Another group traveled to Afghanistan through "the new route": Lahore, Pakistan. They attended prayers at this Lahore mosque pictured directly above.

17, 18

Sana'a, Yemen, is a city trapped in another time. The old city buildings, top, are made of mud brick and trimmed with a white paint made of lye. Inside the old city, young men wait for customers in small stalls, selling everything from daggers to dates. The national pastime is the chewing of *khat*. Young men chew great handfuls of the leaves and allow them to sit, and stew, in their cheeks as pictured above.

Jamia Binora *madrasa* in Pakistan claims to have the largest foreign student population in the country. Young men arrive there to commit the Koran to memory. Ali Khan, below right, is from Georgia. He didn't speak Arabic when he arrived and said trying to memorize the Koran without the language is "like trying to teach a Russian something in Chinese."

نفسي
تبيني
واجيك
وعاتبك
واشتكيك
عيني
بتسأليني
عنك
قلبي يسلم
عليك..

21, 22

Juma al-Dosari was known as "The Closer." The Lackawanna Six said he helped convince them they should go to Afghanistan to train for jihad. Now in U.S. custody in Guantanamo Bay, Cuba, al-Dosari says this is all a case of mistaken identity. He has become so desperate during his incarceration, he has attempted suicide many times, all unsuccessfully. A suicide note he handed to his lawyer is pictured below.

My dear friend Josh ...
finally I found a good chance.
finally I will get my freedom very very soon.
When you receive this letter I will be done.
I will not going to suffere to eny abuse from now on.
How wonderfull the freedom...
finally... I am so happy now...
by the way I just sent you this letter to inform you thats it
also is to late to do eny thing forme now...
enyway thank you Josh. about evry thing, you did for my.

Juma
8-3-2006

How are you my beloved, God Willing you are fine. I would like to remind you of obeying God and keeping him in your heart because the next meal will be very huge. No one will be able to withstand it except those with faith. There are people here who had visions and their visions were explained that this thing will be very strong. No one will be able to bare [sic] it.

The intercept rattled investigators. It parroted the phrasing and concepts used by Osama bin Laden in a speech made in December 2001 in reference to the September 11 attacks.

At the White House, the Lackawanna case had taken on all the hallmarks of a cause celebre. FBI Director Mueller had started including the latest twist or turn from the Buffalo JTTF every morning during his 9 a.m. security briefing with the president. Bush even started asking about it. The pressure mounted on Buffalo to provide fresh information from the First Ward so the director had something to pass on to the president. Calls came in from Washington asking for fresh leads and new tidbits.

The men on Wilkesbarre Avenue knew they were being watched. They began to take evasive action—something that only made them appear even more guilty. They started using code words and would suddenly make U-turns so the FBI agents who were following them would have to give chase.

Needham was finding himself cruising the streets of South Buffalo trying to put together a narrative that would make this spiderweb of connections between al-Qaeda and Lackawanna finally make sense. The young men were certainly acting suspicious, but Needham couldn't figure out if they were really up to something or had just gotten "hinked up," or jittery, because the FBI was everywhere they turned.

Needham was advocating a more low-key approach. "If you want them to relax and maybe do what they'd otherwise do, we should pull back a bit," he said in the summer of 2002. As Needham saw it, if the goal was to collect intelligence, then the FBI had to stop cruising in sedans up and down Steelawanna and Wilkesbarre Avenue. The Yemenis in the First Ward were so close knit, an unfamiliar car immediately attracted attention. If the FBI's goal was to prosecute these guys, Needham was of the opinion that the agents should just pick up the five men who had returned and make their case.

MEANWHILE, Juma al-Dosari, the man who was supposed to have closed the deal in convincing the Lackawanna Six to go to the camps, was shackled to the floor of a cell at Guantanamo Bay. The craggy forty-five-square-mile strip of land on Cuba's southeastern tip had been his home for nearly a year after he was seized in Pakistan at the end of December 2001. Wearing a very tightly fitted pair of goggles, the lenses blacked, and a pair of plastic ear muffs, al-Dosari was put on the plane from Pakistan to Guantanamo Bay, Cuba, in January 2001. He had been deemed an enemy combatant. As far as he could tell, he wasn't accused of anything aside from being present at Tora Bora in the fall of 2001, and even that was in doubt. Al-Dosari said that there were Yemenis and Pakistanis on the border who were turning in anyone they could find for being in Tora Bora. He said he had never been there. His Lackawanna visit and his national tour of various mosques in early 2001 were not mentioned as reasons for his arrest.

Al-Dosari would claim later (with some corroboration) that he was beaten and tortured in his early days at Camp X-Ray in

Gitmo. One incident, a beating by an Immediate Reaction Force (IRF) in the camp, was particularly brutal and became fodder for a disturbing scene in the film *Road to Guantanamo*. Al-Dosari was complaining about some items missing from his cell after an interrogation and was told to get to his knees because the IRF was on its way. The IRF was used to deal with difficult prisoners. Members appear outside cells looking like Storm Troopers out of *Star Wars*, all helmets and riot gear. A large military policeman in full IRF gear leapt onto al-Dosari and began choking him. A military policewoman kept smashing his head against the concrete floor. Al-Dosari lost consciousness as prisoners shackled in neighboring cells looked on. The scene was filmed by the IRF team, which routinely videotaped interactions with prisoners. That particular video later went missing.

British detainees who were later released from Guantanamo Bay reported that al-Dosari was removed from his cell that day on a stretcher. The floor of the cell was so covered in blood, they said, the water used to clean it turned red. Al-Dosari woke up in the hospital tent unable to move, and he was then taken by ambulance to the U.S. Naval Hospital at Guantanamo Bay. A delegation from the Bahrain Interior Ministry visited al-Dosari about a month later. His face was still swollen. The delegation made a formal request to the State Department for an investigation of the beating. Days later, an FBI agent interviewed al-Dosari at Guantanamo Bay's Camp Delta and asked him what had happened. The agent promised to investigate the incident. The military later released a document dated June 7, 2002, which described the FBI agent's interview with al-Dosari and confirmed the details as al-Dosari himself had laid them out. He was later transferred from Camp X-ray to Camp Delta. "Honor Bound to Protect Freedom," the sign announcing the facility reads.

IF THERE WAS ANY DOUBT about how much the American legal landscape had changed since the September 11 attacks, one need only to consider the case of Sheik Abdul Rahman, the man convicted of conspiring to carry out a campaign of bombings and assassinations around New York City in 1993. In that case, the FBI used eight months of surveillance, 125 secretly recorded tapes, a paid informant, and 200 other witnesses. It was a classic sting operation in which an FBI informant befriended the terrorists, won the confidence of Abdul Rahman, and offered technical help in building bombs meant to destroy New York City landmarks and tunnels. The FBI wired the Queens garage where the plotters mixed the chemicals for the bombs and toyed with detonators. The FBI had videotaped the men actually stirring the witch's brew of chemicals before they arrested them. The group was found guilty of sedition. On one of the tapes the FBI played at Rahman's trial, he was heard telling his followers he didn't want to know the details of their plots because he wanted to remain a political leader for Muslims.

After 9/11, law enforcement in America was bound to change. The national mood required the FBI to round up suspicious people first, and ask questions later. The CIA was playing offense, and the FBI was suddenly handling defense. It was nothing less than a complete change of mission for the bureau. Previously geared toward prosecuting committed crimes, it found itself stalking prospective ones. In the age of terror, the FBI had a nearly impossible job. If there was no tolerance for an attack, suddenly everyone became suspect. Most agents will say today, privately, that the major difference is that arrests occur much earlier now than they did the in the past. The Lackawanna Six's proximity to terrorism, having attended an al-Qaeda camp, was reason enough to bring them in.

IN FEBRUARY OF 2002, the Bush administration appointed a young black judge, Michael Battle, as western New York's new U.S. Attorney. Formerly on the bench of the state's family court, Battle was one of those men who was immediately likeable. He had an easy smile, a good sense of humor, and he bristled with intelligence. He clearly relished his new job. He described it to reporters as "his dream job come true."

Battle was a Bronx native and began a love affair with western New York when he attended Ithaca College in the late 1970s. He attended the University of New York at Buffalo School of Law and then began working on civil cases in the legal aid offices in New York City. He came back to Buffalo in 1985 to work in the U.S. Attorney's office. He worked as an assistant public defender for four years and then was elected to the Erie County Family Court in 1996. He was on the bench for five years when the U.S. Attorney post came up. In June 2002, he received a phone call from the FBI's Pete Ahearn, the Special Agent in Charge of the FBI's office in Buffalo. Ahearn asked if he could come by Battle's office for a chat. Battle said he would be happy to talk.

"We've got stuff going on, and if you are going out of town, let us know," Ahearn told Battle after some initial pleasantries.

Battle said he expected he'd be in town for the foreseeable future. He knew better than to get into details. "I had a sense it was [about] counterterrorism because everything else was pretty openly discussed," Battle said later.

Ahearn called Battle two months later, in August, again bearing a sketchy message. "Something is up," Ahearn said, "and it will likely come in the next several weeks. We have a serious matter that may involve al-Qaeda in our own backyard. I wanted to give you a heads up so your staff could be up to speed. We think we've got a pretty good break in the case."

"Okay, I have been listening to this cryptic stuff going on for months. I'll bite," Battle said. "What is going on?"

———

NEEDHAM WAS IN THE KITCHEN serving up his daughter's birthday cake in August 2002 when a call came in from the office. It was Pete Ahearn, Needham's boss. Ahearn needed Needham in Washington, DC, to brief FBI Director Robert Mueller, personally, about the case. The director wanted to hear about the Lackawanna Six from the people most directly involved. As Ahearn saw it, there was no one else in the bureau who knew more about the details of the Lackawanna investigation than Needham. The call made Needham uneasy. Briefing the director personally could be a double-edged sword. Needham wasn't sure if he'd be walking into a maelstrom or something worse. He *did* know, however, he didn't want to go in there less than fully armed. Needham said he would only go if David Britten, the agent heading up the intelligence part of the investigation, could join him.

"Be prepared to tell the director every detail," Ahearn said. "He asks tough questions, be ready for tough questions."

Field agents such as Needham were rarely summoned to brief a director. The fact that they were flying to Washington, DC, for the meeting indicated a level of seriousness that, as far as Needham knew, had not been directed at the Lackawanna Six to that point. The two men were told they would have a two-hour pre-brief with the top brass at the FBI and then thirty minutes with Mueller. They walked into the director's conference room with handouts, and they started at the beginning with the anony-mous letter Needham had received more than a year earlier. "I am very concern [sic]," the letter began. "I am an Arab Amer-ican . . . and I cannot give you my name because I fear for my life. Two terrorist [sic] came to Lackawanna . . . for recruiting the Yemenite youth . . . the terrorist group . . . left to Afghanistan to meet . . . bin Laden and and [sic] stay in his camp for training . . ."

The two agents laid out their concerns about the group, what they were doing to investigate their links to al-Qaeda, and went over the intelligence and legal issues inherent in the case. The group was not planning anything, the agents assured the direc-tor, and they were being watched twenty-four hours a day to en-sure that they didn't. But not all of the six had returned. Elbaneh and Derwish were still at large. Derwish was in touch with some of the men. He had told Goba to destroy his old passport with incriminating country stamps and get a new one. Goba put his passport into a shirt pocket and threw it into the washing ma-chine. He applied for a new passport, telling officials he had ac-cidentally ruined his current one. Agents did not know, precisely, where Derwish and Elbaneh were. Mukhtar al-Bakri was still in Bahrain.

Needham suggested again that they back off a little bit, to give the group some room. Maybe Derwish would return. But Mueller would hear none of it. He wanted surveillance around the clock. "If you are there, you are preventing something," he said. "Buffalo, you are in the hot seat. Just stay with them, stay close. We can't afford for them to slip away and do some-thing."

The briefing lasted about forty minutes, and the director gave the agents his car to get them back to the airport.

Mueller's personal interest in the case increased the pressure on the agents in Buffalo. Needham and the JTTF team decided they had been covert long enough. It was time to rattle some cages. The task force met twice a day to make sure that every lead and every nuance was scrutinized. Then al-Bakri, just days before his wedding, made that fateful phone call to a friend in Lackawanna. Calling to say goodbye, in that dramatic fashion he chose to use, "you won't be hearing from me again," tipped the balance. The order was given. After four months of briefing, President Bush and Vice President Cheney ordered al-Bakri's arrest.

"Can you guarantee me that these guys won't do something?" Bush asked Mueller as the 9/11 anniversary approached.

"We are ninety-nine percent sure that we can stop these guys from doing something," Mueller replied.

That wasn't enough. Ahearn called Needham and said that the moment had come. Al-Bakri was going to be picked up in Bahrain, and Needham's team needed to get ready to start arresting the men who had returned to Lackawanna. The tolerance for waiting until the Lackawanna Six did something had evaporated. Hours later, al-Bakri was ripped from his marital bed and was behind bars, where he immediately confessed to going to Afghanistan to attend an al-Qaeda camp with five other men from Lackawanna. The FBI finally had the makings of a criminal case. When Special Agent Gamal Abdel-Hafiz, who had flown in from Saudi Arabia to interview al-Bakri, called headquarters to tell them what al-Bakri had said, there was pandemonium at the other end of the line. He thought he heard high-fiving. What the FBI still didn't know was whether an attack was about to happen.

"Your e-mail has the world on one foot," Abdel-Hafiz told al-Bakri, describing the level of concern among FBI agents who had read the lines of the e-mail he sent to Derwish—"the next meal will be very huge. No one will be able to withstand it, except those with faith"—so apparently full of menace.

"The what?" al-Bakri asked, blinking in disbelief.

"The whole world on one foot," Abdel-Hafiz repeated.

Al-Bakri continued to make a fitful transition from shock to recognition. He said he had always planned to return home "for a future and go to college and get a nice job," he told Abdel-Hafiz.

"How in the hell are you going to have colleges and future and nice jobs in America if you want to destroy America?" Abdul-Hafiz said.

"Destroy America?" al-Bakri looked genuinely perplexed. "I don't want to destroy America."

Then al-Bakri talked about food, something that seemed to have become an obsession with the Lackawanna Six. He talked about eating at Denny's and a restaurant called the Little Red Caboose that "makes nice subs." Abdel-Hafiz said it didn't strike him as the talk of a jihadist. Instead, it was the discussion of someone who clearly didn't understand what kind of trouble he was in.

———

ABDEL-HAFIZ was still debriefing al-Bakri in Bahrain when Ed Needham got into his car and drove up to the Iroquois Job Corps Center to meet with Sahim Alwan. The men filed into a conference room, and Needham got right to the point.

"We know you were there; we know about al-Farooq," Needham told Sahim. "We know you were only there for like two weeks, and we know about Taseesy."

Alwan felt his heart sink. He nodded slowly. He admitted he and the other five men from Lackawanna had been at the camps.

"I'm going to need a statement," Needham said quietly. "When do you get off of work?"

"In an hour."

"Call me when you get out."

"Am I being arrested?"

"If you hadn't have told me, yes. But I need for you to call me as soon as you get out of work. Bring your passport. We're going to meet. Bring your passport with you."

A statement from Alwan, alongside al-Bakri's confession, was all the FBI needed for arrest warrants. Needham knew that FBI agents were following Alwan 24/7, so he wasn't concerned he was a flight risk. Needham hadn't told Alwan where he had received his information, so there was no use in Alwan denying it. At 6 p.m., Alwan's car pulled into the parking lot of the Small Boat Harbor halfway between Lackawanna and downtown Buffalo. Alwan didn't want to be seen driving to the Bureau, he had told Needham. He locked his car door and climbed into a waiting sedan. Needham was at the wheel. They drove the ten minutes to the FBI building and went in a back way. They wouldn't leave until 11 p.m. that night.

The statement began with a long conversation. Alwan talked about what it was like to be at the camps and recreated the trip as FBI agents took dictation. He talked about staying at the Hotel Faran in Karachi. He talked about the guesthouse and the bus and motorcycles that took the Lackawanna Six into the camp. And for all the talking he did, there was plenty he left out. He said he never live-fired a weapon. "We did dry-firing," he said. He talked about what al-Qaeda taught him about guns and explosives but said he didn't do the topography course that was required. He kept saying he was doing everything he could to leave. Needham and Britten took notes on Alwan's story, had someone type them up, and then asked Alwan if the statement reflected what he knew. He would shake his head, add little details, correct misunderstandings, and the statement would go back to a typist. It took five hours to put together a narrative of what had happened more than a year earlier. Alwan signed the statement, known as a 302, and left just before midnight. What Needham didn't know at the time was how much Alwan omitted. While the agent suspected Alwan was trying to protect his own skin by saying he only dry-fired the weapon, he never suspected that Alwan had met with Osama bin Laden—not just once, but twice. Alwan looked almost relieved when he left the Bureau, Needham recalled. He had been lying for so long; telling the truth must have provided its own release.

"I actually think he felt guilty about lying to us for all those previous months," Needham said later.

CHAPTER 11

FITTING PROFILES

IT WAS AFTER 1 A.M. when Alwan walked through his front door. His wife had waited up. He only managed to tell her the barest of details. He said he thought he was going to be arrested. He didn't explain why. She kept her questions to a minimum. Alwan's mind kept running over what he had told Needham, why he had gone to Afghanistan, and how one spur-of-the-moment decision—because he didn't want to be left out—looked like it was about to change the course of his life. He had always known, deep inside, that decision would come back to haunt him.

After a sleepless night, Alwan rose and went to the mosque to pray at 5 a.m. He noticed a car across the street from his apartment. It followed him, at slow speed, and then parked. The surveillance, at this point, was anything but subtle. Alwan called his supervisor at work to tell him he might be a little late.

"Those were federal agents out here yesterday, weren't they," his supervisor asked Alwan when he called. "I know, I saw the cars. I saw them. Are you getting harassed? What's going on?" Naturally, harassment was his supervisor's first thought.

When Alwan set out for work, he noticed four cars behind him. A voice mail from Needham was waiting for him at the Job Corps center. "Sahim, give me a call."

He dialed the number. Needham was brief. "They are going to arrest you."

Alwan didn't want the kids at the center to see him handcuffed and taken away. "I'll come in. They don't have to come get me. I'll come right in." Needham said the police would be at his house and would give him time to make sure his children wouldn't be there when he was taken in.

The First Ward exploded with activity around 4 p.m. on September 13. Police and FBI agents blocked off streets and swarmed the neighborhood, guns drawn. Residents poured out into the narrow streets to watch the melee. They didn't say a word. They just looked on with disbelief as Alwan and Goba were led out of their respective homes in handcuffs. Goba had recently married and had bought his own home. He had spent every spare moment trying to fix it up for his new bride. Alwan emerged from the house where he had reared three children and where he had, until that moment, grown to be one of the First Ward success stories.

Squad cars filled the narrow streets of the ward, their lights bouncing off the ramshackle houses. Residents were half expecting bloody bodies to emerge, there was so much commotion. They craned their necks for a better view. Police started cordoning off Wilkesbarre and Ingham avenues. As the police tape went up, residents knew in a shadowy ungraspable way, that life as they'd known it had changed.

Mosed was coming out of a deli on Genesee Street and Sherman on Buffalo's East Side. He had just called his mother to tell her he would be home soon. It was about 7 p.m. Four or five unmarked cars screeched up to the storefront. Witnesses said later that agents burst into the store with guns drawn. They arrested Mosed and asked him for the keys to his car. They opened the trunk, presumably looking for explosives or the suicide vest they failed to find in Bahrain when they arrested al-Bakri hours before. The trunk was empty.

They found Yassein Taher in nearby Cheektowaga at a mall. Local police arrested him without incident. His wife Nicole had no idea what had happened. Her toddler son had accidentally locked her out of the apartment. She was trying to cajole him into opening the door. When she finally got inside, there were fifteen messages on her answering machine. "Yassein has been arrested," they all said.

First Ward residents interviewed that night said they knew that the FBI had been watching the neighborhood for months. FBI officials told reporters that the discovery of "the cell" prompted the Bush administration to raise the nation's terrorist threat level to orange, the second highest. The FBI didn't say that one of the key pieces of evidence was al-Bakri's email to Derwish.

"The suspects are believed to have a connection to Arabian Foods, a store on Wilkesbarre that was a target of the raids," the *Buffalo News* reported. "Federal agents removed several boxes from the store Friday night. A senior government official said the Justice Department plans to release more information about the arrests at a news conference in Washington." It was never explained what Arabian Foods had to do with anything. Maybe the name just sounded sinister.

The mayor of Lackawanna, John Kuryak, told reporters that he had known about the FBI investigation for six months. "We just want to reassure everybody in the city that they are safe."

It was starting to get dark when U.S. Attorney Mike Battle got home. CBS News' Jim Stewart was on television. Battle's wife was watching the news wide-eyed. Stewart was broadcasting live from the First Ward. There were police cars behind him, their lights swirling and the sound of helicopter blades overhead. She turned to her husband and simply said, "What did you guys do?"

He shook his head, said he couldn't talk about it, and made himself a sandwich. "My phone rang every ten minutes for the next twenty-four hours," Battle said later.

President Bush provided his own coda on the arrests a day later. "One by one," he said in a press conference with the Italian prime minister at Camp David, "we're hunting the killers down."

The plane carrying al-Bakri would land at Niagara Air Base, in Niagara, at 4 a.m., three days later. Needham and Ahearn were among the agents standing on the tarmac when the young man arrived.

———

THE LEAD STORY in the *Buffalo News* the next morning, September 14, said it all:

> The City of Good Neighbors learned this weekend that five of its neighbors may well be terrorists. And that sent waves of fear across metropolitan Buffalo: fear that terrorists might strike here and fear that the community might strike back against its Arab residents. After the FBI took five Lackawanna men into custody and accused them of attending a terrorist training camp in Afghanistan, many local residents seemed focused on the possibility of terrorism in Buffalo. Yet there was also talk of a boycott of Arab businesses, and the Lackawanna School Board called an emergency meeting to convene today to consider whether it needed to increase security to protect its Arab students.

Suddenly the loyalty and patriotism of the residents of the First Ward was at issue. Were there other terrorists living among the Yemenis in those small clapboard houses? People outside the

Yemeni community began to wonder aloud whether the next wave of terrorism against the United States would show up in small communities like Lackawanna. They worried about terrorism in their own backyards. The Buffalo area suddenly seemed like a perfect terrorism target. There was the Niagara Falls power station and the city's close proximity to the Canadian border. People were kicking themselves for not suspecting they were ripe targets for terror attacks before. The Lackawanna arrests awoke the same uneasy feelings about "the Arabs" that had cropped up right after the September 11 attacks.

Members of Lackawanna's black community renewed talk about organizing a boycott of the Arab-owned delis in the First Ward. They said they didn't want to be sending money to al-Qaeda. Councilman Charlie Fisher of Buffalo said the delis were magnets for weapons trading and drugs. He resurrected his 2001 claims that local delis in Lackawanna and Buffalo might have ties to al-Qaeda. The arrests of the Lackawanna men only seemed to vindicate Fisher and his suspicions. "If someone would have told you six months ago that the first arrests of an al-Qaeda terrorist cell in the country would take place in Lackawanna, people would have called that far-fetched, too. Of course we need to be careful about trampling on people's freedom, but our greatest concern has to be protecting public safety."

———

THE FBI'S CRIMINAL complaint didn't say the men arrested were terrorists, but it didn't have to: that label was provided by everyone from the New York governor to the FBI to the deputy assistant attorney general. The complaint alleged that the young men trained at the al-Farooq camp near Kandahar, the same place that the so-called American Taliban, John Walker Lindh, had trained. It cited bin Laden's anti-American and anti-Israeli speech at the camps and the fact that the Lackawanna men didn't leave the camp even after they knew the nature of its message. Elbaneh, one of their best friends, never returned. That in itself seemed suspect.

Five of the Lackawanna Six were led into the U.S. district courthouse in leg-irons and bullet-proof vests the next morning. The leg-irons were a testament to the severity of the alleged crime, the vests were a reminder that there were lots of people in Buffalo who still thought the best way to deal with terrorists, even alleged ones, was preemptively.

The judge made quick work of the proceedings. It was clear, at that point, the men accused of receiving weapons training from an al-Qaeda camp, including training in the use of Kalishnikov assault rifles, handguns, and long-range rifles, would not be released. The complaint also made much of the presence of Osama bin Laden at the camp. For their "material support" of a terrorist organization, they each faced up to fifteen years in prison. Weapons charges could stiffen the penalty.

The men entered not-guilty pleas. They weren't terrorists, they said. They didn't have lawyers, so the judge entered the plea for them. Their case marked the first time since the September 11 attacks that America was trying suspects accused of having direct ties to al-Qaeda. That made the Lackawanna men more than just suspects. They were symbols. They represented what was, or wasn't, working in the war on terrorism.

"These arrests send a very important message," Governor George Pataki of New York said at a press conference in Buffalo later that day. "The threat of terror is real, and it's not just in far corners of the globe or in large cities like Washington or New York. The threat of terror is out there in every single community."

As reporters sought to understand the threat, Special Agent in Charge Pete Ahearn explained that the FBI's investigation did not find that the men were planning anything. There was no cache of weapons or reconnaissance of targets or even a hint that something darker or sinister was afoot. One of the reporters asked what Ahearn meant when he called the Lackawanna men a cell. "It's a, it's a, it's a trained group of individuals that were trained in Afghanistan. It's an al Qaeda-trained cell. It's a . . ." Then an FBI media spokesperson, off camera, cut him off. That was all they wanted to say about that.

A Washington press conference began at the Justice Department hours later with Deputy Attorney General Larry Thompson. "Terrorism and support of terrorists is not confined to the large cities and metropolitan areas of America; it lurks in small towns and areas as well," he said. "Today's arrests send an unambiguous message that we will track down terrorists wherever they hide."

Before the Lackawanna men even hired lawyers, they became shorthand for homegrown terrorism at its worst. Headlines called them America's first homegrown al-Qaeda cell. They were dubbed the Lackawanna Six even though there were, technically, more than six of them. (Derwish, al-Dosari, and Elbaneh, had he returned, would have made nine.) The story was too sensational to miss. Television satellite trucks lined the narrow streets of the First Ward. Reporters stood with microphones at the ready, chasing anyone who walked by to get an interview. For many people in the First Ward, all this was part of their worst nightmare. Not since Timothy McVeigh blew up the Murrah Building had so many journalists descended on a Buffalo suburb. Reporters from France's *Le Figaro* as well as the *London Times* and major television networks, including al-Jazeera, lined up along Holland Avenue.

Some of the Muslim women who were cornered by the reporters, not knowing what else to do, pretended not to speak English.

THE LACKAWANNA SIX would be a test case on a number of levels: it was the first time U.S. citizens had been investigated for terrorist activity since 9/11, and it was the first time that such a case was built on the new rules for information sharing. Civil liberties groups were crying foul. Agents like Ed Needham were trying to do the right thing but were caught in the middle just the same.

"My first impression was that they were part of a sleeper cell," Mike Battle said later. "I always felt that somewhere along the line they weren't the only guys doing this. The September 11th hijackers might have looked the same way before they actually got on the planes. We don't know."

For Mike Battle, the case was not just about terrorism. It was about race. Lackawanna was at the forefront of America's reaction to Muslim-Americans post–9/11. Suddenly, Muslims were dealing with a wholly negative perception, and, as an African-American, Battle found himself being particularly sensitive to that. "There was a legal life to this case and a political life to it," said Battle. "I wanted to roll the dice on a trial because I was hoping that it would end up making us, as Americans, define our level of tolerance post–9/11, and I wanted to have a case define 'material support,' once and for all. I thought it would put a stake in the ground and be an important marker. If we lost, we could say 'American tolerance for punishing terror suspects is here.' If we won, we could say tolerance is there.' As I saw it, it was win-win."

Battle decided to charge the Lackawanna Six under the Anti-Terrorism and Effective Death Penalty Act of 1996, a law passed in response to Timothy McVeigh's homegrown terrorism attack against the Murrah building. The six were accused of "providing, attempting to provide, and conspiring to provide material support and resources to designated terrorist organizations." The case was not a slam-dunk. There was no evidence whatsoever that the Lackawanna Six were planning to do anything or attack anyone. So they were on trial, in a sense, for what they might have done. There was also nothing in the law itself that specifically barred anyone from attending a terrorist training camp. The law specifically does not stop "a member of one of the designated (terrorist) groups of vigorously promoting and supporting the political goals of the group," Judge Alex Kozinsky of the Ninth Circuit Court of Appeals in California wrote in a 2000 decision. "What the law prohibits is the act of giving material support."

Battle and his team argued that simply by offering themselves as recruits, the Lackawanna Six fulfilled the requirement. "As I saw it, they individually or collectively put themselves in the position of material support," said Battle. To Battle, any money they provided to the camp, whether to pay for a uniform or buy a sleeping bag or flashlight, was tantamount to the kind of support the laws found illegal. Lodging, money, weapons, training, shelter, and false documentation could all count as material support. But because nothing surfaced to indicate that the six did anything for al-Qaeda (besides attend the camps), there was a question about whether Battle would have enough to prosecute.

Battle saw, in the case of the Lackawanna Six, all the earmarks of a conspiracy. He likened it later to a bank robbery. If prosecutors were accusing people of a conspiracy to rob a bank, and they bought the masks and the guns and had a floorplan of the bank, then they could be found guilty of a conspiracy to rob a bank. Material support, in his view, was similar. If the Lackawanna Six went to a camp, took the training, and didn't come back to tell anyone, they were guilty under the statute. This whole question of whether they were a sleeper cell didn't really matter. "It was a place that wasn't necessary for me to go," he said. "The possibility was enough." Given the national mood, even a year after 9/11, it was easy to prosecute terrorists, even before they struck. Even, in other words, they could be deemed terrorists before they became terrorists.

That was not to suggest that Battle wasn't sympathetic to what the six might have felt when they decided to go to the camps. He grew up in a time when the Black Panther movement and Malcolm X's writings were luring young African-American men to explore their own roots. "A lot of us thought about traveling to Africa," he said. "And you could have had the same thing happen, so I understand where they might have been coming from."

THE POSSIBILITY THAT men from Lackawanna may have been siding with Osama bin Laden set nerves on edge. Local schools braced for reprisals. The FBI sent squad cars to the First Ward to protect residents. Vandals smashed windows and dented the hoods of cars parked at a gas station where Faysal Galab sold used cars. Detectives said a baseball bat was used on the vehicles. They said the fact that one of the Lackawanna suspects worked there was "probably a coincidence." The police said they knew only about some harassing phone calls to the Lackawanna Six families after the arrests. A fire broke out in a house on Wilkesbarre Avenue just a few blocks from Goba's apartment, but police said it was probably an electrical fire and they didn't expect arson at the time.

WHAT THE FBI had not revealed publicly was that several suspects in the case were still at large, notably Derwish and El-baneh. Both made the list of the State Department's "Most Wanted Terrorists." The department offered a reward of up to five million dollars for information leading to Elbaneh's capture, making it among the largest rewards ever offered for the arrest of an American citizen in a terrorism investigation. The State Department had lumped Elbaneh together with Osama bin Laden and twenty-five other al-Qaeda operatives. "These people committed terrorist acts resulting in the deaths of thousands of innocent people," a poster read. "These acts include attacks on embassies, hijacking of airlines and their destruction, the attacks of September 11, 2001, and other incidents." Elbaneh had never been charged with any of those things. As far as the FBI knew, all he had done was attend the al-Qaeda camp with the others. The big difference was that Elbaneh, for whatever reason, never returned from Afghanistan. Elbaneh's talk of martyrdom, and the fact that he held an American passport, worried investigators. In the First Ward, residents thought it was overkill. "People say he is so dangerous, but nobody explains why," said one of his brothers. "We're not getting the full story."

By then, the people of Lackawanna's First Ward felt under siege. They felt that the authorities were targeting the entire Yemeni community, seeing everyone through narrowed lids and suspicious eyes. They woke up in the morning with police cruisers parked at cross streets and police helicopters flying overhead. There were house searches and, residents said, officials were cornering their children, interrogating them, encouraging them to inform against their parents or neighbors or friends. Out of nowhere, surveillance cameras appeared mounted on utility poles, trained on the Islamic Center, a local gas station, and on Lackawanna High School. The FBI would say later they were for the community's protection.

If officials wanted to keep an eye on the Yemenis of the First Ward they would have done well to simply put surveillance on Tim Horton's donut and coffee shop down the street from Steve's Pig and Ox Roast on Ridge Road. The young men of the community went there, knowing they would run into a handful of their friends either just hanging around or stopping in while on a half-hour break or a late lunch hour from work. The informal meetings allowed the men of the First Ward to catch up, to discuss without concern about being overheard what was going on in their town. In the fall of 2002, there was a general belief that the Lackawanna Six had been framed, that they were part of a vast conspiracy meant to cover up the real culprits of the September 11 attacks or part of a larger plan to wage war against the enemies of Israel the world over. The scheme was part Bush administration, part neo-conservative, part Israeli intelligence or Mossad.

Months after the arrests, Ahmed, al-Bakri's older brother, saw a lot of holes in the official version of events on September 11. Any thinking man, he believed, would have to question basic facts. Steel melts at 2,700 degrees, he said slowly, but hydrocarbon fires max out at 1,800 degrees. One could see how Ahmed might know the melting temperature of steel—everyone in Lackawanna appeared to know that—but his knowledge of hydrocarbon-fueled fires came from a different place: the roster of conspiracy theory Web sites on the Internet that told young Muslim men, like those in Lackawanna, what they wanted to hear that they were not to blame.

"How is it that the black box flight-recorders were destroyed in the crash but the passport of Satam al-Suqami, one of the alleged American Airlines Flight 11 hijackers was found in pristine condition? Explain that," Ahmed said, nodding knowingly. "It is all a conspiracy. The Bush administration and the Israelis were looking for a way to make Muslims the bad guys, so they staged this whole thing so they would have the excuse they needed to invade Afghanistan and then Iraq. There are just too many things that don't add up. Explain why thousands of Jewish workers in the World Trade Center didn't show up for work?" (That theory is mirrored by the rumor that the reason no one could hail a taxi in New York City on September 11 was because all the Muslim cab drivers were warned by Muslim brothers that the attacks were imminent.)

"There are videos on the Internet," Ahmed said. Other friends and relatives of the Lackawanna Six had gathered around Ahmed to add their voices to the conversation. Some with coffee in hand. Others with the tell-tale powder of a donut on their mustaches. Surrounding Ahmed, supporting his theories with knowing nods, the other young men saw the web of interlocking anti-Muslim forces joining together to create the September 11 attacks.

"The videos show the plane that crashed into the Pentagon was flying low, and then there is a gap in the video and then the plane is gone," another of the Lackawanna Six brothers offered. "It is clear if you look at the video it isn't a plane at all. It is a missile. The Pentagon was hit with a missile. That's why they couldn't find wreckage of the plane, why the hole in the side of the Pentagon wasn't shaped like an airplane at all."

They were very serious about all their theories, intent on show-ing that there was a vast underground war against Muslims that the average American was simply unwilling to see. They would talk like this all afternoon before falling silent, wearing them-selves out thinking through the wealth of conspiracies. Then they would leave Tim Horton's, one by one, to return to their clap-board houses in the First Ward.

FOR THE MEN who had returned to Lackawanna after spending time at the camp, the prospect of being seen as terror-ists or members of a secret cell was nothing short of surreal. Al-Bakri, in particular, was amazed at the turn of events. He couldn't believe anyone could possibly see him as a threat. He was Mukhtar, the guy who loved the Buffalo Sabres hockey team and played soccer. He knew he had no intention of ever attack-ing the United States. He loved America, and certainly, if he were given a chance to explain, he would be able to convince au-thorities that this was all some kind of terrible mistake. One af-ternoon, after the FBI director had come to Buffalo and referred to the Lackawanna Six as a sleeper cell, al-Bakri tried to engage Needham on the issue.

"Why do you think I am a terrorist?" he asked him. "I'm not a terrorist."

"Look at it from my perspective," Needham began. "Did you travel to Afghanistan?"

Al-Bakri nodded.

"Did you go to an al-Qaeda camp?"

He nodded again.

"Did you know an al-Qaeda recruiter?"

More nods.

"Did you train with weapons and explosives?"

"Did you conceal your identity?"

"Did you contact the recruiter after you got back?"

"Did you meet Osama bin Laden in person?"

"Do you think he's one of the most dangerous people in the world?"

Al-Bakri's head kept bobbing.

"So what do you think? If you were me, wouldn't you think you were a terrorist? Can't you see why people would be concerned?"

The logic stopped the young man short, as if he were about to agree. "But you know me," al-Bakri said earnestly. "You know I'm not, right?"

CHAPTER 12

A CONSPIRACY OF SILENCE

Why do a group of young Yemeni Americans, born and brought up in Lackawanna, NY, and in the majority of cases married with children, suddenly leave their otherwise unremarkable lives to spend six to seven weeks in a terrorist training camp, then quietly slip back into roles of middle class America?

—from the government's filing against
the Lackawanna Six

WITHIN HOURS of Sahim Alwan's arrest, his family was on the phone with Buffalo defense attorney Jim Harrington. A distinguished-looking Irishman, Harrington was known for taking on the tough cases other lawyers wouldn't touch. People still talked about his defense of two Sinn-Fein leaders who had been barred from traveling to the United States in 1983. They entered the country anyway, and Harrington managed to get them acquitted. Harrington also defended a man named Johnson Parker who, in 1998, was out on bail for a gun charge in Buffalo and managed to shoot two police officers who had stopped their squad car to question him. The crime was considered so heinous, the District Attorney sought the death penalty. Harrington was lead counsel. He lost the case, but it did indicate something about Harrington: he didn't seem to re-gard anyone as legally untouchable. Whether Alwan's family called on Harrington because there was a vague recollection of these cases, or just because Harrington was the only high-profile defense attorney anybody in the First Ward could name, is un-clear.

Harrington suggested the family come by his office in down-town Buffalo to chat. Alwan's sister, an uncle, and another dis-tant relative showed up. They gave Harrington a broad outline of what Alwan stood accused of. They assured him that Alwan was not like the others the police had accused of going to an al-Qaeda camp: Alwan had a steady job, he was a family man. He was definitely not a terrorist. He had already provided a state-ment to the FBI, they said, and largely admitted to the charges. He had attended the camp, but he left after only ten days once he realized what he had gotten himself into. "He isn't a terror-ist," they kept repeating.

Harrington, a no-nonsense guy, leveled with them right away. "Are you millionaires?" he asked the small assembled group, knowing the answer.

They shook their heads.

"Well, frankly, I don't think you can afford to retain anyone for your brother," he said. "A high-profile case like this one, any attorney is going to ask for a $250,000 retainer, at a minimum. The court will assign him a lawyer. Wait for the court to assign him a lawyer."

The family looked pained. They worried aloud whether Alwan would be assigned a lawyer who could handle this kind of case. Harrington assured them that the judge would only assign a lawyer who had a lot of experience in a federal court. Whomever ended up helping Sahim Alwan, he said, would be a competent lawyer. Still, to make the family feel better, Harrington said that he would make a point of going to the arraignment later that morning so their brother would have someone there monitoring the proceedings. The family left together, thanking him profusely for his advice and counsel.

About a half hour later, Bill Clauss, the federal defender for western New York, strolled into Harrington's office. The two had had a scheduled meeting of the New York State Criminal Defense Lawyers Association. At the time, Harrington was president of the organization, and Clauss a member. Luck would have it that a number of Buffalo's defense attorneys were on their way to Harrington's office that morning. Bill Clauss was the first to arrive.

"Did you hear about these guys charged for terrorism?" Clauss asked, walking in the door. Harrington nodded and said he had already spoken with one of the families. The news coverage suggested that the case was going to be as much about how the men played in the press as it was about the law. Clauss was going to have to find a handful of lawyers to represent the young men. Typically, in cases like this, the magistrate of the court calls the federal defender to represent a client who needs a lawyer in federal court but doesn't have the money to retain one. The federal defender usually takes the first of the accused and then, to avoid conflicts of interest if there are multiple defendants in a particular case, other lawyers take the remaining defendants on a rotating basis. Harrington was on the list of lawyers who accepted that responsibility. By the end of the weekend, a handful of Buffalo's best-known lawyers had signed on to represent the men from the First Ward. The lawyers said later that they viewed their job not to prove their client's innocence—since two of the men had admitted they had attended an al-Qaeda camp—as much as to poke enough holes in the prosecution to draw a better deal. There was no evidence that the men had spoken of or planned an attack. There was no proof they were terrorists. They were guilty only of attending an al-Qaeda camp, and as the lawyers saw it that might not be enough to charge them with helping a terrorist organization.

Harrington and a handful of attorneys put their Saturday meeting on hold long enough to go across the street to the federal courthouse to attend the Lackawanna Six arraignment. It took no time at all to establish that the Yemeni men before the judge did not have the means to retain lawyers. Harrington entered Alwan's not-guilty plea as a courtesy. The judge entered the pleas for the others. The judge assigned Harrington to the Alwan case then and there. Harrington sat down next to Sahim to talk to him for the first time. Alwan looked exhausted. Even so, Harrington was immediately struck by how gentle and articulate he was.

"I just couldn't understand how he'd get mixed up in something like this," he said. "I still don't."

———

DEFENSE ATTORNEY Rod Personius had been enjoying a beer at a local bar just outside of Buffalo when he happened to glance up at the television screen where, even though the sound was turned down, the scrolling headlines said enough: "Al-Qaeda Sleeper Cell Arrested Outside Buffalo." He watched with disbelief as the cameras caught a parade of Lackawanna youth being pushed into squad cars and driven out of the First Ward. As patrons caught sight of the scrolling headlines, the noise in the bar went dead. Drinkers stopped in mid-swallow as the gravity of the headlines started to soak in. Almost exactly one year after the 9/11 attacks, the nation's worst fear was coming to life: the jihad was next door.

"Holy shit," Personius said aloud, uttering what nearly everyone in the bar was thinking. Then, under his breath, he added, "I hope they nail those bastards."

The next day, Personius was in his offices at the Staler Towers in downtown Buffalo when Jim Harrington approached him. He wanted Personius to represent one of the Lackawanna Six. "Are they the real deal, are they really a sleeper cell?" Personius asked him. Harrington said as far as he could tell they were a bunch of kids who got in over their heads. Personius immediately agreed to help.

This was an unusual case for Personius, who was a deceptively gentle, soft-spoken man. A partner at Personius Melber LLP, he tended to focus on white-collar criminal defense and business litigation. He had been an Assistant United States Attorney for the Western District of New York and served as both chief of the Financial Crimes Unit and chief of the Civil Division, so he knew how to prosecute as well as defend. But wading into a terrorism case was a departure.

Two days later, Personius was sitting across from Yassein Taher at Batavia Prison, about forty minutes east of Buffalo. The two men sat on either side of a small desk, and Personius was struck immediately by how young Taher looked. He wasn't frightened or nervous, just very young. Like Personius, Taher was genial and soft-spoken. It wasn't what the attorney was expecting. On television, he had seen six men who looked like foreigners. He half expected Taher to have an accent, or broken English. The young man sitting before him was all-American. He spoke like a typical American kid. He could have been any Buffalo twenty-something.

Personius had decided, prior to being buzzed into the prison, that he wouldn't ask Taher whether the allegations against him were true. He had enough experience at the U.S. Attorney's office to know that the government wouldn't be accusing these kids of going to Afghanistan and an al-Qaeda camp unless they actually had. Personius was certain that the devil was in the details. In his experience, he found that it was a mistake to have a client lay out his version of events from the outset. They often got into a tangle of half-truths before they trusted him, and then they would spend too much time trying to extricate themselves from the original statement. "I didn't know what he would be like, but I guessed that he would have a disinclination to be forthcoming," Personius said later. "That becomes a problem later because once someone tells you a story it is hard for them to change it."

Personius wasn't sure whether the Lackawanna Six were the secret cell the government claimed it to be or, as Harrington said, just a bunch of guys who didn't know any better. Personius couldn't shake the feeling that the timing of the case appeared to be motivated by politics. They had returned from the camp months before the September 11 attacks, and since their return had done precisely nothing to incriminate themselves or suggest they were planning to do so. Could it really be a coincidence that they were suddenly arrested now, so close to the 9/11 anniversary?

———

HARRINGTON MAY HAVE been better prepared for the media maelstrom that was to follow the arrest of the Lackawanna Six than the rest of the attorneys. The Saturday of the arraignment there were only local crews and reporters from the *Buffalo News* sprinkled around the courthouse square. By Sunday, out-of-town journalists had arrived. Newspeople of every description had descended on Buffalo: members of the major wire services, photographers, television crews, reporters from around the world. There was a space designated on Court Street for the tents set up by the networks for their anchors. Another group of reporters were installed on the courthouse stairs. From the looks of it, one would have thought that the crowd in the streets had gathered in expectation of a movie star or famous politician. Everyone wanted to get a glimpse of America's first homegrown terrorists.

Protesters supporting the Yemeni community set up across from the courthouse at the Mahoney State Office Building. Banners reading "Civil Rights Means Innocent Until Proven Guilty," "Collective Punishment is Unjust," and "Stand Together in Defense of the Rights of All" made clear their take on the events. Across the street, a handful of non-Yemenis gathered to shout at the protestors. "You wouldn't be doing this if you had lost someone in the World Trade Center attacks," accused one. Another protester was waving an American flag and wearing a T-shirt with Osama bin Laden labeled as America's Most Wanted. "Go back to where you came from," she shouted to the Yemenis. "We don't want you here." Two muscle-bound white guys with Buffalo accents began arguing with the Yemeni crowd. They suggested they take a flight back to Afghanistan.

The tension was hardly a surprise. Security around the courthouse had reached a fever pitch. Police blocked off streets and put officers in combat gear at the surrounding street corners. The Lackawanna Six were brought to the courthouse in a motorcade of cars with lights flashing and sirens wailing. The scene made it look like the authorities expected al-Qaeda operatives to rappel off the roofs and come up through manholes to break out their brothers-in-arms. Of course, nothing of the sort took place.

Law enforcement officials braced themselves for a surge of protestors. But when the crowd caught sight of the accused, who were thin and young and pained by the attention, with police escorts, the crowd was struck dumb, as though they were amazed to find the accused terrorists in such ordinary human shape. Clad in prison jumpsuits, bullet-proof vests, and handcuffs, the men looked startled by all the attention. They craned their necks as if trying to catch a glimpse of whatever had motivated the crowd to gather. It didn't occur to them, when they first emerged from the police vehicles, that they could be worthy of such commotion.

The *Buffalo News* began covering the Lackawanna Six story as if the men were ungrateful immigrants who were guilty as charged. A September 20 cartoon in its pages depicted a woman in Muslim dress standing by an open mailbox holding a letter. To her left stood two kids. The boy was holding a soccer ball, and the bill of his cap was pointing over his ear, hip-hop style. The speech balloon over the woman said, "It's from your father."

A balloon coming off the letter allowed the readers to view the text:

> My dear wife and children, How are things in Lackawanna? Today we had training on combat techniques and other neat skills that could come in handy some day. Osama bin Laden spoke to us (in person) about the alliance of jihad and how to bring down the U.S. (The Great Satan). I'm very excited.
>
> I'll be home soon and we'll go to a Bills game. We'll buy the wide-screen T.V. you always wanted and start looking for a new car. We have so many choices in America.

Personius was taken aback by all the press coverage: "I had no idea that this case was going to garner this kind of attention. I was very naïve about that. The government was really savvy the way they used the press, the way they leaked particular facts—

that they had met Osama bin Laden or known something about the terror attacks before 9/11—and once they got that momentum against our clients going it was hard to stop it."

It wasn't really until one of Personius's friends at the U.S. Attorney's Office took him aside that he realized just how political the case had become. "Don't expect anything in this case to be normal," the friend told him. "This is being directed from the highest levels. This is not going to be like anything you have done before."

Had this been a typical case, Personius would have likely tried to get the charges reduced to giving federal agents a false statement. The six would serve a sentence in terms of months, not years, because they had not been truthful when asked by the authorities if in fact they had gone to Afghanistan to train at the camps. That sort of defense wasn't going to fly this time. "Don't sit back and wait, get a deal sooner rather than later," a fellow attorney in the U.S. Attorney's office counseled. "Ashcroft is involved, the Department of Defense is involved. Bush is watching this. There is a lot of pressure being brought to bear."

The natural assumption had been that the government had revealed only the minimal amount of evidence to get the young men arraigned. Everyone was waiting for the other shoe to drop: the proof of an intricate terrorist plot derailed, direct instructions from Osama bin Laden to wreak havoc on a western New York border town, bombmaking materials secreted in a garage. The Justice Department was careful not to release too much information too quickly. They spread out the more memorable details. Days after their arrest, newspapers began reporting that the men had not just attended the al-Qaeda camp in Afghanistan but might have been able to prevent the 9/11 attacks. A day or two after that, reporters wrote that the men possessed tapes on suicide attacks and had sent ominous coded emails. Audiences got a steady dose of incriminating evidence that never surfaced inside the courtroom. The media hungrily grabbed the crumbs that fell from the table and suggested darker acts were still to be revealed. The Lackawanna Six came to embody whatever sinister act doomcasters could dream up. Everyone seemed to agree, in a general way, that these men were a sleeper cell and, had it not been for the government's quick work, they might have struck. Of course, there was no evidence of anything of the kind.

The press would only find out after the initial dust settled that America's first sleeper cell was not exactly a collection of fierce jihadists. They would learn later that Alwan faked an injury as a ruse to get out of the camp, that the men were partly motivated to leave because they hated the food, and the camp was too rigorous. Instead, in the early days of the trial, the focus was on the government's version of events, the Kalishnikov rifles they fired, the plastic explosives they learned about, and the conspiracy of silence before and after the September 11 attacks. Though silence wasn't a crime, prosecutors used it against the Lackawanna Six. The judge said there was no law requiring citizens to report attendance at a camp, but he made his position clear. "It's more of an obligation, I suppose, if you're an American citizen, to the citizenry, or to humanity." Heads in the courtroom nodded in agreement. The defendants sunk lower in their chairs.

"They returned to the United States without telling authorities about the planned attacks, which culminated in the deaths of 3,025 people at the World Trade Center and the Pentagon and in rural Pennsylvania," the *Buffalo News* wrote. What the newspaper didn't report was that the Lackawanna Six didn't have any details about the attack aside from Osama bin Laden's cryptic message that forty volunteers were ready to "take their souls in their hands." It wouldn't have been the kind of tip-off from which the FBI could fashion an arrest.

While residents of the First Ward wanted to be supportive in that general way people have of wanting to help people they know, the more they learned of the true nature of the Lackawanna Six's trip, the more troubled they became. For weeks, they had been telling anyone who would listen that the allegations were drummed up, that this was an anti-Muslim witch hunt. Family and friends insisted the six had gone to Pakistan with Tablighi Jama'at, a benign Muslim organization. If the Lackawanna men had been to Afghanistan, they would have known about it. Nicole Frick would say later she didn't know about the trip to the camp until she read it in the newspaper. When it became clear that the six had indeed been to Afghanistan and had indeed trained at an al-Qaeda camp, First Warders were angry at being duped. "They were fools," said Abdul Noman, Taher's uncle and a local soccer coach. "I told Taher to just take the plea. No jury was going to sympathize with him after the September 11th attacks. We all knew that."

The Lackawanna case also had the misfortune of overlapping with another high-profile case—that of the so-called American Taliban, John Walker Lindh. Lindh was working out his plea agreement when the Lackawanna Six were arrested, and, as tidbits of information began to leak to the press, it appeared that the jihadi world was a very small one. Lindh and the Lackawanna Six had overlapped at the outgoing guesthouse in Kandahar. Lindh recalled overhearing some Americans in one of the guest rooms talking about a restaurant they wanted to go to and the food they were going to eat once they left. While the group didn't speak to Lindh or meet him directly, Lindh had had a roommate in college who had been from western New York, and he recognized the accent in the conversation he overheard at the guesthouse. The Lackawanna defense attorneys were concerned that Lindh might be providing information about the Lackawanna Six to benefit his own plea bargain just as their attorneys were building a case. As far as Personius could see, the timing "couldn't have been worse."

———

FEDERAL PROSECUTORS used al-Bakri's email about the "big meal" as the foundation of their case. Because the email sounded so sinister, for prosecutors it was the perfect ticket to ensure the men would not be released on bail. Al-Bakri told the FBI that the email referred to "what he believed to be a planned attack by al-Qaeda upon Americans," said prosecutor William J. Hochul. "We submit that this is an indication of Mr. al-Bakri's continuing knowledge and certainly dissemination of a possible al-Qaeda attack, terrorist attacks upon American citizens."

The prosecutor wanted the government's case to unfold like a sinister movie of young Muslim men who were prepared to do anything for their cause. He painted a picture of a sleeper cell, a small army of Osama bin Laden's warriors posing as normal American boys until called upon. "We all know that regrettably on September 11th, 2001, Mr. bin Laden activated persons who had lived in the United States," the prosecutor told the court. "They, in some cases, had gone to school here and had attended flight training in this country, in order to commit the most dastardly terrorist act ever upon United States soil." The implication, of course, was that there was little difference between the nineteen suicide hijackers and the handful of men who sat at the front of the courtroom wearing expressions of anxiety and defeat.

The defense attorneys insisted there was no evidence of a grand al-Qaeda design but simple twenty-something bravado. Osama bin Laden was not a household name in the narrow streets of the First Ward before the 9/11 attacks. In the most for-giving of scenarios, the men who traveled to Afghanistan did so out of a sense of adventure, and once they realized that the trainees in the camp were leveling their sights on America, they left. "These guys had no idea what they were getting into," Har-rington said later.

Like most talented criminal-defense attorneys, Harrington and Personious excelled at shifting the focus of their trials from the behavior of their clients to the actions of the investigators, police, or other suspects in the case. FBI searches of the men's homes had yielded little. There was not a cache of weapons or secret bombmaking chemicals. Instead, they discovered an an-tique Derringer in one house and a videotape that, depending on whose side one was on, was entitled "An Invitation to Jihad" or "A Call to Jihad." And in Taher's apartment was a file folder marked "personal." Inside was a paper that appeared to make the case for martyrdom missions. The nine-page document, taken from some Internet Web site, laid out the definition of martyr-dom operations and their effect on the enemy:

> Martyrdom or self-sacrifice operations are those performed by one or more people, against enemies far outstripping them in numbers and equipment, with prior knowledge that the operations will almost inevitably lead to death . . . The form this usually takes nowadays is to wire up one's body, or a vehicle or suitcase with explosives, and then to enter amongst a conglomeration of the enemy, or in their vital facilities, and to detonate in an appropriate place there in order to cause the maximum losses. We have found, through the course of our experience that there is no other technique which strikes as much terror into their hearts, and which shatters their spirit as much.

Taher said it was part of a larger tract that compared Catholicism and Islam, two issues that were a constant point of contention with his wife, Nicole. Personius said that the prosecutors only read the most inflammatory parts aloud. They didn't, for example, explain that the document appeared to be focused on Russian fighting in Chechnya. It wasn't anti-American. But that hardly mattered. The prosecution was seeking to paint Taher as a potential suicide bomber. "Taher was doing the best among them until they found that note. For Yassein," Personius said later, "that changed everything. Yassein wasn't becoming a suicide bomber. He was just trying to understand a controversial interpretation and aspect of the Islamic faith. These kids were wrestling with their identity and how to be a good Muslim in America. This trip was supposed to be all about that, not terrorism."

Defense attorneys thought the evidence presented was thin enough that they could plant at least a seed of doubt in a critical juror's mind if the case ever went to trial, though everyone seemed sure that it wouldn't come to that. The government wanted a deal, something that would give it a win on the war on terror without having to completely tip its hand and reveal what it knew, and didn't know, about the recruitment of the Lackawanna Six.

The prosecutor used the theater of the situation, the drama of a sleeper cell, to full advantage. The courtroom was filled to bursting with FBI agents. They lined the seats in the jury box; Ed Needham was in the front row. The presence of so many agents was meant to suggest that there were reams and reams of evidence against the defendants. Each man and woman represented some new item, some incriminating fact that would show that these men should not only be denied bail but jailed as well. Harrington, Personius, and the other Lackawanna Six lawyers doubted that the government had collected all that much concrete evidence against their clients, though they couldn't be sure: discovery, an accounting of what the other side intended to present, was almost non-existent. Every witness the defense asked to talk to, every fact they attempted to check, was quickly swathed in a blanket of secrecy. Their requests for interviews with Juma al-Dosari in Guantanamo or Kamel Derwish were summarily dismissed in the interest of national security. This was, of course, precisely what the overflow crowd wanted to hear. Each new turn in the narrative, every allegation made, only confirmed their deepest suspicions about the Lackawanna Six and reflected badly on the Yemeni community in Lackawanna more generally. The residents of the First Ward had so vehemently defended this group from the start, every revelation seemed to imply that Lackawanna's Yemenis couldn't be trusted either.

The *Buffalo News* editorial pages focused on their conspiracy of silence. "Even if they were innocent dupes who thought they were going to Afghanistan to learn more about Islam, and whether or not they were disturbed by what they heard, they sided against America with their silence. Whether based on belief or fear, an indifference or failure to recognize evil or the seriousness of bin Laden's threats, they made a decision not to warn law enforcement officials of a threat to this nation's security," its editorial read. "That should carry a price, albeit one not nearly as severe as the one paid by thousands of their fellow Americans on 9/11."

What the prosecution papered over was that it wasn't a crime not to say something to officials just as it isn't a crime to say things against America or to be anti-Israel. The lectures in the Wilkesbarre Avenue apartment weren't illegal either. Even traveling to Pakistan and Afghanistan, as the men did, wasn't beyond the pale. But in the post–9/11 world, all six Muslim men doing all of this was suspect. "The big problem for us was that, even though they went to the camps before 9/11, we couldn't unring the September 11th bell," Personius said. "The community, even a jury, could never step back in time to see that they went to a camp before the towers fell. And that made this a very tough case."

The defendants had roots in the Yemeni community of Lackawanna, the government said, but by not telling authorities about their trip to the camp "the defendants failed to demonstrate ties to the American community, let alone their allegiance to the American community." When al-Bakri heard this, he cried.

————

HARRINGTON FIGURED that if any of the men were to get out on bail it would be Sahim Alwan. He had, after all, cooperated with the government. He had standing in the community, and he was first out of the camp. He didn't flee when he was told he would be arrested. But the media had already dubbed him a terrorist, Harrington said, and he would carry that distinction with him wherever he went. "Mr. Alwan has already been punished unfairly, he now has a giant scarlet T written across his forehead," Harrington told the court. "It is a label he will carry with him for the rest of his life."

The courtroom was packed with supporters from the Yemeni community as Personious and Harrington attacked the government's charges. Friends and relatives were willing to put up $2.2 million in property and cash for bail, they told the judge. The community could raise up to $5 million, if necessary.

The defense lawyers said the young men were victims of what is known as false-flag recruiting. They had been lured to the camp under other guises. They were not a sleeper cell. A group had to be operational to get that kind of distinction. They needed to begin reconnaissance on a target, pick participants. That never happened with the Lackawanna Six, even though the FBI had been observing them for more than a year.

The prosecutor said that was beside the point. Crucially, he suggested that had the government captured the attackers before 9/11 and asked them what they were training for, they probably would have had the same answers the Lackawanna Six provided. It was a suggestion that could not be completely dispelled—there were no surviving hijackers to test it out on. The government kept drawing the parallel between these six and the 9/11 hijackers, and it seemed to be working.

"My purpose in attending the camp was to see what it was all about," Alwan said in a statement he read in federal court in September. "After I realized the crazy radical mentality of the people at the camp, I decided to leave."

As the defense saw it, attending the al-Farooq camp could not, in and of itself, be seen as a violent crime. "It is like charging someone with a thought crime," said Personius. "You prosecute for attending a training camp, even though there's no evidence there was any plan for a terrorist act."

"This was like filing charges against suspected Communist Party sympathizers during the McCarthy era of the 1950s," another lawyer said. "People were prosecuting them for being members of the Communist Party, without taking any overt action. Eventually those charges were all thrown out."

"You need something more than just going to a camp," Harrington told reporters. "These young men were driven to the camp, it was heavily guarded, you were not free to leave. Even if you could leave, you wouldn't know where you were."

Ed Needham was in court every day, hanging on every word. He was genuinely concerned the men would get out. The media frenzy surrounding the case, as he saw it, could make it go either way. "The argument was that they knew about explosives, and the camp they went to was al-Qaeda, so it seemed like a no-brainer," said Needham later. "But to deny them bail the lawyers just needed to convince the judge they weren't a flight risk and weren't violent, and they could make that argument."

The hearing lasted three days. None of the men was offered bail.

———

ABOUT THIS TIME, a phone solicitation began popping up on answering machines all over Buffalo.

"You've probably heard that our local authorities have detailed six allegedly trained al-Qaeda terrorists," it began. "We believe that the goal of this terrorist cell was to detonate briefcase-sized dirty bombs right here in western New York.

"Our division is responsible for delivering crisis kits to every household in western New York," it continued. "We need for you to call us back at our local headquarters here in Buffalo. We cannot stress the importance of getting back to us enough."

Law enforcement officials started looking into complaints about the telemarketing company a couple of days after the recorded messages for special "crisis packets" started going out. Residents said the recordings from a Buffalo company called Bio-Fend seemed like the real thing. They asked if it was true that the sleeper cell in Lackawanna was planning to set off suit-case-sized dirty bombs before the FBI foiled their plot. No one, as far as law enforcement could tell, ever bought a kit, so it was hard to tell if the calls were meant as a scam or as a way to taint the jury pool. New York's Attorney General Eliot Spitzer got a court order dissolving Bio-Fend several months later.

A FEDERAL GRAND JURY indicted the Lackawanna Six in October 2002. They stood accused of making a clandestine trip to Afghanistan where they heard a speech from bin Laden, listened to lectures about suicide attacks, and learned how to fire automatic weapons in an al-Qaeda training camp. The two-page indictment presented their actions as a conspiracy and as providing material support to a terrorist organization. Personius and Harrington had a nagging feeling that there was nothing they could do in the current environment to help their clients. They were in a new legal world in which the accepted rules of justice were being rewritten and revised.

Lackawanna was the first major case to test a law enforcement system that had morphed from an establishment whose mission was to solve terrorist crimes to one meant to make sure they didn't happen in the first place. That meant they used new antiterrorism tools, from enhanced surveillance to interrogation of enemy combatants, that the defense never would have access to. Questioning Derwish and al-Dosari might have allowed the defense to prove their clients had been duped into traveling to Afghanistan. The prosecution said they couldn't find Derwish, which was true. They had a more tenuous reason to deny access to al-Dosari. It was widely known that he was being held at the U.S. military base in Guantanamo Bay, Cuba, though there were still no prisoner lists released at the time. The Justice Department refused to acknowledge where he was. The defense had to build a case with one hand tied behind its back.

CHAPTER 13

A TIME OF FIRE

A MONTH LATER, anyone looking for Kamel Derwish would have had to go to the hills and scrub of Ma'rib province in Yemen. On November 3, 2002, he was sitting in the backseat of a truck in a small convoy of SUVs speeding across the desert. Qaed Salim Sinan al-Harethi, considered al-Qaeda's top operative in Yemen and the likely mastermind behind the attack on the USS *Cole*, was also in the backseat. Evidently, Derwish's inability to keep the Lackawanna Six at the al-Farooq camp for the duration had not affected his standing among the terrorist operatives. He was keeping company with some of the most notorious members of the organization. One would have to expect that Derwish's thoughts could not have been any further from Lackawanna and the men whom he had befriended months before. He was on to other things. It is unclear whether he knew the six had been arrested just weeks earlier or whether he even cared.

Seen from above, the thin line of cars carrying Derwish and al-Harethi looked innocent enough—just dots moving on pinkish sand. The group turned off a busy highway onto a more remote road slicing through the hills. A man in the front seat was talking on a satellite phone. The SUV was quiet but for his conversation and fans from the air-conditioning.

Half a world away, a handful of intelligence officers in the Counter-Terrorism Center in Langley, Virginia, were sitting in front of a bank of computer screens watching a grainy video. It showed a bird's-eye view of the convoy's progress across the dunes. Another group of intelligence operatives in Djibouti, in eastern Africa, were tuned into the same picture, toggling the joystick on the remote controls of a Predator drone as it circled above. The camera in the aircraft was providing both groups with a live feed of the events on the ground. The quiet hum of its engine would have been indistinguishable above the whirling air-conditioning in the cars. And even if it hadn't been, the man in the front seat shouting into a satellite phone to another al-Qaeda operative he was trying to meet in the Yemeni desert would have drowned out any outside sound. The al-Qaeda leaders were trying to use what few landmarks the area provided to meet a soldier in the field. "We're right over here . . . ," the conversation went. What the man in the car didn't know was that the operative with whom he was speaking was in U.S. custody and had no intention of meeting him.

CIA Director George Tenet was watching from headquarters in Virginia. He gave a nod and returned his gaze to the screen before him. A Hellfire missile screamed from the Predator drone. Eighteen pounds of high explosives slammed into the convoy. The Hellfire had originally been designed to blow up Soviet tanks. It made short work of al-Harethi's car. He was the "high value target" the Bush administration had slated for elimination. The only American within a hundred of miles of the attack, and just as completely obliterated by it, was Kamel Derwish.

A CIA officer arrived at the convoy while it was still smoldering. He sifted through the bits and pieces of metal and then took out a knife and, picking through the charred remains. He carefully extracted DNA from a femur. They assumed it was

that of Kamel Derwish. Derwish's uncle in Lackawanna provided the DNA sample needed for a match. Publicly, there
would be questions later whether Derwish was actually in the
convoy. To have affirmed his death would have meant admit-
ting that the murder of an American, without charge or trial,
was sanctioned by the Bush administration and that would
mean the administration had taken the war on terror to a new
level: it had decided that it could summarily kill an American
citizen. And while there was little doubt, given the company he
was keeping, that Derwish had connections to al-Qaeda, in
killing him officials had murdered the one man who could clarify whether the Lackawanna Six were really a sleeper cell or half
a dozen confused friends who had gotten in over their heads.

On another level, the targeted assassination of Derwish was
pre-emptive justice of the most dire variety. Amnesty International called it a death sentence without a trial. "If this was the
deliberate killing of suspects in lieu of arrest, in circumstances in
which they did not pose an immediate threat, the kills would be
extrajudicial executions in violation of international human
rights law," the group said after the killing. Law enforcement in-
siders said they were focused on killing al-Harethi and were not
concerned about the collateral damage—killing other al-Qaeda
members who might be with him.

When Mike Battle learned of the killing, he was shocked. It
showed just how keen American leaders were to strike back at al-
Qaeda after the September 11 attacks. What made this different
was that the strike happened outside any formally recognized
war zone. The killing smacked of political assassination. Many
critics compared it to Israel's targeted killings in the West Bank.

There were legal issues raised by the attack as well. Before the
killing of Derwish, the United States had considered acts of terrorism largely in judicial terms—law enforcement officers

arrested perpetrators who were then given access to the due process of law. It was proof of America's insistence that it hold itself to a higher standard. They may be murderers, but Americans still allowed them to have their day in court. Lethal force had previously been a last resort used only when armed suspects resisted arrest. But in this case, as the convoy sped across the desert, an arrest wasn't part of the plan. Apart from al-Harethi, none of the men in the convoy had even been charged with a crime.

"We all would like perfection," Secretary of Defense Donald Rumsfeld said about the use of pre-emptive military strikes. "We'd all like all the dots connected for us with a ribbon wrapped around it. Americans want evidence beyond a reasonable doubt. You want to be able to be certain that you know before anyone's punished." But Rumsfeld dismissed that option. "We've got the wrong model in our minds if we're thinking about punishment."

U.S. government officials still refuse to comment about Derwish specifically. Intelligence officials would not speculate whether the reports that he was in the convoy were true. When U.S. and Yemeni authorities initially planned the operation, they had decided to release a joint statement about the attack. That didn't happen. The Bush administration announced it unilaterally in time for Election Day on November 5. The Republicans, running on an anti-terrorism platform, kept their majority in the House of Representatives and the Senate.

———

TWO MONTHS LATER, the first of the Lackawanna Six gave up any hope that he might be able to make a pre–9/11 argument of innocence in a post–9/11 world. In a plea agreement, Faysal Galab admitted to providing material support to a terrorist organization. The Lackawanna-born, American-educated, father of three admitted in a nineteen-page plea agreement in January of 2003 that he and the others had traveled to Afghanistan knowing that what they would be doing was illegal. He confessed to buying a uniform at the Kandahar guesthouse, receiving weapons training, and performing guard duty at the camp. He said that he had heard bin Laden speak, and the leader of al-Qaeda had talked about the bombings of the American embassies in Kenya and Tanzania and said that "40 men were on a mission to attack America." For all this, Galab got seven years. His attorney was quick to point out, however, that he didn't know that 9/11 was coming. "No specifics were given, he didn't hear anything about 9/11," his attorney said.

The special agent in charge of the Buffalo FBI office, Pete Ahearn, agreed that Galab didn't know about 9/11 in advance. Nor could he have prevented it. But as he saw it, just going to the camp was enough to damn him. "For any American citizen to go over there and participate in a training program like that, I think is unconscionable," said Ahearn.

Galab's plea took Harrington, Personius, and the other defense attorneys by surprise. The defense lawyers had agreed among themselves only to speak to prosecutors as a group, assuming they could get their clients better deals if they stood united. Galab's attorney made a deal without consulting them.

Once that happened, it was only a question of time before the others followed. Ten weeks later, Shafel Mosed and Yahya Goba, took a similar deal. Concerned that they might be charged with treason or that the government would pursue the death penalty or make them enemy combatants, the two men pled guilty to a felony charge of material support. Mosed faced eight years. Goba, because he seemed to be more in charge of the operation, was sentenced to ten years.

U.S. Attorney Battle wouldn't comment on whether treason charges were the next shot his office intended to fire. He denied he ever threatened to send them to Guantanamo as enemy combatants. He didn't need to. The threat was unspoken: Juma al-Dosari was already there, after all.

With Derwish dead and Jaber Elbaneh still at large in Yemen, the remaining members of the Lackawanna Six—Mukhtar al-Bakri, Yassein Taher, and Sahim Alwan—agonized over what to do next. In their hearts they felt they weren't terrorists. Taking a plea suggested that they were. Their families wanted them to fight. Their lawyers warned they could end up with weapons charges as well as material support, adding fifteen years to their sentences. Enemy combatant status would mean the twenty-somethings could end up in a military brig without the benefit of a jury trial. There were few good choices.

Harrington and Personius sincerely believed their clients did not fully comprehend the trouble they had stumbled into. Jihad, as they understood it, didn't involve the United States. At most they would have been recruited to fight in Chechnya or Bosnia against Russians or Serbs. Taher told friends before he left that he might end up in the former Yugoslavia, fighting against the Orthodox Christians, standing shoulder to shoulder with other Muslims. He and the others were simply looking for a way to feel a few cuts above an ordinary Muslim. Harrington and Personius said their clients were naïve. They genuinely thought it had been a religious trip with a military component—not the other way around. During their time in Afghanistan, they felt something they hadn't felt since they ruled the soccer field in high school: important. That was intoxicating enough for them to paper over the initial reservations they had about being there. They focused instead on how this was turning them into better Muslims.

"This trip was sold as a way for them to get back to Islam," Personius said later. "It began with a huge guilt trip about how they were too American and had bought too much into the Western way of life. The trip was supposed to remedy that. There was never any suggestion that this was going to move into attacks against America. I was careful when I talked to Taher about his decision, though. Part of me really wanted to take this to trial, but another part of me said that there was no way a jury would see this objectively. Before the September 11 attacks, there were lots of people in America who didn't know exactly who bin Laden was. I don't think I really did. It wasn't something I focused on, and I considered myself pretty much up on current affairs. So it isn't crazy to suggest these guys didn't understand who bin Laden was or what al-Qaeda was all about. But trying to convince a jury that was the case would be pretty hard. People forget what they did or didn't know before the attacks. Now it is a whole new world."

Sahim Alwan, the last-minute addition to the Afghanistan trip, finally pled guilty to material support three months after Galab's plea, in April of 2003. Harrington said that, in the end, Alwan felt bad enough about what he did that he felt he deserved to be punished. In a quiet voice, Alwan told the court that he had met and spoken with bin Laden twice but never heard about his plans for terrorism and was never asked to take part in any terrorist acts.

The item that made the headlines in the papers the next day, however, had less to do with Alwan's plea than another morsel he offered up to the court: seven additional men from Lackawanna had been ready to go to Afghanistan and train at al-Farooq. They were supposed to leave when the first six had returned. He named names. He said the men who had been part of the second wave balked only after Alwan came back and told them how difficult the training was. Then the September 11 attacks derailed any travel plans the new men had made. Kamel Derwish's recruitment campaign had been very successful.

Ed Needham said later that if the FBI had not received an anonymous letter from someone in the First Ward, it might never have known about Derwish's activities. The author of the letter never came forward. But investigators were sure it was a young man in the Yemeni community who had sat in on the Wilkesbarre Avenue meetings and had been frightened by what he heard or saw. Clearly, it had been someone who had read between the lines of Derwish's discussions and saw them more clearly for what they were: a call to jihad in a small town full of young men eager to belong to something, anything, even if that something turned out to be al-Qaeda.

Alwan would say later that he knew going to the camp would get him into trouble, but he did it anyway. "I was naïve. It was dumb," he told the news program *Frontline*. "It's just like you know, hey let's go steal that car. It's wrong, you know, excitement, you know. You do it, and then you realize it was wrong. I think back and think, what the hell did you do? If I could change anything in my past, it would be that trip."

Harrington was hoping a prime-time interview with Alwan, the most articulate and homespun of the Six, would provide some counterbalance to the terrorist sleeper cell stories coming out of Washington. As soon as the interview aired, however, Harrington and the others knew it wouldn't be enough. The American public had already decided. The Lackawanna Six gave human shape to greatest fear in post–9/11 America: that the enemy might well be among us.

———

PERSONIUS DIDN'T WANT Taher to take a plea. It interfered with Personius's sense of right and wrong and his basic belief in the American system of justice. He was convinced that these guys from the First Ward were not terrorists, and Taher, as amiable and uncomplaining as he had ever been, didn't deserve to spend a decade in prison simply because he had made one bad decision. Yassein Taher's brothers had been in and out of prison for smuggling and drug running for years. Somehow Yassein had been able to stay out of that and lead, comparatively, a responsible life. Going to the camp was something his brothers might have done, but not Yassein. For him, it wasn't part of some larger pattern; it was an anomaly. Personius felt he could convince a jury of that much: Yassein wasn't a terrorist wannabe. He was a kid looking for a purpose, and unfortunately Derwish was able to prey upon that.

What was more, the way the government handled the case had gotten Personius's back up. There was too much political pressure. He couldn't talk to Battle or his team without hearing that they would need to check with officials in Washington. Leaks to the press from the prosecution were selective, damaging, and often downright false. Innuendo was used to create a groundswell of negativity against the Lackawanna Six.

"I felt like our system for meting out justice had stopped functioning the way it should," Personius said later. "The government was scared to be wrong about Yassein and the rest of them, and that fear, in my opinion, made it impossible for the system to work properly. Part of me really wanted to test all this in court, to see if a jury would buy the government's version of events. Another part of me didn't want to see Yassein spend his whole life in jail if we didn't prevail. It was a really tough choice."

Ultimately, Taher took a plea deal. It was April 2003. Personius told the court that he had advised his client not to take the deal. "It was the first time in twenty-five years of being a defense attorney that my client went against my advice to turn down a plea agreement," Personius said later. "In the end, Yassein took the deal because of Nicole and Noah. He didn't want to risk going to jail for thirty years. The government was saying if he didn't take the deal they would file weapons charges and possibly treason against him. That could have produced a thirty-year minimum sentence or even the death penalty. Once Yassein was sure Nicole thought he should take the deal, he did. It was really important to him how she felt about it."

Certainly the pressure had been mounting on Taher. The prosecution told reporters that if the case went to trial, there was a witness who would testify that around February 2001 Taher was surfing pro–Osama bin Laden Web sites. The witness would also testify that Taher had made occasional comments supporting the al-Qaeda leader. Taher denied it.

Personius, for his part, was furious. He said the allegations were part of a strategy out of Washington to portray the Lackawanna Six as tintypes of the 9/11 hijackers. President Bush, Attorney General John Ashcroft, and FBI Director Robert Mueller had taken to referring publicly to the Lackawanna Six as America's first homegrown sleeper cell.

"You did in this case what the government claims you did—is that right?" the judge asked Taher, as he stood before him in April 2003.

He nodded. "Yes, sir," he answered.

Taher said he knew before he ever left Lackawanna that he would be training with al-Qaeda, and that it was against the law to do so. At the al-Farooq camp, Taher said, he was trained in the use of four weapons, including rocket-propelled grenades.

Almost a dozen women stood behind him in the courtroom. They were dressed in abayas and hajibs so their feelings would have been difficult to read were it not for the fact that one could hear them snuffling beneath their veils.

The last of the Lackawanna Six to sign a plea agreement was the first to be arrested: Mukhtar al-Bakri. The groom roused from his wedding bed in Bahrain came to court wearing a red sweater with a large American flag on the front. He described to the court his conversation with bin Laden.

"I just told him that I was there without my parents knowing," al-Bakri said, quietly. "He told me to send them a letter and let them know I was okay."

He sounded more like a truant schoolboy than a traitor.

———

PERSONIUS SAID LATER that the case was an exercise in frustration. The defense never knew how far Washington was willing to go: "They were bandying about the death penalty for these guys," one of the defense attorneys said later. "It was ridiculous. These kids were clearly idiots. They weren't traitors."

The Lackawanna case showed just how much the legal landscape had changed after 9/11. Defendants' choices were stark: either plead guilty, face the possibility of imprisonment without trial, or possibly death. The prosecutors never offered evidence that the Lackawanna Six were planning to do anything. Then again, in the age of pre-emptive justice, they no longer needed to.

"The administration did a magnificent job of politicizing this case from the get-go," Personius asserted. "In subtle ways, they were able to take advantage of the climate in the country to influence the thinking of our clients. Bush still calls them a sleeper cell and for the life of me, I don't understand why. Don't cells plan things? Case targets?"

To be fair, U.S. Attorney Mike Battle never referred to the Lackawanna Six as a sleeper cell. He didn't think they were one. And speaking about the case later, after the agreements had been signed and the men had been in jail for months, Battle admitted that legal landscape had shifted since 9/11, and now the advantage was with the prosecution. Attorney General John Ashcroft was personally involved in the Lackawanna Six case, and made clear he wanted stiff sentences—agreements that would send a message. Galab's attorney had asked for five years for his client. Ashcroft had been pushing for a minimum of ten years for the whole group. Battle got it down to seven.

"We're living in a time of fire," Abdul Noman, Taher's uncle and former soccer coach, said when asked about the case. "We Muslims now have to be extra careful of everything we do, and everything we say. It isn't safe to be a Muslim in America anymore. Nine-eleven has changed it all for us."

His nephew, in his own way, had been right to curl up in a ball on the floor the morning the planes hit the towers. He knew the moment the planes exploded that life as Muslims in America knew it had changed. He was now, as a Muslim, going to be hated and loathed. There was nothing he could do to change who he was, and he would always be suspect.

THE LACKAWANNA SIX had been behind bars for months when the Yemeni police finally brought in Jaber Elbaneh. He was the only one of the men from the First Ward who had never returned to Lackawanna. He had been on a wanted poster and at the top of the FBI's fugitive list for nearly a year. There was confusion as to whether the Yemenis had swooped down and arrested him or if he had actually just turned himself in. Investigators in the United States said he had been driving a taxi in Sana'a for months. The FBI began negotiating for his extradition. They mused aloud about whether he would end up at Guantanamo Bay with Juma al-Dosari. There was a hefty reward for his return. The trouble was that Yemeni authorities began to fight over the money: five million dollars went a long way in Yemen.

As they argued over who had captured Elbaneh, there was an internal debate as to who was responsible for what: the discussion took on the tenor of a real-estate transaction instead of a law enforcement victory. There was a perception among Yemeni officials that if they held onto Elbaneh long enough, the price on his head might rise. So as secret negotiations continued behind the scenes between the United States and the Yemeni government, Elbaneh sat in Yemen's special national security jail.

Yemen's main intelligence arm, the Political Security Office (PSO), runs the national security jail. It sits just blocks away from a new Taco Bell, Kentucky Fried Chicken, and Burger King food court in downtown Sana'a. The PSO is a low-slung building, all square and concrete encircled in razor wire. It is supposed to be the most heavily guarded facility in the country, as close as Yemen came to running one of America's so-called supermax prisons. Behind its walls were some of Yemen's most notorious government detainees. Another of the men linked to the USS *Cole* attack, Mohammed Hamdi al-Ahdal, was behind bars there. Dozens of other al-Qaeda suspects were also locked up there. While Elbaneh's friends were killing time in a medium-security prison not far from Buffalo, Elbaneh was put together with more than a dozen suspected al-Qaeda operatives. If the Lackawanna man was not a terrorist before he went into prison, he would certainly be very familiar with several of the world's leading ones after his incarceration.

In early 2006, women in a mosque down the street from the PSO started complaining about noises coming from under the mosque. They told leaders of the mosque that the sounds were so loud they had difficulty concentrating on their prayers. It sounded like scraping, they said. The elders told them they would look into it. They never reported back. A month later, on February 3, 2006, the reason for all that scraping became clear. Nearly two dozen prisoners from the PSO staged an escape of Hollywood proportions. The prisoners dug a tunnel 143 feet long out of the facility. It came up through the floor of the women's bathroom in the mosque. PSO officials claimed the tunnel was carved out of the earth with a broomstick and a sharpened spoon tied to the end of a spade. The prisoners were very canny, a Yemeni official said. "They hid their project from the guards," he told a television news crew from Sana'a. They had apparently kicked a soccer ball around in the basement of the prison to mask the noise of the digging. What the officials didn't talk about was that the prisoners had started barring guards from the basement more than a month earlier. For inexplicable reasons, the guards acquiesced. Officials also couldn't explain the enormous mounds of dirt that were quite obviously piled around the basement. "Let's just say we're pretty sure that it was an inside job," said one FBI agent investigating the escape. FBI agents joked that Elbaneh was part of the Yemeni government's "catch and release" program.

Leading the group out of the PSO, the man who played the role Steve McQueen made famous in the 1963 movie

The Great Escape, was Jamal al-Badawi, another suspect in the *Cole* operation. Al-Badawi woke the prisoners at about 4:30 a.m. on February 3, and one by one they crawled through the long tunnel. They chose a Friday, a Muslim holy day, when the prison authorities were more lax about accounting for prisoners. The group popped out in the woman's bathroom of the mosque and disappeared into the early morning darkness.

While it was unclear just how much outside help the prisoners had in their escape, FBI officials said it was awfully suspicious that they knew precisely where to dig to come up under the tiles of a nearby women's bathroom. The FBI suspects officials at the PSO were involved, and much of the digging was probably done by al-Qaeda sympathizers at the mosque.

When news of the great escape broke in the United States, authorities in Buffalo were hoping it was part of an elaborate ruse to finally turn Elbaneh over to the American authorities and collect the reward. The Yemeni government's help in the war on terror had always been somewhat ambivalent. They did just enough to keep the Bush administration at bay but not enough to actually be seen as a partner in the fight. They often put al-Qaeda suspects under a liberal house arrest, hauling them into the PSO when it suited them politically. For U.S. law enforcement, it was endlessly frustrating. For individual jihadists, it offered one of the world's last safe havens. Three years earlier, al-Badawi had managed to escape during a prisoner transfer. He was quickly recaptured, and Yemen officials tried then, unsuccessfully, to claim a multimillion-dollar U.S. reward when he was re-arrested. The negotiations were still underway when al-Badawi slipped away a second time.

When news of Elbaneh's daring tunnel escape reached Lackawanna's First Ward, residents were quietly pleased. Ever since the arrests, they had felt bullied. Searches by the government seemed unnecessarily heavy-handed. There was a constant FBI and police presence in the neighborhood, as if there was a presumption of guilt. It was only a matter of time, they felt, before someone else among them would be accused of being a terrorist. Because of that, they saw Jaber Elbaneh's escape as a win for the home team, one for the good guys.

CHAPTER 14

IDEOLOGICAL DETONATORS

NO ONE WILL EVER quite understand why the Lackawanna Six went right to the precipice of radicalization but didn't dive in. It was not a big step from al-Qaeda camp to bonafide religious warrior. But for some reason, most of the young men didn't take that leap. None of them appeared to be actively plotting to attack anything. None of the men signed a pledge to Osama bin Laden. And none of them seemed eager to put what they had learned at al-Farooq to use.

Investigators said Derwish may have envisioned something other than al-Qaeda membership for the Lackawanna boys. He may have thought that they could be part of his own private army, a small jihadi contingent striking targets out of Yemen. There was some logic to his plan. The Lackawanna Six had all been proud of their Yemeni heritage. The family trips to their villages had created an enormous sense of nationalist pride in all of them. Where Derwish miscalculated was in thinking that he could scrub a lifetime of living in America from six men in just a matter of weeks. Derwish had left Lackawanna as a boy, so he hadn't counted on the hold America had over the young men. While one of his recruitment strategies was to accuse the men of being too American, too entrenched in Western ways, in fact, Derwish was prescient in that respect. He assumed their aimless lives in Lackawanna would be easy to leave. In the end, nearly all of the recruits could hardly wait to get back to them.

The FBI was twice lucky in the Lackawanna case. For whatever motive—patriotic concern or some unknown score-settling or grudge—someone in the Yemeni community of the First Ward decided to tell the authorities about Derwish and his recruiting scheme. That was their first break. The second was that ultimately, the Lackawanna Six were willing to flirt with jihad but remained too American to commit to it. It was a thin thread for law enforcement to hold onto.

But luck isn't strategy. The war on terror needed to be part of something bigger. That's why terrorism task forces preferred to use Raed al-Banna as a case study for how best to wage it.

He was a thirty-two-year-old Jordanian who was turned away at Chicago's O'Hare International Airport in July 2003 when border officers saw him possessing "multiple terrorist risk factors." He spoke fluent English and was a lawyer, but they denied him entry anyway. Something about al-Banna just was not right. Fast forward to February 2005 and a suicide car bombing that killed 132 people in Hilla, Iraq. Investigators fingerprinted the bomber's severed hand, still chained to the steering wheel of the wrecked car. (Those who sponsor suicide bombers often chain their wrists to the wheel to ensure they don't change their minds.) The Hilla suicide bomber was none other that al-Banna. Authorities see that episode as validation of their anti-terrorism strategy.

They also saw the grisly murder of filmmaker Theo van Gogh in November of 2004 as instructive. Dutch Moroccan Mohammed Bouyeri emptied a magazine of bullets into van Gogh's body and then spiked a letter to the filmmaker's chest, promising a new holy war in Holland. The letter warned of "screams that will cause chills to run down a person's back and make the hairs on their heads stand straight up . . . People will be drunk with fear, while they are not drunken. Fear will fill the air on the Great Day," it said. "I know that you, America, will go down. I know definitely you, Oh Europe, will go down. I know definitely that you, Oh Netherlands, will go down."

The letter sent a frisson of horror through Holland, which in the winter of 2004 liked to think of itself as the liberal and tolerant heart of Europe. The FBI saw the killing as proof that radicalized Muslims could strike anywhere. The Dutch themselves were less convinced that Islam was really the culprit. While they worried about people like Bouyeri in their midst, they also recalled the no less shocking murder of Pim Fortuyn in 2002. He, like van Gogh, was anti-immigrant and controversial. But Fortuyn was killed by a lone radical vegan. His name? Impeccably Dutch: Volker van der Graaf. The Dutch were a little uncomfortable about making the Muslims among them immediately suspect. They had come to The Netherlands in the 1960s and 1970s and certainly by now were part of Dutch society, not fighting it. The Dutch felt more comfortable wondering if Bouyeri was a bonafide jihadi or, like van der Graaf, an angry young man whose anger had attached itself to a convenient cause and a high-profile killing. Certainly, jihad couldn't happen here.

The Dutch liked to think, with an air of satisfaction, that they lived in the finest, most progressive and evolved nation in the world. They naturally assumed that the Muslims that lived among them thought so, too. The murder of Theo van Gogh suggested otherwise and that was a truth many in The Netherlands preferred not to see. It meant Holland's liberal utopia wasn't that at all. That's why it was easier to think of Bouyeri as an anomaly—a crazed young man instead of an indication that jihad had come to The Netherlands.

The FBI saw it as an omen. It called young men like Bouy-eri "Pepsi jihadists," men from the "Pepsi generation" who saw redemption in relgious violence. It was a disturbing trend: it meant a small number of young transplanted Muslims were open to jihad without necessarily ever really training for it.

For Ed Needham, the July 7, 2005, rush-hour bombings in London hit uncomfortably close to home. The working-class area of Beeston in the suburbs of Leeds where the bombers lived was not unlike Lackawanna. It was a place that offered very little hope for young men looking for work and opportu-nities. The British bombers were friends and bonded not in an apartment but at the Iqra Learning Center, a bookshop on Bude Street in Beeston that neighbors said never seemed to sell any books. It became a meeting place where a lot of young Muslim men from the neighborhood transformed themselves from clubbers to devout followers of Islam. People in the neighborhood, just as they did in Lackawanna, appreciated the change. The men seemed to emerge from the Iqra center on a straighter path. Three of the four suicide bombers who donned backpacks full of explosives and blew themselves up attended prayer sessions at Iqra. To hear Ed Needham tell it, the biggest difference between the Lackawanna Six and the London bombers was that the FBI was lucky enough to get a letter tip-ping them off before the Lackawanna men had a chance to do anything. Another explanation was that the men in Beeston had more resolve than the Lackawanna men. They were never able to muster the gumption to do much of anything besides play soccer. There was always the frightening prospect that if Derwish had picked six men who were angrier or more disaf-fected, the outcome would have been completely different.

Certainly, the cast in the London bombing bears some similarity to the Lackawanna Six. Mohammed Sidique Khan was a thirty-year-old school teacher and married father of an eight-year-old daughter. He grew up just a block away from the bookstore and then moved to another neighborhood nearby. Shahzad Tanweer, twenty-two, was crazy about sports. He worked behind the counter at his family's fish-and-chips shop and used to live just around the corner from the bookstore. Hasib Hussain, eighteen, was a successful business student at a nearby vocational school. He lived minutes away from the store. And, finally, there was Jamaican-born Muslim convert Germaine Lindsay. He lived about 150 miles from Beeston. But investigators saw him as different from the other bombers. Lindsay, unlike the other young men, was on a terrorist watch list. Investigators suspected he led the group, but they had never been able to link Lindsay to al-Qaeda in the same way the FBI was able to do with Kamel Derwish.

When the backpack bombs ripped through the trains and buses of London, friends of Tanweer and Hussain said they couldn't believe the pair could be involved. Both were friendly, nice men. They had been a little wild in their younger years, but more recently they had settled down. They had made a trip to a madrasa in Pakistan and seemed to find an inner peace there. Now they had religion in their lives. When investigators checked if they had attended an Islamic school, there was no record of their being there. It was unclear whether they actually went to Pakistan to study or whether that was a cover story for something else. What investigators do know was that the men used a bathtub to mix up TATP, the dangerous and unstable explosive used in the attack. It was the same kind of explosive shoe bomber Richard Reid had put in his shoes when he intend to blow up a flight from London three days before Christmas in 2001.

For Ed Needham in Buffalo, Bouyeri and the Leeds bombers didn't seem very different from the young men he rounded up in western New York. The van Gogh murder and the London attacks only hardened Needham's belief that the FBI couldn't have waited for the Lackawanna Six to actually plan a mission. "We just couldn't take the chance," Needham said later in comparing the cases. "We just can't afford another al-Qaeda-type attack, and we have to try to intercept and prosecute the people who could strike out against us. Do I think they were going to do that? Probably not. But what if I was wrong? What would happen if they had a bad day? What would they do if some al-Qaeda member called them and asked them for a place to stay or a ride from the airport? Are we really sure they wouldn't help with that? I wasn't."

This was, of course, part of the murkiness and complexity of the battle against terrorism. The FBI had arrived at the conclusion that one couldn't afford to wait until a cell was operational: they had to act first, ask later. As Needham saw it, there hadn't been more homegrown terrorism in America because law enforcement had managed to catch plots before they had gained much traction.

"If you wait until the fuse is lit, you're waiting too long," FBI Director Robert Mueller said. "A sleeper cell can become operational in a blink of an eye."

But that kind of vigilance comes at a cost. The FBI was always trying to juggle civil liberties with its new mandate to prevent another 9/11.

SHAHEEN RASSOUL, a graduate student in Santa Fe, New Mexico, considered himself an artist. It wasn't the great masters or even modern well-known works that caught his fancy. Instead his mind drifted to enormous art installations in public squares—great masses of twisted steel or colorful murals with round cartoon figures. He saw artwork as a way to inspire entire communities. Art didn't need to be about radicalism or, even in late 2002, provide a visual protest against the war in Iraq. His vision of art was more innocently expressive. His favorite story about art revolved around a man in Paris who had attached a paint nozzle to his bicycle before pedaling quietly through the streets of Paris, releasing the color in random squiggles where people on the Champs-Elysées or Avenue Foch would least expect them. The lines would begin without explanation and then end just as suddenly.

Rassoul wanted to create something like that—a pleasant and whimsical artistic surprise for Santa Fe where he lived. So, on a lazy afternoon, he decided to do just that: create a massive anonymous public art project. That decision set off an unexpected series of events that would change his life forever.

What Rassoul didn't grasp when he decided to create art for the people of Santa Fe was that in 2002 nerves were still jangling over the 9/11 attacks. In a largely unplanned way, the way most people fall in love, many Americans had become nervous when it came to Muslim men or men they thought looked Muslim. The drums of war had whipped up the citizenry, and they had taken to stereotyping. Shaheen Rassoul was not Muslim, but because he was from Afghanistan, that made him a marked man. Common sense suggested targeting young Muslim men—Yemenis, Afghanis, men from the Middle East. Five years after the September 11 attacks, it was unclear where common sense morphed into racial profiling. And the inability to find that bright line made everyone question not just others but themselves as well. Those who were against profiling said America couldn't fight terrorism with racism. But, given the circumstances, what was the alternative?

In the wake of the London bombings in 2004, an article by Paul Sperry, a Hoover Institute fellow and former homeland security official in Washington, appeared in the op-ed pages of the *New York Times*. He was endorsing racial profiling. He wasn't alone. Columnist Charles Krauthammer echoed Sperry's call in the *Washington Post*. Sperry suggested that law enforcement officials and subway commuters needed only to be on the lookout for "young men praying to Allah and smelling of flower water." Eyes ought to be peeled, he said, for "a shaved head or short haircut" or a recently shaved beard or moustache. Men who looked like that were "the most suspicious train passengers." Krauthammer, for his part, took aim at the random bag checks program in the New York City subway. He said it was a waste of effort and resources. He recommended security officials should concentrate on "young Muslim men of North African, Middle Eastern, and South Asian origin."

Both men argued that profiling young Muslim men was no less radical than insurance companies charging higher premiums for young male drivers. Those were the people most likely to have accidents, and, consequently, they ought to pay more to be insured. So, too, with terrorism and young Muslim men. The 9/11 attacks were carried out by nineteen young Muslim men and their Muslim brothers. Muslim men were also responsible for the Madrid train bombings, the *Cole*, the twin embassy bombings in Africa, the First World Trade Center bombings, and the London bombings.

And there were other, smaller cases. In 2005, the FBI arrested five men, including two fathers and sons, in Lodi, California, forty miles south of Sacramento, because they, too, had allegedly received terrorist training in Afghanistan. Their secret mission was to carry out attacks on hospitals and large food stores in the United States. One of the men was an ice cream truck driver.

Their neighbors said he never aroused suspicion. "We always bought ice cream off his truck," they said. "They were friendly neighbors."

Two months after discovering the group in Lodi, the FBI uncovered an al-Qaeda recruitment operation in New Folsom State Prison, just miles from where the so-called Lodi Cell was uncovered. According to an *ABC News* report, Saudi-trained extremist imams were stirring up inmates and hoping to use them for terrorist operations once they were released from prison. They reportedly began planning to attack three National Guard facilities, the Israeli consulate, and a handful of synagogues in the Los Angeles area. The attacks were supposed to take place on the fourth anniversary of the September 11 attacks. The plan wasn't so far-fetched. Richard Reid, the convicted "shoe bomber," converted to Islam after he met a radical imam in a British prison.

Former Chicago gang member Jose Padilla ended up in an al-Qaeda camp and was subsequently arrested for allegedly planning to set off a dirty bomb. (He was never charged for this, however.) Amassing a huge army of religious conspirators would seem far-fetched were it not for the fact that such dangerous converts seemed to be all around. Prison officials are now keeping a closer watch on their prison imams.

The steady drumbeat of such news, fresh reports of enemies potentially lurking within, helped buttress the Bush administration's contention that it needed bigger, better crime-fighting tools to combat the enemy. The USA Patriot Act was supposed to be one of those weapons, a way to fight fire with fire, to go beyond the terrorism laws put in force after Timothy McVeigh's Murrah Building attack. What the administration had been less vocal about, however, was the fact that the Patriot Act had been used almost exclusively to pursue nonterrorism cases. Nearly two-thirds of the searches relying on the Patriot Act had been money-laundering offenses.

As of May 2004, the Patriot Act had led to 310 charges against individuals and 179 convictions. Only a small number of those cases, however, could be described as being about terrorism. One instance uncovered evidence of bribery and corruption involving strip clubs in Nevada. Another focused on sex crimes against children. The Justice Department released a report in July 2004 extolling the virtues of the Patriot Act, but it detailed only seven examples in which the act was used against foreign terrorist activity and fewer than four sets of convictions or guilty pleas involving fewer than twenty individuals.

What the Patriot Act did do, at a time when regular crime in America was at record lows, was open a new front in the battle against evil. The Arab Muslim was the new target, and the new enemy looked, if one were to generalize, an awful lot like the Lackawanna Six and, as it turns out, Shaheen Rassoul. Law enforcement wasn't just chasing shadows on a screen. These were plausible prejudices based on the evidence before them. And that was why, very often, young men like Rassoul why many Muslims, in their own way, did have a low-grade sense that they were under fire. In black communities in America the men often say that they are "born suspect," simply because they are black. In post–9/11 America, Muslims were born suspect too.

———

TO THIS DAY ADAMA BAH is not sure why the U.S. government thought that she posed a threat to national security. Until FBI agents arrived at her family's brownstone apartment in Brooklyn in March 2005 and arrested her, Adama was just a typical sixteen-year-old. She spoke with her friends on the phone for hours. She liked boys. She volunteered at a local hospital, spending hours reading to children in the cancer ward. She liked to draw. The only thing that might have set her apart from all her classmates at the Heritage School in East Harlem was the fact that when in public, she chose to wear an abaya and hajib.

For Adama Bah, the wardrobe choice was motivated by parental respect. But to those who didn't know her, the dark dress suggested something more sinister. In post–September 11 New York City, it appeared to be a conscious political statement. It seemed to carry with it a whiff of anti-Americanism and religious extremism. And those generalizations and a handful of unfortunate coincidences led law enforcement to believe Adama Bah was ready to put that choice into stark relief. They thought she would become the nation's first suicide bomber.

The New York Police Department began taking new aim at homegrown terrorists in 2004. The hydra-like world of Islamic extremism sent the New York Police Department's counterterrorism unit into crash courses in Islam. It focused on how radical imams sought to recruit and motivate young Muslims. It tried to identify possible threats bubbling below the surface. Officers began attending an Islamic ideology academy, gathering in an unmarked Brooklyn warehouse where local academics came to teach courses such as "The Evolution of Militant Sunni Ideology." The officers studied how different groups had twisted the Koran to serve their own purposes. The idea was to give the NYPD officers a context in which to interview Muslim suspects or spot trouble before it began. The NYPD hired the academics as consultants to scour intelligence gleaned from informants, surveillance reports, and the department's terrorism hotline. It helped organize a cyber unit, a group that penetrated overseas chat rooms to troll for clues on possible future attacks.

In New York, one of the groups that had caught the attention of both the NYPD and the FBI was a small radical Muslim group called the Islamic Thinkers Society. Based in Queens, the Thinkers, as they were known, were a handful of young Muslim men who made national headlines after they distributed pro-jihad flyers in the days immediately following the 9/11 attacks. They had an unambiguously anti-American message. They stomped on an American flag while shouting that it represented a "crusader war on Islam"; their Web site included a mock advertisement for a video game they call "Mujahideen Strike II," which had an airplane crashing into the World Trade Center and an ax cutting the Statue of Liberty in half. They have been a fixture on the corner of 37th and 74th Streets in Queens, New York, every Sunday for years. The FBI had had the group under surveillance for two years. In that time, although the Thinkers had exercised the broadest definition of their freedom of speech, members had not broken any laws.

The FBI's concern was not so much their message as their overseas connections. In particular, the FBI was concerned about members of the group visiting a cleric in London named Abu Hamza. Hamza, a forty-five-year-old Egyptian-born engineer, was one of the most controversial Muslim figures in Britain. The leader of the Supporters of Shania group in London, Hamza came to prominence in 1999. That's when five Britons of Pakistani origin were sentenced to prison in Yemen after their plot to blow up the British consulate in Aden was discovered. Hamza's teenage son and stepson were among the group of men convicted. Prosecutors said the men had gone to Yemen to carry out the mission at Hamza's urging. Hamza denied the allegations.

Missing a hand and an eye, both of which he said he lost while tackling a landmine in Afghanistan, Hamza was the leader of the Finsbury Park Mosque in north London. The mosque had visits from a who's who of jihadis: the London subway bombers had prayed there, as had would-be shoe bomber Richard Reid, and Zacarias Moussaoui. Moussaoui was the so-called twentieth hijacker who had nearly crossed paths with the Lackawanna Six at the Hotel Faran in Karachi. Hamza denied any involvement in terrorism.

Both the NYPD and the FBI discovered all this after the Patriot Act made it easier to track email traffic to and from suspected terrorists. The Patriot Act changed the warrant requirements for those kinds of taps. As long as the information that would be obtained was likely to provide fodder for an international terrorism investigation it was permissible to track the electronic traffic. Traditionally, one could only get a wire tap by showing probable cause that a specific crime had been committed. Technology was also helping the fight. Law enforcement had started using computer programs that could actually monitor the source of all incoming calls. The content of the phone call wasn't necessarily revealed, but the fact that officials knew it took place allowed the NYPD and FBI to build what they called "spiderweb networks" of suspects and their friends. Those matrices allowed law enforcement to look at everyone the suspect contacted, everyone those people contacted, and so on. That's how the FBI was able to piece together the connections between Derwish and al-Qaeda and to confirm that several of the Lackawanna Six were still contacting Derwish after they returned from the camps.

For the NYPD, the computer program had been tremendously effective. It helped them foil a plot to bomb the Herald Square subway station during the Republican National Convention in 2004. Herald Square is a shopping area in Midtown Manhattan not far from Madison Square Garden where the convention was held. The NYPD tracked two men who had been visiting an Islamic bookstore the NYPD had identified as "an environment of concern." Religious leaders at the bookstore had allegedly coaxed them into a terrorist mission, and the pair had intended to strap backpacks full of explosives to their backs and detonate the packages on the train. It was, Police Commissioner Ray Kelly told the *New York Times*, "a classic case of homegrown terrorism. They had no connection to any international organizations that we knew of, but we saw things that indicated they were going to take things into their own hands and we caught them before that happened."

The online sleuthing was more art than science, however. People blustered more on the Internet than they might otherwise in person. They said things but never intended to follow through. "You have to understand what you are supposed to react to," one investigator explained.

Law enforcement officials react with alacrity to something they call an "ideological detonator," a person who incites others to murder. And while FBI agents would only talk about Adama Bah's case in the most general terms, it appeared that she and another sixteen-year-old named Tashnuba Hayder were red-flagged because they appeared to have exactly that—an ideological detonator. They thought Hayder had convinced Adama Bah to do something violent.

Before 9/11, Adama Bah would never have been accused of being a terrorist. She was not a fiery figure. She didn't extol the virtues of Islam or castigate America or its foreign policy. She never tried to convert friends to her religion. She had no interest in discussing politics. Instead, by all accounts, she was a bubbly, energetic young woman who just happened to wear an abaya to school. Her friends said she used to be a whirlwind of conversation, but after her arrest she weighed her words. Not permitted to talk to reporters or anyone about her case as a condition of her release, she returned to school having to pretend nothing had happened. She had to act as if she hadn't been incarcerated for two weeks or hadn't been held incommunicado from her parents or hadn't been accused of wanting to strap a bomb to her waist and blow something to bits.

The FBI came to the door of the Bah family's small apartment in Bushwick, Brooklyn, and told Adama and her father that they needed to come with them. Initially, the two understood the charges were related to immigration irregularities. The Bah family moved to New York from Guinea when Adama was just three years old. They had started in a one-room flat and slowly did what they could to live some portion of the American dream. There were bad jobs that led to better ones. There were apartments in bad neighborhoods followed by small houses in good school districts. Somehow the Bah family had gone from that to fielding accusations. Agents told her that they knew that she was a suicide bomber in the making.

"They were accusing Adama of being a potential terrorist and it was so unexpected because she's a kid that's like any other kid," said Dennis Quinyonez, a senior at the Heritage School. His girlfriend, who did not want to be named, had been Adama's best friend since elementary school. Everyone was scared to talk about Adama, she explained, and her parents had told her to stay out of it. Quinyonez agreed to act as her mouthpiece and spokesman. "Adama was doing good in school and everything and wasn't bothering anyone. She was friendly, like no one would have ever thought of the FBI accusing her of anything. And then, just like that," he snapped his fingers, "they picked her up and threw her in jail. She didn't do nothing."

NYPD and FBI officials had clashed on this case. While NYPD had had an eye on Adama's friend, the Bangladeshi girl named Tashnuba Hayder, officers didn't think Adama Bah was a threat. They thought they could continue to watch her. The FBI, they said, misread what were at best fuzzy signals.

Tashnuba Hayder was a home-schooled, religious young woman who had become devoutly Muslim and radical. She was described by one FBI agent as "really bad news." Bah and Hayder knew each other, but only tangentially. They both babysat the same children. But, partly because of Internet and phone-call surveillance, Adama Bah was swept up in a net of circumstantial evidence. Her mistake: even knowing Tashnuba Hayder.

Soon after Adama arrived at the detention center in Berks County, Pennsylvania, officials were telling her that Section 411 of the Patriot Act made even an unknowing association with terrorists a deportable offense. Section 412 of the law allowed the Attorney General to order a brief detention of aliens without a court ruling that the person was a threat. Adama had no idea why the FBI was telling her all this.

FBI and NYPD officials had flagged Tashnuba Hayder as one to watch in January of 2005. She came to their attention when she began appearing in a chat room frequented by members the Thinkers with a link to the Finsbury mosque. Some of the chat room conversations indicated Tashnuba Hayder was looking to create a name for herself in New York Muslim circles. Hayder had apparently mentioned suicide bombing in passing. A short time later, authorities picked up both girls.

There are more questions than answers in the case. All the hearings were closed. All the FBI declarations sealed. Lawyers for Hayder and Bah were not permitted to reveal government information. James Margolin, an FBI spokesman, would not comment on the cases. What was known, though, was that Tashnuba

Hayder was deported with her parents back to Bangladesh. Officially, she was deported for immigration irregularities.

Adama Bah's story was clearly more complex. Officials released her after six weeks in the Berks County facility. No charges were filed. Natasha Pierre, Bah's lawyer, said that the outcome spoke for itself. "She should never have been detained in the first place," Pierre said, adding that she was under a gag order so had to be careful about what she said. "She is innocent, she is more than innocent. She doesn't know anything and didn't do anything wrong."

NYPD officials familiar with the case said they never would have arrested Adama Bah. There just wasn't enough there. "Should the two girls have been monitored? Absolutely," one NYPD counterterrorism official said. "But the FBI jumped the gun. They saw something in the chat room that looked like the beginnings of a plan and they jumped to conclusions. Are we better off that Tashnuba is no longer here? Yes, probably. But we certainly can't say the same thing about arresting Adama Bah."

Adama told her friends that she was furious at the turn of events, though she was careful not to speak too loudly out of concern that the FBI would suddenly find some irregularities in her immigration status or that of her father's. FBI officials insisted that she had mulled over becoming part of a suicide attack on New York City, even though she never wavered from telling them that this was all some kind of mistake. NYPD officials familiar with the case said it looked like Hayder had claimed Bah was willing to do some sort of terrorist act just so she could seem like she was a recruiter. Bah knew nothing about it and said she was a victim of the worst kind of racial profiling. She was arrested, she told her friends, simply because she wore an abaya.

SHAHEEN RASSOUL had arrived in America when he was just three years old. He departed Afghanistan, literally, on his mother's back, fleeing across the Khyber Pass just as the Russian army was entering Kabul. Emotionally, Shaheen Rassoul had never really rid himself of his homeland. He found himself drawn back. When he graduated from college, he went to Tajikistan as a school teacher, something Juma al-Dosari had said he had done when he was in Afghanistan. A succession of other in-country assignments followed until Rassoul found himself director with an American aid organization setting up emergency shelter relief in Tajikistan. Eager to learn more about aid and development, Rassoul started applying to graduate schools. He looked at international affairs programs at Georgetown and Columbia and figured he would get a master's degree and return to Afghanistan to finish what he had started. While he waited for the next phase of his life to begin, he enrolled in a law and economics course at a local community college and moved into an artist's studio behind his stepfather's home in the Sunlit Hills section of Santa Fe. Rassoul accepted that for 2002, at least, his life would remain in transition.

It was during one of those long, slow afternoons in his apartment waiting for graduate school acceptance letters that Rassoul found a leggy stencil lying on a table. It looked part frog, part human. The arms and legs were hinged, like an Indonesian shadow puppet. The figure was oddly headless. Rassoul thought it looked like a cross between a frog and an alien. He idly began moving its lanky limbs into various poses—sometimes arms and legs above the torso, other times making the little figure look like it was running, or arms and legs akimbo. Then inspiration struck. Why not paint outlines of this stencil around Santa Fe? The project would thrust Rassoul into the artist tradition he had dreamt of. He would be like that lone Frenchman pedaling a bicycle along the streets of Paris to paint squiggly lines that no one could explain. Just the thought of it made him grin. Maybe, he thought to himself, the mysterious frogman would get a mention in the local paper.

Rassoul started work the next day. The orange outline of his frogman appeared on a downtown sidewalk with no fanfare or explanation. Shaheen could not have been more pleased. He stood back and admired his handiwork. He thought the figure looked comical, harmless, funny. To others it might have looked more sinister: it looked vaguely like the chalk lines police draw to outline corpses at a crime scene, except, of course, this one was shaped like a frog.

About the same time Rassoul embarked on his secret project, he met a girl. Molly Howitt was twenty-three and a recent graduate from Bennington College, where she majored in ceramics. As much as she loved art, Howitt was practical enough to know that she couldn't live on an artist's earnings. So she learned sign language, earned a teaching certificate, and started working at a school for the deaf. Her parents were also in the academic field but in a wholly different way. Her father was a well-known political science professor at Harvard University, and her mother practiced biochemistry there. An artist's education wasn't exactly what they had in mind for their daughter.

Mutual friends in the Santa Fe artist community had introduced Shaheen to Molly, and by all indications the fit was a good one. They both appreciated art. They were both fiercely intelligent. And they both wanted to do something for people who were less fortunate. It was such a good combination that just weeks into their relationship Shaheen decided to tell Molly about his role in the mysterious appearance of frogmen all over town. Rassoul was careful not to create too many of the little figures—that would have diminished their effect. Instead, they appeared in small bright orange groups, infrequently enough that they lived safely behind the line of quirky and steered clear of public menace. Shaheen wanted to tell Molly about the frogmen in a special way. He decided he would paint some of them right outside her house. They would be like a coded message that would not only let her know about his project but also hint at how he felt about her. The perfect night for the revelation, he decided, would be after the two cooked a chicken curry dinner for their friends at Molly's house.

The party could not have been better. Everyone had fun, the chicken curry was great, and around 11 p.m. Shaheen excused himself and told Molly he had to go home. She wondered whether she had done something wrong. She had expected him to stay. She kissed him goodbye and watched him walk down the street toward his car. Twenty minutes later, armed with a can of orange spray paint and rubber gloves, Rassoul was tiptoeing back down Buena Vista Avenue. He decided he would paint four or five of the figures on the sidewalk outside her apartment and leave a little Indonesian jewelry box with flowers on her car. It was meaningful and romantic, he thought. She would discover the frogs in the morning, would put two and two together, and then the new couple would have one more bond, one more little secret to share.

He had painted four of the five frogmen on the sidewalk and was focusing on the whisper hiss of the spray can when the scene abruptly changed from quiet and contemplative to chaotic. The street exploded in sound and light, a police SUV and regular squad car roared up from behind, lights blazing. Shaheen stood up wondering who the police might be chasing. When they stopped just ahead of him, he tossed the spray can and stood at attention. He looked down at his hands. He was wearing latex gloves. Reflexively, he clasped his hands behind his back like a small child. Then, thinking that looked suspicious, he shoved his hands in the pockets of his shorts. The latex clung to the material and almost squeaked to a stop as he thrust his hands out of sight.

Rubber gloves had become a necessary component in his work. Painting at night in a hurried way, Rassoul had more than his share of accidents. He had sprayed himself in the face more times than he could count because he couldn't see the directional nozzle in the dark. Sometimes he returned home from painting with a patch of orange in his hair. His car was a testament to his deficiencies. There were smudges of bright orange around the ignition. Orange dripped from the latch on the hatchback. The rubber gloves were meant to make his spray-can shortcomings that much less obvious. And now he here he was, in the middle of the night, standing on the street with his hands in his pockets facing a phalanx of officers, wondering why he ever thought rubber gloves were a good idea at all.

Shaheen tried to seem nonchalant. "I was just in the neighborhood having dinner at my girlfriend's house," he began. He felt his mouth go dry.

The officers asked for her address. Shaheen froze. He and Molly had been dating for two weeks, but he didn't know the address. He looked up the street hoping that the number would magically come to him, appearing through the haze of his panicked thinking. Instead he started to stammer. He noticed the police had moved in closer. He saw the insignia of the Santa Fe Police Department on sleeves. Some plainclothes cops had joined them.

Their questions whizzed toward him like gunshots. Where was his car? Where was his identification? Who was his girlfriend again? What was he doing there so late at night? Shaheen tried to breathe. His wallet, he said, was in the car, but he'd be happy to get it. They nodded and slowly climbed back into their vehicles, the spotlights still trained on the young man as if any moment he would foolishly make a run for it. He found himself alternately putting his latex-gloved hands behind his back or inserting them into a pocket. The police drove slowly along beside him, blue and red lights still turning. Shaheen was uncomfortably aware that the neighborhood was lighting up. People were peering through blinds and shades as the cars inched up the road.

Shaheen reached into his silver Saab and extracted his wallet, throwing the rubber gloves on the floor of the front seat as he did so. He could see his whole story was falling apart. He was starting to think that even the truth sounded implausible.

"We had a call about a prowler and a barking dog," one policeman said, approaching him. "Do you know anything about that?"

Shaheen shook his head and held his driver's license in an outstretched had. "Why were you wearing gloves," another cop said, eyeing him warily.

"My friends and I were doing some painting," Shaheen stammered. The officers looked dubious. They asked if they could search his car. Shaheen, who only days earlier was sitting in a lecture about civil rights at a nearby community college, suddenly got the idea that he would put theory into practice.

"No," he said flatly, "you can't search my car."

Bad idea, he thought to himself as soon as he said it. He felt the entire tone of the conversation change. He was in handcuffs moments later.

"If you want to play tough, we'll play tough with you," one officer said.

As the metal closed around his wrists, Shaheen decided to come clean about his art project.

"Look, I'm not a prowler. In fact, I was painting on the sidewalk. Those frogmen all over town, well, those are mine."

The policemen blinked at him in disbelief. They cocked their heads as if they weren't quite sure what he was talking about or as if he had been speaking another language that they needed to translate before processing. Then they put him in the back of a squad car. One young officer looked at him curiously. "That wasn't a very smart thing for you to say," he said.

Rassoul was handcuffed in the back of a squad car when he was introduced to Special Agent Chris Warner of the FBI. A big, clean-cut man, Warner had evidently decided to play good cop to the Santa Fe policemen's bad one. He transferred the still-cuffed Rassoul into his Town Car and gave him a weak grin. Did he want heat? Music? Rassoul nodded slowly. Soft rock came wafting out of the speakers as heat began pouring into the back seat. Rassoul's arms and wrists were starting to ache. It was hard to see what the officers were doing outside. They had positioned the spotlight from the squad car so Rassoul could only make out shadows swarming around his Saab. They were clearly rifling through his car, literally taking it apart. Door panels lay on the sidewalk. Occasionally he could see them removing something and putting it on a nearby lawn. Rassoul was making a quick mental inventory of what they might find in his car.

His heart sank. It suddenly dawned on him why these men were so interested. Photographs from his trips to Afghanistan were in his car. Months earlier, he had been moving offices for his employer in Afghanistan. Tajik colleagues who had never been to Kabul saw this as a rare opportunity to play tourist. The group had ended up on Chicken Street, an old marketplace in Kabul where vendors sold knickknacks, arts and crafts, woodwork, and old Soviet guns. The visiting group dressed up

like mujahideen and posed for photographs. They strung ban-
doliers of bullets over their shoulders. They held old Kalashnikovs in menacing positions. They put on headscarves and
mugged for the camera in that way that only tourists do. If they
had been in Cody, Wyoming, they would have been dressed as
Buffalo Bill, complete with Winchester rifle; if they had been in
Nevada, they might have put on prospector's clothes. Then the
officers discovered his passport, a document full of visas from
every jihadist haven known to man. Turkey. Kazakhstan. Korea.
Afghanistan. Pakistan. Rassoul saw himself embodying their
worst fears. And all this was unfolding before his eyes while soft
rock hummed from the radio.

"We're going to have to take you to the precinct," one of the
officers said, getting into the car. The frogmen hardly seemed to
matter anymore.

Molly Howitt was awakened by pounding on the front door.
"Open up, FBI." Her heart was in her mouth. Had she heard
them correctly? It was 5 a.m., and her dinner party had ended
only hours before. She staggered to the door and opened it.
The men filled her entryway and immediately started asking
questions. They kept asking about Shaheen. He says he's your
boyfriend, they said. Howitt nodded. What is his last name,
one officer said. She blinked at him, wide-eyed. She searched
her memory. Suddenly, she couldn't even remember Shaheen's
last name. How could she not know her boyfriend's last name?
The agents asked her if Shaheen had ever touched her computer. She thought for a moment. She had a new computer. He
had helped her load the software. Is that what they meant?
Howitt felt herself getting defensive and protective. They asked
if Shaheen had ever been alone with her computer. She
thought hard. It never occurred to her to think about it in
those terms.

The agents' questions began rearranging everything she knew about Shaheen Rassoul. They began talking about al-Qaeda and whether he had mentioned it; could he be a member? She stopped short and cocked her head. She didn't know what al-Qaeda was. But clearly they thought Rassoul was some sort of terrorist. They asked if he was obsessed with planes. Did he like flight simulator games? In fact, Shaheen *was* obsessed with planes. And then for a brief moment, just a flash, Howitt's mind drifted toward a far-fetched possibility. For a second she thought, Oh My God, what if I am Shaheen's cover? Then the thought evaporated.

She asked where Rassoul was. All the agents would say was that he was being detained. When the agents finally left, an hour later, she watched them drive away from behind the curtain. On the pavement outside her house she saw five painted frogmen. Shaheen Rassoul was the secret frogman artist of Santa Fe, not a terrorist. At that moment, her alarm in the bedroom sounded. It was 6:30. She had to leave for work.

SPECIAL AGENT WARNER was sitting across from Rassoul in the Santa Fe police station. He had a flyer in his hand. "So what do we have here?" he asked, laying it on the table before Rassoul. It was a flyer for a protest against the war in Iraq. It showed a pile of skulls, and sitting atop the drawings was a photograph of Defense Secretary Donald Rumsfeld's head. Rassoul shifted uncomfortably. He couldn't believe this was why he was sitting in a police station under interrogation.

"I can see how this doesn't look very good," he said. "But is it against the law to have a flyer?"

Warner narrowed his eyes. He asked Rassoul if he wanted to hurt Rumsfeld.

Rassoul was confused. "No, of course not. If I had a meeting with Rumsfeld I would want to question him, I guess."

The agent asked what Rassoul knew about the defense secretary.

Rassoul tried to think. He didn't know anything more than anyone else knew about Rumsfeld. Then, largely out of nervousness, he began to get chatty, trying to figure out what they were getting at. "I know Rumsfeld has a house in Taos," he began helpfully. "I know his daughter lives in Santa Fe and his granddaughter lives here and goes to some special school."

His answers evidently made the situation worse. The agents asked to search his house, the little studio behind his stepfather's place in Sunlit Hills. Agents and police officers piled into unmarked cars and drove to Rassoul's place with him, sitting in handcuffs, in the back. They took his computer, his CDs, and DVDs, and then told Rassoul that he was under arrest on suspicion of prowling and defacing public property. An hour later, he was in the local jail.

His sister and Molly arrived late that afternoon to post bail. Rassoul emerged looking ragged in the same shorts, T-shirt, and Teva sandals he had been wearing the night before. He went home that night with Howitt. The two cooked dinner and ate in silence. They were numbed by the day's events and went to bed without a word.

They were awakened the next morning by the sound of a telephone ringing. Rassoul picked it up.

"Hey Shaheen, what are you doing?" It was Agent Chris Warner, and it was the first of dozens of phone calls he would make to keep tabs on Rassoul.

Even though Shaheen's story was clearly checking out okay—he had indeed been with an aid agency and had been doing all the things he had told the FBI he had been doing in

Afghanistan—he couldn't seem to convince Warner and his superiors that this was one big misunderstanding. Warner's phone
calls came with alarming regularity, reminding Rassoul and
Howitt about the gravity of the situation in which they found
themselves. And while Warner's phone calls were always
cheery—"Hey, Shaheen, what did you do today?"—there was
clearly something slightly frightening about them.

The fact that weeks after Rassoul's arrest the FBI was still calling seemed to bring Rassoul and Howitt closer together, almost
as if they were circling the wagons against an unseen enemy. The
two had a vague sense that their lives were on hold until this pall
of suspicion passed. Rassoul didn't feel like he could visit friends
in Afghanistan without drawing undue suspicion to himself. He
was dutiful about calling the FBI office when they had questions, as if he were a parolee trying to convince his case officer
that he had really turned over a new leaf.

Eventually, Shaheen said later, the FBI must have come to the
conclusion that he was really as innocent as he looked. But by
that time he had been visiting the FBI offices in Santa Fe for
three and a half months. He and Special Agent Warner had
forged an odd bond; they talked about politics and current affairs. Yet the FBI refused to completely go away. Warner said his
superiors wanted Rassoul to take a lie-detector test. Then,
Warner promised, it would all be over.

Apparently the case of the frog artist of Santa Fe had reached
the highest levels of government in Washington, Warner told
Rassoul. "I think this case has reached Rumsfeld, maybe even the
president's desk," Warner told Shaheen. While he didn't say, precisely, that the case had been politicized, it was clear it had been.

Rassoul began to research lie-detector tests, and the more he
discovered, the more uneasy he became. The tests were often not
accurate and Rassoul was worried that if he didn't pass the test,

somehow failed it even though he was telling the truth, his situation would get worse, not better. After weeks of weighing his options, Rassoul agreed to take the test. Warner assured him that it would just include some general questions and wouldn't be a problem. Rassoul got the impression that Warner was as fed up with the investigation as he was.

A Mr. Sterling came all the way from the FBI's Oklahoma bureau to administer Shaheen Rassoul's lie-detector test. Sterling was spindly and bespectacled and expressionless. He opened Rassoul's shirt and attached electrodes to his chest. Another set were put on his forehead. Others were attached to his fingers. He asked Rassoul a list of what he called benchmark yes or no questions: his birthdate, place of birth, mother's name. Rassoul could hear the needles scratching on the rolls of paper. He was sure he had failed already. He felt some sweat drip down his back.

Sterling left the room and briefly left Rassoul to his own devices. Shaheen began playing with the machine. He stared at it first. The needles moved accusingly. Then he changed his breathing to see how the machine would react. The inky needle scratched across the paper. He held his breath. The machine didn't seem to like that either.

Once Sterling returned, he moved the machine out of Rassoul's line of sight and began asking questions.

"Don't elaborate your answers," he said. "Just answer yes or no."

Rassoul inhaled and nodded.

"Do you or anyone you know harbor any malice toward America?"

Rassoul swallowed hard. That wasn't the kind of general question he was expecting.

"Do you belong to any terrorist organization?"

"Have you ever wanted to hurt anyone?"

Rassoul felt a general sense of agitation, a sort of interior fizzing, as he threw up defenses against an invader that he was convinced had already found its way in. He couldn't help listening to the snapping and scratching of the needles on the polygraph. He was sure he was failing.

Two days later, Shaheen picked up his cell phone. Warner was on the line. "You did fine on the test," was all he said.

Much relieved, Rassoul had just one other thing to do to make the whole incident go away. He wanted to get the prowler charge lifted.

NESTLED IN THE TREES at the end of a long dirt road in the Buena Vista district of East Santa Fe, there sat a long ranch house. An enormous American flag flapped out front. Rassoul drove along the road, stopping to ask neighbors for directions. He needed to speak to the lady of the house who, the police report said, had complained about a prowler the night the police had picked him up. Rassoul wanted to see if he might get her to drop the charges—to explain that it was all some sort of misunderstanding.

Shaheen drove his silver Saab slowly down the drive, hoping that he would find someone home. He was greeted instead by an enormous white dog. And the dog, at least at first, didn't seem to like him. The animal came bounding off the porch running right at him. Shaheen picked up a stick and threw it. The dog seemed to make a small canine calculation, shifted his weight, and charged after the branch. All of a sudden, Shaheen Rassoul was his new best friend. They played fetch for a short time as Rassoul made his way to the front porch. The entry was lined with a series of sliding glass doors. Rassoul cupped his hand at the brow and peered inside, looking to see if his knocking inspired some movement. There appeared to be no one home. Then he looked down at the police report to make sure he had the correct address. He scanned the sheet: the victim information said the prowler report was filed by a woman. She weighed 165 pounds and her name . . . Rassoul followed along the page with his finger and then suddenly felt sick.

"Victim's name," the report read, "Rumsfeld, Valerie."

Shaheen felt his stomach spasm. He looked at the roof of the house for the first time. There were a dozen antennas. He started to feel woozy. He wondered if he was being watched. His mind raced to odd places. He had just played fetch with the dog Donald Rumsfeld played fetch with . . . He walked away from the house trying to look nonchalant and slowly climbed into his car. He dialed Special Agent Chris Warner's number.

"Chris, you are not going to believe this . . . ," Shaheen began, explaining where he was. Warner cut him off. "Shaheen, get the hell out of there."

As if in slow motion, Rassoul drove down the dirt road and began putting the pieces of this investigation together. The reason his case seemed so important to the FBI wasn't just because he was Afghani but because he had been painting odd frogs, unbeknownst to him, just three blocks from Donald Rumsfeld's daughter's house. All those little details he knew about the secretary of defense's daughter—that she had a house in Santa Fe and a daughter that went to school there—random bits of information he thought nothing of sharing, had only confirmed the worst suspicions that somehow he was targeting Rumsfeld's family.

Those frogs, perhaps they were a coded message for others who were laying in wait in the shadows. Suddenly, it all became clear.

Oddly, Rassoul wasn't resentful that he had been targeted, profiled in the worst way. "The burden is on us, young Muslim men, to show that we don't pose a risk," he said. "There is a profile, and we know what it is. It is just the implication of that that's new to me." Rassoul, in an odd way, supported profiling. He said young Muslim men had been behind the terrorists' attacks on the United States, so it was only natural to suspect they would deliver blows in the future.

A judge in Santa Fe ended up sentencing Rassoul to forty-eight hours of community service for spray painting. He wrapped Christmas presents at the Salvation Army to do the time. The FBI has him on a terrorism watch list. He is used to being stopped at the airport. He said he is much more careful about everything now that America, for him, has become a country where "you can be spray painting one minute," he said, "and be a terrorist the next."

CHAPTER 15

BILLS FANS OR JIHADISTS?

ETWEEN SEPTEMBER 2001 and September 2006, according to a New York University report, the government
indicted 417 people after terror investigations. Nearly three
hundred of them ended up being indicted for nonterror crimes
like fraud or immigration violations. Of the 143 actually indicted on federal terrorism charges, some eighty-two are pend-
ing, thirteen were dismissed, and nine were acquitted. Of the
thirty-nine that were convicted, thirty-six were found to be supporting terrorism, like the Lackawanna Six. Of course, "supporting terrorism" had come to have a rather broad definition and
didn't require any intent to commit a criminal act in the United
States at all. This was part of the strategy to prevent terrorism
from happening before, in FBI Director Mueller's words, "the
fuse was lit."

Four people among these suspects were actually convicted of
terrorism charges. Richard Reid, the infamous shoe bomber, got
a life sentence for his foiled attempt to blow up a plane over the
Atlantic Ocean. A Maryland man, Masoud Khan, was convicted
of traveling to Pakistan so he could fight alongside the Taliban
against U.S. forces. He also received a life sentence. Two others,
Ahmed Abdel Sattar and Ali Timimi, were convicted of conspiring to kill and kidnap in a foreign country as well as encouraging others to attend terrorist camps, respectively. They also were

given life sentences. None of Timimi's followers ever actually attended a terrorist camp, so his sentence was considered, at best, controversial. Still, there have been four terrorism convictions by jury trials, and a handful of Americans heard the facts and concluded, at least in the cases of these four men, that they were guilty of terrorism.

The number of arrested and convicted says something about how the rules of justice have changed in America. The story of the Lackawanna Six is a snapshot of the war on terror taken from the level of the sidewalks in a small, depressed town. It provides a way to look at the application of justice during an extraordinary period in American history. The treatment of the Muslims who gathered at the mosque on the corner of Wilkesbarre Avenue and Washington Street, and the smaller group who returned to Goba's apartment up the street for pizza and more fervent discussions, is a test for the rules of justice in America post–9/11. For the people who embrace the logic of the global war on terror, the emergence of domestic terrorism plays into their biggest fears. If the threat is here at home, then it becomes doubly difficult to confront, and there is no length to which the country shouldn't go to fight it. For others, who see terrorism as rooted in poverty, social alienation, and economic discontent, as much as it is to the ideology of Osama bin Laden, holding America to the highest standards of fairness seems more important than ever. Selectively abandoning civil liberties and due process to battle the war on terrorism gives the terrorists a win. They end up changing America simply by threatening it.

The way America ended up treating the men from Lackawanna—Derwish, Goba, Taher, Alwan, Galab, al-Bakri, Mosed, and even Elbaneh—provides a measure by which we can see how much this country has changed. Was the Lackawanna Six really a sleeper cell if its members weren't planning a crime?

Were they really Yemenis, as they were routinely described, when all of them were American citizens? Did their case mean that they could be both dedicated to the overthrow of America as members of al-Qaeda as well as fans of the Buffalo Bills? The Lackawanna Six provided a view into how elastic justice in America had become after 9/11.

A year after sentencing, Nicole Taher had finished her nursing studies and was a floor nurse at a local hospital. She worked long back-to-back shifts so that she could have three or four days off at a time to spend with Noah and, for a time, so that she could manage the long drive, one or twice a month, to visit Yassein at Loretta Prison in Altoona, Pennsylvania. Taher shared a cell with five other men. They cooked Halal food together, studied the Koran and, by virtue of their circumstances, became fast friends. The only difference Nicole saw in Yassein, the guy voted friendliest of their high school class, was that he had become stronger. He was lifting weights, he told her, to pass the time. When Nicole took Noah to visit his father, the boy would climb all over his dad. Nicole was always struck by how much her son looked like her husband. "He's a little white Yassein," she said.

Most of the time, Noah seemed like a normal little boy, blithely unaware of the controversy that enveloped his father. But there were moments when it was clear his father's incarceration weighed on him. When there had been a mock presidential election in his first grade class, Noah blacked out Bush's name and put a huge crayon arrowed next to Kerry. "I hate Bush," he declared. "He put my daddy in jail."

Nicole had trouble arguing with his logic.

The Lackawanna Six had been promised, as part of their plea agreements, that they would be jailed close to home so their families could continue to visit them. So it was with some surprise that they discovered in December 2006 that they were going to be moved to a maximum security prison in Terre Haute, Indiana, along with a hodgepodge of other terrorism inmates—most of whom were Arab Muslims.

The idea was to have all of America's terrorists in one location so their phone calls, mail, and interactions with other prisoners could be closely monitored. Every conversation, under prison regulations, had to be in English. The prison was considered a step below a supermax facility like the one in Florence, Colorado, where the so-called American Taliban, John Walker Lindh, and the twentieth hijacker, Zacarias Moussaoui, had been moved. Seventeen inmates were placed in the new terrorism unit. They were housed in the prison's former death row. Among those seventeen were five of the Lackawanna Six.

"They are all on the same cell block now; they can talk to each other," said Rod Personius. "It's ironic. You'd think they would want to keep these guys apart. Instead, four years after they were arrested for being America's first sleeper cell, they are all together again. You have to wonder, maybe the government thinks they weren't so dangerous after all."

TEN DAYS AFTER the London bombings in July 2005, Juma al-Dosari, who the Lackawanna Six had described as the man who helped them decide to go to the camps, handed his lawyer a twenty-page diary laying out the abuse he claimed he had suffered while under U.S. custody in Guantanamo Bay. He had been there since the end of 2001. According to al-Dosari, his treatment had been beyond demeaning. He said women had played with his genitalia while he was restrained, that he was watched when he went to the bathroom, and that the guards started to pull the hairs of his beard out one by one. There was no official record or corroboration of his claims.

"I wonder how my ailing heart could bear such memories," al-Dosari wrote in his diary. "I wish all this could be obliterated out of my memory and imagination. From the darkness of prison and from the depth of detention centers I inscribe my suffering . . . my pain . . . my sadness, an endless story, the suffering of years and months. From here, from behind horrific bars I write these lines of the life I spent and continue to spend in American detention camps." Al-Dosari continued to insist it was all some mistake.

His lawyer, Joshua Colangelo-Bryan, said that he never had a fire-and-brimstone conversation with al-Dosari about Islam or religion. He was more mild-mannered than that. Al-Dosari once asked Colangelo-Bryan if he were Jewish. "Joshua seemed like a Jewish name," he said. His lawyer explained that he wasn't Jewish, though it had been a popular name on the Upper West Side of New York City where he had grown up.

Al-Dosari cocked his head thoughtfully. "I heard that the best lawyers were Jewish," he said, then quickly added, "but I am sure you are a good lawyer, too."

Colangelo-Bryan laughed and assured al-Dosari that he was.

Though FBI agents continued to refer to al-Dosari as "the Closer," the accusations leveled against him in his file at Guantanamo, known as the Summary of Allegations, said nothing at all about Lackawanna. He has been in jail for five years for, ostensibly, being "present" at Tora Bora.

"If he was really the Closer and a recruiter for al-Qaeda, why aren't they coming out and accusing him of it?" said Colangelo-Bryan. "Maybe it is because they can't prove it. I can't find anyone who says al-Dosari was an extremist or pushed those sorts of views on others. And he says that it would be crazy to just show up in some town like Lackawanna and suddenly think he'd recruit a bunch of men who didn't know him. It doesn't make sense."

By 2006, Juma al-Dosari had been in prison without charge, trial, or hope of release, for five years. He was a psychologically broken man who had succumbed to terminal hopelessness. That October, Colangelo-Bryan arrived from New York City to have another chat with his client. The two men had developed an easy rapport. There were jokes shared, and al-Dosari liked to test out his newly acquired English idioms on his young attorney. Most of the expressions he picked up were inner-city lingo that he had learned from the guards. Colangelo-Bryan said the conversations were particularly poignant because al-Dosari would apologize for the profanity as soon as it came out of his mouth, blushing and clapping his hand to his lips, giggling.

The October encounter began as their meetings usually did. They went back and forth, each asking how the other was doing. Al-Dosari handed his lawyer an envelope and said he wanted to discuss the contents of it with him later. Colangelo-Bryan assumed the envelope contained another installment of al-Dosari's diary. Then al-Dosari excused himself to go to the bathroom. To do so, guards had to come into the cell, unshackle him from the floor, and then allow him to shuffle over to the toilet. They generally left the room when this happened. The guards locked him in, as was the usual practice. A few minutes passed and there was not a sound from al-Dosari. Colangelo-Bryan was expecting him to call the guards back in. When that didn't happen, Colangelo-Bryan peered in to check on him. He went to the attorney-client side of the cell and through the mesh he could see an odd pattern of color on the floor. He watched it grow and it slowly dawned on him what it was. He looked up and saw something hanging from the wall and then after a moment he realized it was his client. Al-Dosari was hanging by his neck from a braided sheet. He had also managed to cut a gash in his arm. He had written two Arabic words on the wall in blood: I'm innocent.

Colangelo-Bryan started to panic. He started yelling for the guard, banging on the door. He was locked on the wrong side of the cell and could only watched helplessly as the guards cut through the noose and put al-Dosari, now unconscious, on the floor. They hustled Colangelo-Bryan out the door as they tried to revive his client. Ten minutes later al-Dosari was being carried out of the cell on a bloody stretcher.

"I feel very sorry for forcing you to see a human who has suffered too much, dying in front of your eyes," he had written in a suicide note to his lawyer. "I know it is an awful and horrible scene, but there was no other alternative to make our voices heard by the world from the depth of the detention center except this way in order for the world to re-examine its standing and for the fair people of America to look at the situation and try to have a moment of truth with themselves."

Al-Dosari would attempt suicide three more times—all the attempts were unsuccessful. He had fallen into the judicial void, denied any rights whatsoever, and yet given no charges to answer for. He had become one of the disappeared.

THEN THERE WAS DERWISH, killed instantly with five companions by the Hellfire missile fired from the unmanned Predator drone. It still isn't known if Derwish was a target of the attack or an accidental casualty. What is clear is that he perished in a desert a hundred miles east of Sana'a, Yemen, a country with which the United States was not at war. The attack was described by the Swedish Foreign Minister Anna Lindh as "a summary execution that violates human rights." It fact, it likely violated quite a few laws. It is unclear if the Predator drone had permission to fly in Yemeni airspace at all, let alone to initiate a military attack. The Yemeni government had scant authority over the region in which the attack took place anyway. Since the attack was initiated at Langley, and controlled out of Djibouti, it was a clear invasion of sovereign airspace. The Yemeni government has been vague about how much it knew about the attack. Putting all that aside, there is something alarming about the fact that the U.S. government approved the assassination of one of its own citizens without trial or, some would say, much in the way of evidence. Derwish had committed no greater crimes, that we know of, than the other men who came from Lackawanna. Yet he died brutally at the hand of his own government.

After his death, U.S. authorities began to question whether he was, in fact, in the vehicle at all, clearly embarrassed at the precedent they might have set. He had not merely disappeared; it was as if he had never existed at all.

Derwish's story is largely finished, but the story of al-Dosari and the men now at Terre Haute prison continues. The question is whether the men who emerge from prison will return to Lackawanna as fervent Yemenis or chastised Americans. Will they be Bills fans or energized jihadists? Will their experience of the rough end of American justice make them better Americans, or will it have succeeded in making them the very thing that America tried to protect itself from when it locked them away: a bitter, implacable enemy from within?

"NOT STONES,
BUT MEN"

LITTLE HAD CHANGED in the FBI's Buffalo field office since the arrest of the Lackawanna Six. Investigators maintained a constant presence in the First Ward. Residents chaffed under all the scrutiny. Many of the Yemeni-Americans had good things to say about Ed Needham, however. All the families of the Lackawanna Six seemed to think that Needham was trying to do the right thing. He kept his promises, and he seemed genuinely concerned about how the families were getting along.

Needham is still a special agent with the FBI assigned to the Buffalo field office. In 2003, the Buffalo Joint Terrorism Task Force won the Service to America Award, the FBI Director's Annual Award for Excellence, and the Attorney General's Award for Excellence. The glass eagle Needham won as part of the AG award hangs in his kitchen.

Mukhtar al-Bakri was moved to the Communications Management Unit at Terre Haute, Indiana, in December 2006, with the rest of the Lackawanna Six. He will be eligible for release, assuming time off for good behavior, in February 2011.

Kamel Derwish died in the deserts of Yemen, but the U.S. government has yet to admit, on the record, that he was killed by U.S. forces or a Hellfire missile in November 2002. His uncle and family members in Lackawanna have chosen not to file a wrongful death suit.

Yahya Goba has been instrumental in helping U.S. authorities bring cases against other suspected al-Qaeda members, including Chicago gang member Jose Padilla and Australian Joseph Thomas (known as Jihad Jack), who was charged for receiving funds from al-Qaeda. Authorities are looking at reducing Goba's sentence, but as it stands today his earliest parole date is February 2011.

Yassein Taher was moved to the Special Terrorism Unit at Terre Haute, Indiana, in December 2006. The long distance from Lackawanna has made it virtually impossible for his wife and son to visit him. He is eligible for release in about April 2009. His lawyer, Personius, said Taher hasn't changed a bit since he went to prison. He is still cheerful and, unlike many inmates, never complains about the conditions. "He is just doing his time," Personius said.

Nicole Frick is a nurse at a local hospital in Lackawanna. She is shy and doesn't like to talk about the events surrounding the Lackawanna Six and her husband. What is clear is that to this day she thinks her husband didn't deserve to go to jail. He was naïve, but going to an al-Qaeda camp before 9/11 and going afterward, in her view, were two totally different things.

Sahim Alwan feels so guilty about going to the al-Qaeda camp that he has resigned himself to doing his jail time without any argument. He has told friends he thought he deserved what he got. He should never have attended the camp, he said. He, too, was moved to the Terre Haute facility in late 2006. His wife and three children are unable to visit because the distances are just too great. He is eligible for release just two days before Christmas, in December of 2010.

Shafel Mosed is in Terre Haute, Indiana, and is eligible for parole in February 2011.

Faysal Galab is on the same cellblock in Terre Haute as his friends from Lackawanna. He received the lightest sentence, seven years, and is eligible for parole in August 2008. His behavior in prison hasn't been stellar, though, and that could delay his release.

Juma al-Dosari was released from Guantanamo on July 16, 2007, along with sixteen other Saudi prisoners. The Saudi government flew his family from eastern Saudi Arabia to Riyadh to greet his flight from the United States. The reprieve had come just in time. In June of 2007, al-Dosari had tried to commit suicide by cutting a hole in his stomach. Evidentally, in the end, al-Dosari did not appear to be as dangerous as the authorities made him out to be. His file never contained a direct reference to Lackawanna.

Monsignor Robert Wurtz, the man leading the charge for Father Baker's sainthood, died without his mission accomplished in December 2006. The new leader of Our Lady of Victory has said that Baker's sainthood will be one of his top priorities.

Rod Personius is still involved with Yassein Taher's case and talks to Nicole about once a month. Most of his practice in Buffalo has returned to white collar crime. He believes that the system failed the Lackawanna Six.

Jim Harrington still speaks to Sahim Alwan every so often and is still working in criminal defense in Buffalo. He is still convinced the Lackawanna Six were railroaded.

Mike Battle was elevated from U.S. Attorney for western New York to a job in Washington at the Justice Department as director of the Executive Office for United States Attorneys. Ironically, it was Battle who personally called the eight U.S. attorneys to fire them, though he was not involved in the decision-making process. He remained above the fray as that controversy played itself out in Washington. He was, essentially, the messenger. He is now a lawyer at Fulbright & Jaworski, in Washington, DC.

Jaber Elbaneh was recaptured by Yemeni officials in May 2007 after his daring great escape. The United States is still seeking his extradition.

NOTES ON SOURCES

For background on al-Qaeda, Osama bin Laden, and the progression of the Lackawanna Six case, three sources were particularly invaluable: Lawrence Wright's *The Looming Tower: Al-Qaeda and the Road to 9/11*; Rohan Gunaratna's *Inside al-Qaeda*; and the investigative reporting of Matthew Purdy and Lowell Bergman, who wrote a longish piece for *The New York Times* in October of 2003 entitled "Unclear Danger: Inside the Lackawanna Terror Case." While all are cited here, these works in particular were so helpful it would be impossible to give them their full due by simply putting them in an alphabetical list of sources. For anyone looking to read more on the subject of jihad, these three pieces of journalism would be an excellent place to start.

Abbas, Azmat. "The Making of a Militant," *The Herald* (Pakistan), July 2003.

———. "Men With a Mission," *The Herald* (Pakistan), July 2003.

Abdo, Geneive. "Panic Mongers Could Not be More Wrong," *The Houston Chronicle*, September 10, 2006.

Abu Mus'ab. Letters to Abu Mohammed in reply to his injury about the status of jihad. July 26, 2002.

———. Letter to Al-Sahal al-Mumtan Leadership during the Islamic insurgency. Date unknown.

Ali, Saleem. "Islamic Education and Conflict: Understanding the Madrassahs of Pakistan," paper presented at the U.S. Institute of Peace, June 23, 2005.

Al-Maqdasi. "Jordanian militant sympathetic to al-Qaeda," *Interview with al-Jazeera in which he spoke against Arab regimes.*

Anderson, Dale. "Officials are Relieved as Schools Remain Calm," *The Buffalo News*. September 19, 2002.

Anderson, Jon Lee. *The Lion's Grave: Dispatches from Afghanistan* (New York: Grove Press, 2002).

Archibold, Randal. "Prosecution Sees Setback at Terror Trial in California," *The New York Times*, April 10, 2006.

———. "In California Terror Case, a Mistrial for a Father, but a Son is Guilty," *The New York Times*, April 26, 2006.

Armstrong, Karen. *Islam: A Short History* (New York: The Modern Library, 2002).

Arquilla, John, and David Ronfeldt. "The Advent of Netwar (Revisited)," in Russ Howard, ed., *Terrorism and Counterterrorism* (New York: McGraw Hill, 2003).

Bailles. "Going to the Source: Why Al Qaeda's Financial Network is Likely to Withstand the Current War on Terrorist Financing," *Studies in Conflict in Terrorism*, Vol. 27, 2004.

Bamford, James. *Body of Secrets: Anatomy of the Ultra-Secret National Security Agency* (New York: Anchor Books, 2002).

Bar, Shmeul. "The Religious Sources of Islamic Terrorism," *Policy Review*, June–July 2004.

Becker, Maki. "Peace Bridge Arrest Tied to Terror Plot," *The Buffalo News*, June 5, 2006.

Beebe, Michael, Dan Herbeck, and Lou Michel. "Relatives Insist Terror Suspects Duped," *The Buffalo News*, September 18, 2002.

———. "Outside Courthouse, Media Circus is a Sideshow to Terror Hearing," *The Buffalo News*, September 19, 2002.

———. "Suspects Plead Not Guilty," *The Buffalo News*, October 23, 2002.

Bernstein, Richard. "What is Free Speech, and What is Terrorism?" *The New York Times*, August 14, 2005.

———. "Despite Terror, Europeans Seem Determined to Maintain Civil Liberties," *The New York Times*, July 8, 2005.

Blanchard, Christopher. "Al-Qaeda: Statements and Evolving Ideology," Congressional Research Service, November 16, 2004.

Bloom, Mia. *Devising a Theory for Suicide Terror, Dying to Kill: The Global Phenomenon of Suicide Terror* (New York: Columbia University Press, 2004).

Bortin, Meg. "Polls Find Discord Between Muslim and Western Worlds," *New York Times*, June 22, 2006.

Borum, Randy, and Michael Gelles. "Al-Qaeda's Operational Evolution: Behavioral and Organizational Perspectives," *Behavioral Science Law* 23, 2005.

Bravin, Jess. "As Justices Weigh Military Tribunals, A Guantanamo Tale," *The Wall Street Journal*, March 28, 2006.

————. "White House Will Reverse Policy, Ban Evidence Elicited by Torture," *The Wall Street Journal*, March 22, 2006.

Broder, John. "Federal Victory in Terror Case May Prove Brief, Experts Say," *The New York Times*, April 27, 2006.

Brookhiser, Richard. "Will the Melting Pots Help America's Muslims?" *The New York Observer*, July 2005.

Buffalo News Editorial Board. "The Crime of Silence," *The Buffalo News*, January 15, 2003.

Bush, George W. "The Nature of the Terrorist Threat Today," address to a Joint Session of Congress and the American People, September 20, 2001.

Buruma, Ian. *Murder in Amsterdam: The Death of Theo van Gogh and the Limits of Tolerance* (New York: Penguin Press, 2006).

Brzezinksi, Matthew. *Fortress America: On the Front Lines of Homeland Security* (New York: Bantam Books, 2005).

Caldwell, Christopher. "After Londonistan," *New York Times Magazine*, June 25, 2006.

————. "Daughter of the Enlightenment, Ayaan Hirsi Ali," *The New York Times Magazine*, April 3, 2005.

Cardinale, Anthony. "Worried Area Muslims Condemn Outrages," *The Buffalo News*, September 12, 2001.

————. "Expert Calls Lackawanna Group Dire Example of Radicals' Allure," *The Buffalo News*, May 23, 2003.

Campbell, Kurt. "Globalization's First War?," *Washington Quarterly*, 17:14, Winter 2002.

Clarke, Richard A. *Against All Enemies: Inside America's War on Terror* (New York: Free Press, 2004).

————. "Finding the Sleeper Cells. The London Attacks Can Show Us What to Look For." *The New York Times Magazine*, August 14, 2005.

Coll, Steve. "Ghost Wars: The Secret History of the CIA, Afghanistan, and bin Laden from the Soviet Invasion to September 10, 2001," *Naval War College Review*, June 22, 2005.

————. "Citizens: The Talk of the Town," *The New Yorker*, June 5, 2006.

Condren, Dave. "Residents Urged to Avoid Stereotyping Muslims," *The Buffalo News*, September 13, 2001.

Cooperative Research, profile on Kamel Derwish and Timeline. Internet posting.

Court transcripts, "United States of America vs. Yahya Goba, Sahim Alwan, Shafal Mosed, Yassein Taher, Faysal Galab" and "USA v. Mukhtar al-Barki." Detention hearing, September 18, 2002.

Cowell, Alan. "Police Name 2 of 4 Men Linked to Bomb Attempts," *The New York Times*, July 26, 2005.

————. "British Seek New Laws to Confront Terror," *The New York Times*, July 18, 2005.

Crenshaw, Martha. "Why America: The Globalization of Civil War," *Current History*, December 2001, 425–432.

————. "The Effectiveness of Terrorism in the Algerian War," in Crenshaw, ed., *Terrorism in Context* (University Park: Penn State Press, 2001).

Crouch, Gregory. "Suspect in Killing of Dutch Filmmaker Maintains His Silence," *The New York Times*, July 12, 2005.

————. "Man on Trial Accepts Blame in Dutch Killing," *The New York Times*, July 12, 2004.

Dalrymple, William. "Inside the Madrassas," *New York Review of Books*, December 1, 2005.

Delpeche, Therese. "The Imbalance of Terror," *Washington Quarterly*, 25:1, Winter 2002.

De Winter, Leon. "Tolerating a Time Bomb," *The New York Times*, July 16, 2005.

Dickey, Christopher. "Jihad Express," *Newsweek*, March 21, 2005.

Dishman, Chris. "Terrorism, Crime and Transformation," *Studies in Conflict and Terrorism*, Vol. 24, No. 1, 2001.

Dolnik, Adam. "All God's Poisons: Reevaluating the Threat of Religious Terrorism with Respect to Non-conventional Weapons," in Russ Howard, ed., *Terrorism and Counterterrorism* (New York: McGraw Hill, 2003).

Downey, Tom. "The Insurgent's Tale: A Veteran Foot Soldier Reveals His Role in Jihad," *Rolling Stone*, December 5, 2005.

Dwyer, Jim. "US Counters 9/11 Theories of Conspiracy," *The New York Times*, June 2006.

Emerson, Steven. *American Jihad: The Terrorists Living Among Us* (New York: Free Press, 2002).

Esmonde, Donn. "Tensions Rise Under Media's Spotlight," *The Buffalo News*, September 18, 2002.

———. "Silence Sealed Fate of Six," *The Buffalo News*, May 21, 2003.

"Factual Review for Return to Petition for Writ of Habeas Corpus by Petitioner Juma al-Dosari," in the United States District Court for the District of Columbia.

Fattah, Hassan. "Some Yemenis Back Fugitive Terror Figures," *The New York Times*, February 16, 2006.

———. "Longtime Haven for Arabs Now Must Ask: Why Us?" *The New York Times*, July 10, 2005.

Federal Bureau of Investigation, transcriptions of 302 statements from the Lackawanna Six, unnamed sources and Juma al-Dosari, transcribed in 2002.

———. Interview notes, Juma Mohammad Abdull Latif al-Dosari, classified and unclassified versions. October 2004.

———. Investigative Summary Regarding the Buffalo Subjects, March 2004.

Finnegan, William. "Defending the City," *The New Yorker*, July 25, 2005.

Fitch, John A. "The Human Side of Large Outputs, Lackawanna—Swamp, Mill and Town, The Survey," *A Journal of Constructive Philanthropy*, Volume XXVII, No.2, October 7, 1911.

Flynn, Stephen. *America the Vulnerable: How Our Government is Failing to Protect Us from Terrorism* (New York: HarperCollins, 2005).

Ford, Peter. "Europe's Rising Class of Believers: Muslims," *The Christian Science Monitor*, June 30, 2005.

"Chasing the Sleeper Cell, Interview with Sahim Alwan," *FRONTLINE*, October, 17, 2003.

Garcia, Michele. "Yemeni Cleric Called Dangerous; Prosecutors Playing on Stereotypes, Defense Lawyer Says," *The Washington Post*, March 4, 2005.

Golden, Tim. "Jihadist or Victim: Ex-Detainee Makes a Case," *The New York Times*, June 15, 2006.

Golden, Tim, and Don Van Natta, Jr. "US Said to Overstate Value of Guantanamo Detainees," *The New York Times*, June 21, 2004.

Goodstein, Laurie. "Muslim Leaders Confront Terror Threat Within Islam," *The New York Times*, September 2, 2005.

Graham, Alexander. "Too Many Americans Are Asleep at the Switch," *The Buffalo News*, December 1, 2002.

Grier, Peter. "How the Patriot Act Came in From the Cold," *Christian Science Monitor*, March, 3, 2006.

Griswold, Eliza. "The Next Islamic Revolution," *The New York Times Magazine*, January 23, 2005.

Gryta, Matt. "Apology Sought from Fisher over Deli Incident," *The Buffalo News*, December 7, 2001.

Gunaratna, Rohan. *Inside Al Qaeda: Global Network of Terror* (New York: Columbia University Press, 2002).

Hanley, Boniface. "Servant of God, Monsignor Nelson Baker (1841–1936), Our Lady of Victory Homes of Charity," Lackawanna, New York.

Herbeck, Dan. "Two of Six Men Admit Being at Terror Camp," *The Buffalo News*, September 20, 2002.

———. "Prosecutors Seek to Prevent Release of Alwan on Galab's Claims," *The Buffalo News*, January 15, 2003.

———. "Five Lackawanna Suspects Beg for Bail," *The Buffalo News*, December 31, 2002.

————. "Federal Grand Jury Indicts Lackawanna Six," *The Buffalo News*, October 22, 2002.

————. "Under Pressure," *The Buffalo News*, October 1, 2002.

————. "Suicide Bombing Document Found," *The Buffalo News*, October 1, 2002.

————. "Intrigue Surrounds Lackawanna Suspect," *The Buffalo News*, September 27, 2002.

————. "Homes Tied to Alleged al-Qaeda Backer Raided," *The Buffalo News*, September 26, 2002.

————. "Lackawanna Suspect Takes Plea," *The Buffalo News*, January 11, 2003.

————. "Denial of Bail Upheld for Five of Lackawanna Six," *The Buffalo News*, January 17, 2003.

————. "Alwan Spoke with bin Laden," *The Buffalo News*, January 25, 2003.

————. "Lackawanna Man Admits Assisting al-Qaeda," *The Buffalo News*, March 25, 2003.

————. "Second Suspect Admits Aiding Terrorist Group," *The Buffalo News*, March 24, 2003.

————. "Defendants Feel Pressure for Plea Deals," *The Buffalo News*, April 6, 2003.

————. "Alwan Prepared to Become Fourth to Take Guilty Plea," *The Buffalo News*, April 8, 2003.

————. "Fifth Lackawanna Six Defendant Takes Plea Deal," *The Buffalo News*, May 13, 2003.

————. "Al-Bakri Last of Suspects to Plead Guilty," *The Buffalo News*, May 29, 2003.

Higgins, Andrew. "Islamic Threats to Dutch Politician Bring Chill at Home," *The Wall Street Journal*, May 17, 2006.

Hirsh, Michael, Mark Hosenball, and Rod Nordland. "The Tunnel Rats of Terror," *Newsweek*, February 20, 2006, 41.

Holstun, Jim. "Lackawanna Mosque Watch–2003," *The Buffalo Report*, February 1, 2003.

Hosenball, Mark. "Bombers Next Door: Four Dead and Four Others Safely in Custody, But British Police Worry This is Only the Beginning," *Newsweek*, August 8, 2005.

Howard, Russell, and Reid Sawyer, eds. *Terrorism and Counterterrorism*, revised and updated edition (New York, McGraw-Hill, 2003).

Isikoff, Michael, and Karen Breslau. "Storm Clouds in California: Did the Fed Find Qaeda Trainees Out West?" *Newsweek*, June 20, 2005.

Jonsson, Patrik. "New Profile of the Homegrown Terrorist Emerges," *Christian Science Monitor*, June 26, 2006.

Juergensmeyer, Mark. "The Logic of Religious Violence," in Russ Howard, eds., *Terrorism and Counterterrorism* (New York: McGraw Hill, 2003).

Kamp, Karl-Heinz, Joseph Pilat, and Jessica Stern. "WMD Terrorism: An Exchange," *Survival*, Winter 1998–1999.

Karon, Tony. "Yemen Strike Opens New Chapter in War on Terror," *Time*, November 5, 2002.

Kellman, Rich. "Quest For Baker Sainthood Might Get Boost," WGRZ News, January 6, 2005.

Kessler, Ronald. *The Bureau, The Federal History of the FBI* (New York: St. Martin's Press, 2003).

Kifner, John, Susan Saches, and Marc Santora. "Traces of Terror: The Buffalo Case; After 3 Days of Testimony Some Gaps are Unfilled." *The New York Times*, September 23, 2002.

Kramer, Jane. "The Dutch Model: Multiculturalism and Muslim Immigrants," *The New Yorker*, April 3, 2006.

Krebs, Valdis. "Mapping of Terrorist Network Cells," *Connections* 24 (3): 43–52, 2002.

Kurth, James. "Confronting the Unipolar Moment: The American Empire and Islamic Terrorism," *Current History*, December 2002, 402–408.

Kwiatkowski, Jane. "Devoted Tourist's Sainthood Could Focus Worldwide Attention on Lackawanna," *The Buffalo News*, December 26, 2000.

Leiken, Robert S. "Europe's Mujahideen: Where Mass Immigration Meets Global Terrorism," *Backgrounder*, April 2005.

Leweling, Tara. "Exploring Muslim Diaspora Communities in Europe," *Strategic Insights*, Volume IV, Issue 5, May 2005.

Lipton, Eric. "In Zeal to Foil Terror Plots, Cases May Be Missing Important Element, Lawyers Say," *The New York Times*, July 9, 2006.

————. "Recent Arrests in Terror Plots Yield Debate on Preemptive Action By Government," *The New York Times*, July 9, 2006.

Lobe, Jim. "Sovereignty Takes Major Hit in Yemen, Mauritius," *InterPress Service*, November 8, 2002.

Locy, Toni, and Kevin Johnson. "How the US Watches Terrorist Suspects," *USA Today*, February 11, 2003.

Lyall, Sarah. "In Britain, Migrants Took a New Path: To Terrorism," *The New York Times*, July 28, 2005.

————. "Britain's Plans for Addressing Its Muslims' Concerns Lag," *The New York Times*, August 18, 2006.

————. "London Bombers Visited Earlier, Apparently on Practice Run," *The New York Times*, September 21, 2005.

————. "3 Main British Parties to Back Tougher Antiterrorism Laws," *The New York Times*, July 27, 2005.

MacFarquhar, Neil. "Pakistanis Find US an Easier Fit Than Britain," *The New York Times*, August 21, 2006.

Mahler, Jonathan. "The Bush Administration v. Salim Hamdan," *The New York Times Magazine*, January 8, 2006.

Meyer, Brian. "Terror Arrests Leave Community with Mixed Emotions," *The Buffalo News*, September 15, 2002.

Michel, Lou, and Jay Rey. "Sales Pitch on Terror Stirs Complaints," *The Buffalo News*, October 19, 2002.

Mueller, Karl, et al. "Striking First: Preemptive and Preventative Attack in US National Security Policy." Prepared by the United States Air Force for the Rand Corporation.

National Strategy for Combating Terrorism, Washington, DC.

Nordland, Rod. "Terror for Export: Iraq is the Base for a New Generation of Jihadists," *Newsweek*, November 21, 2005.

Packer, George. "The Moderate Martyr, A Radically Peaceful Vision of Islam," *The New Yorker*, September 11, 2006.

―――. "Knowing the Enemy: Can Social Scientists Redefine the 'War on Terror'?," *The New Yorker*, December 18, 2006.

Palmer, David Scott. "The Revolutionary Terrorism of Peru's Shining Path," in Martha Crenshaw, ed., *Terrorism in Context* (University Park: Penn State Press, 2001).

Pape, Robert. *Dying to Win: The Strategic Logic of Suicide Terrorism* (New York: Random House, 2005).

Pasciak, Mary, and Niki Cervantes. "Innocent Targets in Arab-Americans Caught in Emotional Backlash," *The Buffalo News*, September 16, 2001.

Pepper, Tara, and Mark Hosenball. "A Deadly Puzzle: Searching for Skill-Set Operatives Who Recruited and Supplied the London Bombers," *Newsweek*, July 25, 2005.

Pilch, Richard. "The Threat of Biological Terrorism Reevaluated," in Russ Howard, ed., *Terrorism and Counterterrorism* (New York: McGraw-Hill, 2003).

Pillar, Paul. "Counterterrorism After al-Qaeda," *The Washington Quarterly*, Summer 2004.

Pipes, Daniel, and Khalid Duran. "Muslim Immigrants in the United States," *Backgrounder*, August 2002.

Plea agreements from five of the Lackawanna Six as filed in the United States District Court for the Western District of New York.

Powell, Michael. "No Choice But Guilty: Lackawanna Case Highlights Legal Tilt," *The Washington Post*, July 29, 2003.

Purdy, Matthew. "Our Towns: Puzzling Over Motives of the Men in the Lackawanna al-Qaeda Case," *The New York Times*, March 30, 2003.

Purdy, Matthew, and Lowell Bergman. "Where the Trial Led: Between Evidence and Suspicion; Unclear Danger: Inside the Lackawanna Terror Case," *The New York Times*, October 12, 2003.

Raban, Jonathan. The Truth About Terrorism, *New York Review of Books*, January 13, 2005.

Ranstorp, Magnus. "Terrorism in the Name of Religion," in Russ Howard, eds., *Terrorism and Counterterrorism* (New York: Mc-Graw Hill, 2003).

Reich, Walter. "Terrorist psycho-logic," in Walter Reich, ed., *Origins of Terrorism: Psychologies, Ideologies, Theologies, States of Mind* (Washington: Wilson Center Presss, 1998).

Rieff, David. "Their Hearts and Minds? Why the Ideological Battle Against Islamists is Nothing Like the Struggle Against Communism," *The New York Times Magazine*, September 4, 2005.

Risen, James. *State of War: The Secret History of the CIA and the Bush Administration* (New York: Free Press, 2006).

Risen, James, and Marc Santora. "Threats and Responses: The Terror Network; Man Believed Slain in Yemen Tied by U.S. to Buffalo Cell," *The New York Times*, November 10, 2002, p. A17.

Rodenbeck, Max. "The Truth About Jihad," *New York Review of Books*, August 11, 2005.

Roy, Olivier. *Globalized Islam, The Search for the New Ummah* (New York: Columbia University Press. 2005).

———. "Why Do They Hate Us? Not Because of Iraq," op-ed, *The New York Times*, July 22, 2005.

Rubin, Elizabeth. "In the Land of the Taliban," *The New York Times*, October 22, 2006.

Sandler, James. "Chasing the Sleeper Cell. Kamal Derwish: The Life and Death of An American Terrorist," *FRONTLINE*, posted October 16, 2003.

Santora, Marc. "Threats and Responses, The Suspects; Visit to Qaeda Camp Makes 6 Suspects Dangerous, U.S. Insists," *The New York Times*, September 21, 2002.

Sageman, Marc. *Understanding Terror Networks* (Philadelphia: Penn Press, 2004).

Sanger, David. "Waging the War on Terror: Report Belies Optimistic View," *The New York Times*, September 27, 2006.

Savage, David. "No Trials for Key Players, Government Prefers to Interrogate Bigger Fish," *Los Angeles Times*, May 4, 2006.

————. "Moussaoui Case is Latest Misstep in Prosecutions," *Los Angeles Times*, March 14, 2006.

Sawyer, Reid. "The Madrid Attacks—A Case Study," in Russell Howard, ed., *Terrorrism and Counterterrorism* (New York: McGraw-Hill, 2003).

Schlesinger, Robert. "In Djibouti, US Special Forces Develop Base Amid Secrecy," *The Boston Globe*, December 12, 2002, A45.

Sciolino, Elaine and Stephen Grey. "British Terror Trial Traces a Path to Militant Islam," *The New York Times*, November 26, 2006.

Scheuer, Michael. *Imperial Hubris: Why the West Is Losing the War on Terror*, Brassey's (Dulles, VA: Potomac Books, 2004).

Schulman, Susan. "Five Area Men Held as al-Qaeda Suspects," *The Buffalo News*, September 14, 2002.

————. Friends Say Detainees Lived 'All American' Lives, *The Buffalo News*, September 15, 2002.

Schwartz, Peter. "The Art of the Long View," in *Strategy and Force Planning* (Newport: Naval War College, 1997), 29–44.

Schwedler, Jillian. "Islamic Identity: Myth, Menace, or Mobilizer?" *SAIS Review*, Volume XXI, No. 2, Summer/Fall 2001.

Sikand, Yoginder. *Bastions of the Belivers: Madrassas and Islamic Education in India* (New Delhi: Penguin India, 2005).

Sivan, Emanual. "The Clash Within Islam," *Survival*, Volume 45, No. 1., Spring 2003.

Smith, Craig. "Muslim Group in France is Fertile Soil for Militancy," *The New York Times*. April 27, 2004.

Sprinzak, Ehud. "Rational Fanatics," *Foreign Policy*, September 2000.

Stern, Jessica. "Getting and Using the Weapons," in Russel Howard, ed., *Terrorism and Counterterrorism* (New York: McGraw-Hill, 2003).

————. "The Covenant, the Sword, and the Arm of the Lord," in Jonathan Tucker, ed., *Toxic Terror* (Cambridge: MIT Press, 2000).

————. "The Protean Enemy," *Foreign Affairs*, Volume 82, No. 4, July/August 2003.

Stewart, Rory. *The Places in Between* (New York: Harcourt Books, 2004).

Sullivan, Stacy. "The Minutes of the Guantanamo Bay Bar Association," *New York Magazine*, June 26, 2006.

Taibbi, Matt. "Ken Schroeder's Lost Weekend. The Lackawanna Six Case: A View from the Cheap Seats," *The Beast*, Issue 10, October 11:24, 2002.

Tan, Sandra. "Change of Heart," *The Buffalo News*, October 22, 2001.

———. "Meeting at Yemeni Hall Fosters Dialogue," *The Buffalo News*, October 17, 2002.

———. "For Those Who Care Most, A Day of Intense Emotions," *The Buffalo News*, October 9, 2002.

———. "Interfaith Event Shows Solidarity With Muslims," *The Buffalo News*, October 2, 2002.

———. "Security Concerns Prompt School Board to Keep Two on the Job," *The Buffalo News*, October 16, 2002.

———. "Yemenites Wary Over Lackawanna Six Sentences," *The Buffalo News*, April 20, 2003.

Temple-Raston, Dina. "Murder in Holland Brings Terror War Home to the Dutch," *New York Sun*, November 8, 2004.

———. "The Dutch 9/11 Sends Leaders to Safe Houses," *New York Sun*, November 9, 2004.

———. "Hundreds Mourn Murdered Filmmaker Theo van Gogh in Amsterdam," *New York Sun*, November 10, 2004.

———. "Terror Cell in Holland Raided by Police in 14-Hour Siege," *New York Sun*, November 11, 2004.

Thomas, Vanessa, and R. J. Pignataro. "Muslims Mourn Man Killed in Yemen," *The Buffalo News*, November 11, 2002.

Thompson, Carolyn. "Escape of Suspected al-Qaeda Trainee Puzzles Relatives," The Associated Press, February 13, 2006.

Toobin, Jeffrey. "Killing Habeas Corpus, Arlen Specter's About-Face," *The New Yorker*, December 4, 2006.

Tucker, David. "What's New about the New Terrorism and How Dangerous Is It?" *Terrorism and Political Violence*, Autumn 2001.

Unknown author. "Reasons for Suicide Martyrdom," found in the apartment of Yassein Taher after his arrest.

Unknown author. Portions of the anonymous letter to the Buffalo office of the FBI, June 2001.

Unknown author. *The Encyclopedia of Jihad.* Translation from original text. Camp structures.

Unknown author. *A Brief History of Bethlehem Steel Corporation*, produced by Public Affairs Department, Bethlehem Steel Corporation.

Unknown author. *Al-Qaeda Bylaws.* The original document consisted of nineteen pages written in Arabic. April 18, 2002.

United Press International. "Father Baker Miracle Investigation Begun," November 27, 2005.

U.S. Department of State. *Patterns in Global Terrorism* (Washington, DC: Government Printing Office).

Vogel, Charity, and Dan Herbeck. "Overviews of al-Bakri Offer Sharp Contrast," *The Buffalo News*, September 17, 2002.

Waldman, Amy. "Seething Unease Shaped British Bombers' Newfound Zeal," *The New York Times*, July 31, 2005.

Wallace-Wells, Benjamin. "Private Jihad: How Rita Katz Got into the Spying Business," *The New Yorker*, May 29, 2006.

Warner, Gene. "Cars Vandalized at Route 5 Gas Station," *The Buffalo News*, September 20, 2002.

Weaver, Mary Anne. *Pakistan: In the Shadow of Jihad and Afghanistan* (New York: Farrar, Straus & Giroux, 2002).

Weimann, Gabriel. *Terror on the Internet* (Washington, DC: United States Institute of Peace Press, 2006).

Weiser, Benjamin, and James Risen. "The Masking of a Militant. Special Report: A Soldier's Shadowy trail in the US and in the Midest," *The New York Times*, December 1, 1998.

Western District of New York. District Court of the United States, indictment, *The United States of America vs. Yahya Goba, Shafal Mosed, Yassein Taher, Faysal Galab, Mukhtar al-Bakri, and Sahim Alwan*, May 2002 grand jury.

———. Criminal Complaint against Yahya Goba, Shafal Mosed, Yassein Taher, Faysal Galab, Mukhtar al-Bakri, and Sahim Alwan.

Witlock, Craig. "Terrorists Proving Harder to Profile," *The Washington Post*, March 12, 2007.

Wiktorowica, Quintan. "The New Global Threat: Transnational Salafis and Jihad," *Middle East Policy*, Volume VIII, No. 4, December 2001.

Wiktorowicz, Quintan, and John Kaitner. "Killing in the Name of Islam: Al Qaeda's Justification for September 11," *Middle East Policy*, Summer 2003.

Wright, Lawrence. "The Master Plan: The New Theorists of Jihad, Al-Qaeda is Just the Beginning," *The New Yorker*.

Wypijewski, JoAnn. "Living in An Age of Fire," *Mother Jones*, 2003.

Zawahiri, Ayman. "Call to Muslims to Recognize Shame and Bad Conditions of Their Lives," Internet and letter posting. June 2005.

Zremski, Jerry. "Local FBI Team Cited for Fighting Terrorism," *The Buffalo News*, October 16, 2003.

The 9/11 Commission Report: Final Report of the National Commission on Terrorist Attacks Upon the United States (New York: W. W. Norton, 2004).

ACKNOWLEDGMENTS

My deepest thanks to all the people who took the time to help me pull together the threads of a story that had been largely misunderstood and was constantly changing. There were hundreds of people who provided information, added insight, offered advice or patiently listened to yet another story about my trips to Yemen, Pakistan, and Afghanistan. This project spanned three years. The idea for the book took shape after a rash of terror-related arrests in this country sparked a conversation at a dinner party about racial profiling. Some of my Muslim friends in attendance said that given what had happened on September 11, they were resigned to the fact that they would inspire suspicion wherever they went. After the London attacks, a friend told me about a rather well-known Middle Eastern screenwriter who had taken to packing his daily work belongings in a clear plastic bag. He wanted everyone on the Tube to see that he clearly wasn't carrying explosives. I finished the book in mid–2007, soon after the Lackawanna Six were moved to a special unit in a prison in Indiana and the trial of Jose Padilla, the so-called dirty bomber, began in south Florida. By that time, Americans were beginning to question not only the war in Iraq but also the way the Bush administration had conducted its war on terror.

By definition, a book about ordinary people in a small community of a small town depends on the kindness of strangers. The Yemenis in Lackawanna's First Ward are close-knit and intensely private. My greatest debt is to the people there who put aside their suspicions of me and allowed me to pepper them with pointed questions about being Muslim in America after the 9/11 attacks and about the Lackawanna Six, a subject that is sensitive, even today. They shared their feelings and recollections about the men (many of whom were they counted as friends or brothers or nephews or husbands or fathers), how they went to Afghanistan, the prejudice they experience today in America, and the decline of Lackawanna. They talked with me, showing not just a great deal of patience, but unending generosity. They took me into their homes, introduced me to their families, and allowed a non-Muslim outsider to rummage around in their lives and poke into an episode that, for many, still haunts them. Without their help, this book would never have been possible. Many of these people prefer to remain anonymous. They do not want to garner the attention of law enforcement or their neighbors in the community. We often met outside of Lackawanna, in malls or coffee shops, so that no one would know we were meeting. Whether there really was such a risk in speaking to me is unclear. What I do know is that dozens of these people overcame their own fear—whether real or imagined—to try to educate me about what happened and how it affected them.

While some people in Lackawanna might not agree with the conclusions I have drawn about their town and the story of the Lackawanna Six, I hope they conclude that I have been fair in trying to portray their trials during a difficult time.

In particular, I would like to thank Nicole Frick, members of the Taher family, and high school friends of the Lackawanna Six who were willing to speak with me and provide a background and a better picture of the six as young men. Brothers and friends of Mukhtar al-Bakri were also very generous with their time and open about their opinions about how difficult it is to be a Muslim in America today. FBI officials—including Paul Moskal, Ed Needham, and Peter Ahearn—always found a way to make time for me when I came to Buffalo. Moskal and Needham allowed me to bounce my theories off them and helped me calibrate my conclusions as did my good friend Jean Strauss, who also read the manuscript and provided helpful fixes and suggestions.

I was in and out of Buffalo several times a month for two and a half years and then spent the early part of 2007 living in Allentown to finish the project. People there could not have been nicer or more accommodating including Nick Gilmour, who helped me survive a

Buffalo winter when ice had formed inside my apartment windows and a dog and an electric blanket seemed to be the only things between me and freezing to death.

In Yemen, I would like to thank the various volunteer guides who tried to help me understand what it is like to live in Yemen, the Yemen America Language Institute, The Sana'a Institute for Arabic language, Pamela Jerome for her discussion on local architecture, and officials with the American Embassy in Sana'a. For help with the Pakistan leg of the trip, special thanks to Janice and Shaheen, and their friend Nadeem Babar, who was a constant helpful presence as was the ever-enthusiastic Tammy. Mahim Maher and Abbas Naqvi from the *Daily Times* went above and beyond the call of journalistic duty. They never tired of questions and showed a foreigner a part of Pakistan that visitors rarely get to see. Thanks, too to the people of Moosa Colony who patiently answered pointed questions about a suicide bomber in their midst, the elders at Jamia Binoria International, and the Khan brothers and their fellow students who were gracious and good humored when asked personal and probing questions. In Afghanistan, special thanks to Shaheen Rassoul and Molly Howitt, Adrian Edwards at the UN Assistance Mission, Hassina Sherjan, and, last but not at all least, our guide and fixer Qais Azimy, who found a way to make a somewhat dangerous trip incredibly fun. He is one of my favorite people in Afghanistan, and I hope he will be a friend for a long time to come.

My agent, John Thornton, always provided the encouragement I needed when I wondered about the wisdom of this project and my ability to tackle it, as did my editor, Clive Priddle, who pushed me to come to sharper conclusions about a story that was moving as I was reporting it. His patience, good humor, and sense of when to just get out of the way and let me follow the story, were an unbeatable combination. George Orwell once wrote that he didn't know what he thought about something until he wrote about it. Similarly, I had to write much of the book before it became clear that it was likely that the rough justice the Lackawanna Six experienced could succeed in turning a bunch of scofflaws into the very thing of which America is so frightened: bitter enemies from within.

My copy editor, Lori Hobkirk, did a careful job finding my errors of commission and omission, and my good friend George Hager, who has cheerfully read every one of my books and saved me from myself on numerous occasions, is one of my favorite people on the planet. His attention to detail—the nits and tics that he loves to find and point out—has forced me to become a better writer, and I will forever be indebted to him. Special thanks, too, to Konrad Fiedler, who is always willing to sign onto my crazy schemes, and his parents, who so far haven't held it against me for constantly putting their son in peril. And finally, I would like to thank Hubert Faure for his uncanny ability to say the exact right thing at the exact right time. It is a gift that I hope one day to develop.

Joan Didion, in an essay about her editor Henry Robbins, said that a writer's friend "not only has to maintain a faith the writer shares only in intermittent flashes but also has to like the writer, which is hard to do. Writers are only rarely likable." I am fortunate to have a cast of people in my life who manage to do that and more, and for that I will be eternally grateful. I never forget how lucky I have become.

INDEX

PublicAffairs is a publishing house founded in 1997. It is a tribute to the standards, values, and flair of three persons who have served as mentors to countless reporters, writers, editors, and book people of all kinds, including me.

I.F. STONE, proprietor of *I. F. Stone's Weekly*, combined a commitment to the First Amendment with entrepreneurial zeal and reporting skill and became one of the great independent journalists in American history. At the age of eighty, Izzy published *The Trial of Socrates*, which was a national bestseller. He wrote the book after he taught himself ancient Greek.

BENJAMIN C. BRADLEE was for nearly thirty years the charismatic editorial leader of *The Washington Post*. It was Ben who gave the *Post* the range and courage to pursue such historic issues as Watergate. He supported his reporters with a tenacity that made them fearless and it is no accident that so many became authors of influential, best-selling books.

ROBERT L. BERNSTEIN, the chief executive of Random House for more than a quarter century, guided one of the nation's premier publishing houses. Bob was personally responsible for many books of political dissent and argument that challenged tyranny around the globe. He is also the founder and longtime chair of Human Rights Watch, one of the most respected human rights organizations in the world.

·   ·   ·

For fifty years, the banner of PublicAffairs Press was carried by its owner Morris B. Schnapper, who published Gandhi, Nasser, Toynbee, Truman, and about 1,500 other authors. In 1983, Schnapper was described by *The Washington Post* as "a redoubtable gadfly." His legacy will endure in the books to come.

Peter Osnos, *Founder and Editor-at-Large*